For the Love of Mike

For the Love of Mike

More of the Best of Mike Royko

FOREWORD BY ROGER EBERT

THE UNIVERSITY OF CHICAGO PRESS

CHICAGO AND LONDON

The University of Chicago Press, Chicago 60637
The University of Chicago Press, Ltd., London
© 2001 by The University of Chicago
All rights reserved. Published 2001
Printed in the United States of America

10 09 08 07 06 05 04 03 02 01   1 2 3 4 5
ISBN: 0-226-73073-5

Library of Congress Cataloging-in-Publication Data
Royko, Mike, 1933–
For the love of Mike : more of the best of Mike Royko / foreword by Roger Ebert.
p. cm.
ISBN 0-226-73073-5 (alk. paper)
    1. Chicago (Ill.)—Social life and customs—20th century. 2. United States—Social life and customs—1971– 3. United States—Social life and customs—1945–1970. 4. Royko, Mike, 1933– I. Title.
F548.52 .R654 2001
977.3'110432—dc21   00-050303

♾ The paper used in this publication meets the minimum requirements of the American National Standard for Information Sciences—Permanence of Paper for Printed Library Materials, ANSI Z39.48-1992.

CONTENTS

Foreword by Roger Ebert   *xi*
Introduction   *xix*

1
BRAINSTORMS

MARCH 7, 1973   How Slats Lost His Cymbals   3

MARCH 13, 1980   Vegas in Akron?   5

SEPTEMBER 24, 1980   Jay's Bottom Line   8

NOVEMBER 27, 1980   Pilgrims' Progress   11

JUNE 3, 1981   Love Lost in Lingo   13

FEBRUARY 20, 1987   A Devilish Night for Oral Roberts   15

APRIL 2, 1987   A Word About Debate "Poopery"   18

MAY 15, 1989   A Smile a Day . . . Can Be Sickening   21

FEBRUARY 16, 1990   There Go Another Wasted Three Pounds   23

JANUARY 24, 1996   Treatment of Crabs? Some of Us Don't Have Leg
to Stand On   26

2
CUB CAPERS . . . AND GAMES
WE PLAY

APRIL 7, 1969   "Ungreatful" Cub Fans   31

MARCH 23, 1976   At Long Last, the Cubs Again   33

APRIL 20, 1980   A Farewell to Cubs   35

APRIL 9, 1981   When Ya Gotta Go   39

APRIL 8, 1986   For It's 1, 2, 3 Maalox at the . . .   42

MARCH 12, 1987   Read On, Gluttons for Punishment   44

AUGUST 8, 1988   Cub Fans, Let's Be Careful Out There   46

AUGUST 25, 1989   Rose Can Count On the Memories   48

OCTOBER 5, 1993   Three Ex-Cubs Assure Spurning of Atlanta   50

JUNE 8, 1995   Yes, Golf Tantrums Are for Males Only   52

3

AND JUSTICE FOR ALL

MARCH 16, 1965   The "Truth" in Selma   57

MARCH 19, 1965   The "Truth" in Chicago   59

MAY 28, 1968   Fascism Isn't Accidental   61

DECEMBER 24, 1968   For Too Many, There's No Joy   63

JANUARY 28, 1970   One Word Tells All: Outrageous   65

JULY 22, 1970   Bureaucracy—a Nightmare   67

FEBRUARY 17, 1976   For Metcalfe, a 1936 Replay   69

NOVEMBER 18, 1979   Wrong Mom? Tough!   71

MARCH 11, 1981   He Deserved It   73

JUNE 11, 1982   Baseball's Black Eye   76

OCTOBER 21, 1983   Helms' Ranting Reminds Us How Far We've Come   78

SEPTEMBER 21, 1990   Where Good Sense Is in the Minority   80

APRIL 4, 1991   This Story May Not Have Happy Ending   82

JUNE 23, 1994   Lincolnshire Makes Lunch a Real Hassle   84

4
CHASING THE CHANGING SCENE

FEBRUARY 20, 1967   High-Rise Lobby: The Old People Just Don't Fit In
89

AUGUST 10, 1970   Skirt the Issue and Live Longer   91

AUGUST 27, 1970   Lib Gawkers Tiresome Talkers   93

MARCH 31, 1976   Mary Pickford's Old "Error"   94

MAY 2, 1978   It's Love at First Click   96

JANUARY 10, 1980   Survival of the Fairest   99

MARCH 20, 1989   Something's Fishy at the Old Ballpark   101

APRIL 11, 1991   It's Same Old Song Sung with a Twist   103

NOVEMBER 1, 1994   Happiness Floats in a Bowl of Misery   105

SEPTEMBER 13, 1996   Where Have All the Protesters Gone Concerning
Iraq?   107

5
POLITICS AIN'T BEANBAG

NOVEMBER 8, 1968   Nixon Halfway to a Mandate   111

SEPTEMBER 17, 1971   Now, About That Book . . .   112

FEBRUARY 16, 1973   What's Behind Daley's Words?   114

OCTOBER 19, 1973   A Law City Should Keep   116

JUNE 10, 1974   Mr. Ambition at Your Service   118

JANUARY 8, 1980   Slip off the Old Block   120

MAY 7, 1984   Land of the Free, Home of the Fix   123

MAY 17, 1988   Alderman's Brain Is a Museum Piece   125

AUGUST 17, 1988   Bush's Selection Really Hits Home   127

MARCH 27, 1991   Hail a Taxidermist for This Public Body   130

MARCH 17, 1992   Hillary Clinton Is Fair Political Game   132

NOVEMBER 4, 1992 Bush's Wish Isn't Voters' Command   134

NOVEMBER 10, 1995 Democrats Just Got Boost from GOP Without Even Trying   136

6
MY KIND OF TOWN

MAY 16, 1968 Slats Grobnik, Sidewalk Man   141

SEPTEMBER 9, 1968 The True Story of Twinkies   143

JUNE 16, 1969 Change Bugs an Old Square   144

JULY 10, 1970 So, It's Over and Out, Roger!   146

APRIL 12, 1973 A Requiem for a Tavern   147

JANUARY 21, 1976 Ladies Miss Goat's Flavor   150

AUGUST 28, 1990 If Only the Acorn Could Play It Again   152

NOVEMBER 21, 1995 Even a U.S. Senator Can Botch a Recipe for Success   154

7
RAGING AGAINST THE NIGHT

DECEMBER 19, 1966 Lakefront Isn't a Wasteland Yet—But It Will Be   159

APRIL 8, 1968 Trace of Hope Was Lacking   161

JUNE 7, 1968 Laugh It Up, It's Violence   163

APRIL 14, 1971 Fred Hampton at the Ballot Box   165

JANUARY 24, 1973 Hollow Ring of Peace   167

SEPTEMBER 16, 1975 Nero Would Love Chicago   169

MARCH 4, 1976 Busing a Whip to Flog Liberals   170

FEBRUARY 5, 1981 Talk Won't Save Life   172

APRIL 8, 1981 Feel Guilty? Me?   175

MARCH 26, 1991 After All, This Is What We Fought For   178

SEPTEMBER 25, 1992   War's Toll Doesn't End with Last Bomb   180

8
THE TROUBLE WITH EVERY-WHERE ELSE

JUNE 3, 1982   Hicks Get Their Licks   185

JUNE 27, 1982   Iowa's the Real Pits   188

APRIL 9, 1984   Just Take Your Oranges and . . .   190

AUGUST 20, 1984   Regional Tastes Hard to Swallow   193

OCTOBER 5, 1990   Thank You, Cubs: The Pressure's Off   194

JANUARY 20, 1994   Take Off Your Mittens, Count Your Blessings   196

9
NOW, WAIT A MINUTE

JULY 20, 1966   Ringing Dissent to Criticism of Justice Douglas   201

FEBRUARY 21, 1968   Bonnie 'n' Clyde—the Sad Side   203

JANUARY 27, 1978   Short-Legged Dog Has Snow-Fooling Problem   205

NOVEMBER 20, 1979   Fun with Khomeini   207

MAY 16, 1990   Fulfilling Advice for Wellesley Grads   210

SEPTEMBER 28, 1990   So Much to Hate, and So Little Time   213

MAY 6, 1992   Bush Needs Liberal Doses of History   215

SEPTEMBER 1, 1993   '68 Convention-al Wisdom All Wrong   217

FEBRUARY 9, 1994   Time to Be Color-Blind to All Words of Hate   219

MARCH 25, 1994   Using Short Form? Try Briefs Deduction   222

10
MEDIA MUSINGS

DECEMBER 20, 1973   An Exclusive—in Club News   227

APRIL 26, 1981   Come Clean, *Post*   229

JANUARY 29, 1992   *Star* Gives Public Just What It Wants   231

APRIL 7, 1993   Rodney King and a Double Standard   234

JUNE 8, 1994   Second Thought on That Invite: Oh, Forget It   236

MAY 21, 1996   Will "Gotcha" Crowd Go After Questions in Admiral's Death?   238

NOVEMBER 7, 1996   If Media Say It's Over, Why Should Voters Play Around?   240

11

HERE'S LOOKING AT ME, KID

OCTOBER 4, 1967   Riverview Park: A Coward's Tale   245

MARCH 21, 1969   How to Beat an Aching Back   247

JUNE 2, 1969   Who Actually Creates Gaps?   249

FEBRUARY 8, 1972   Acute Crisis in Identity   250

DECEMBER 20, 1976   That Old, Gray Area   253

OCTOBER 24, 1978   He's Loser by a Nose   255

OCTOBER 26, 1978   Lookin' Fine? He Nose It   258

JANUARY 11, 1980   Farewell to Fitness   260

JUNE 24, 1982   Why Rude Is Shrewd   262

OCTOBER 9, 1985   Condo Man Back Down to Earth   265

AUGUST 21, 1987   Windshield Wiper Lets in Some Light   266

JUNE 13, 1995   Oh, the Humiliation a Dad Must Endure   268

FOREWORD

If a journalism society decides they should put up a plaque to Mike Royko, I know where it should go. It should go in the southeast corner of the fourth floor of the *Sun-Times* building, at 401 N. Wabash in Chicago. In that corner, from the 1960s until the *Chicago Daily News* folded in 1978, a standard office partition, steel below, glass above, about shoulder height, defined the space within which Mike Royko wrote the best newspaper columns of his time.

The partition did not go all the way to the ceiling. I think it probably had a door, although I can't remember one because, if there was one, it was always propped open. There was room inside this corner space for Royko's desk and a couple of filing cabinets. He wrote on an old manual typewriter—not his own, just one from the office pool, with keys that stuck and ribbons that jammed.

His office was piled high with newspapers, books, letters, souvenirs, coffee cups, ashtrays, gimcracks, and ties that he had taken off and thrown in the corner. It also contained a holy relic: the wooden city room hat stand from the old *Daily News* building on Wacker, which he brought along when the paper moved into the new building on Wabash.

Mike sat in a swivel chair with his back to the river, and there was a straight-backed chair for his visitors. He had a lot of visitors. Mike could have written his column at anytime from anywhere and his editors would have been happy to have it, but he spent an eight-hour day, sometimes longer, at the paper, where he was the soul of the *Daily News* and the honorary soul, by osmosis, of the *Sun-Times*. No journalist in Chicago was more respected by his colleagues. Any time of the day, if you glanced back there, you would see someone standing in the door of the cubicle or sitting inside. It might be one of his Leg Persons, who had their own desks just outside. Or a press agent like the boxing promoter Ben Bentley or Danny Newman from the Lyric Opera. Most likely it would be a fellow reporter. Mike always had time to talk. Always. Even when he was in the middle of a column, he had time to talk. Not once in all the years did I ever walk in on Mike and have him look up with that harassed look all news reporters know, and shout that he was "on deadline!" Deadlines could wait. "Whaddaya know?" he'd ask.

Mike of course was *always* on deadline. He always had a column to write. He was the most prolific of columnists, turning out five a week at such a high level that you could keep publishing books like this one until you had reprinted all of them. In more than 30 years, I never once heard anybody look up from one of his columns and say, "Royko wrote a bad column today." Sometimes he made people mad, sometimes you might think he was out of his mind, but he never wrote a bad one.

In those days the city rooms of the two papers shared the fourth floor. They had separate but equal facilities, except that the men's room of the *Daily News* had real bars of soap, and the men's room of the *Sun-Times* had liquid soap you tapped out of a dispenser. Office lore had it that the real soap was a concession wrung from Marshall Field III when he bought the *Daily News* from John S. Knight. The city rooms of the two papers were separated by a glassed-in no-man's-land called the wire room, ruled by copy boys/dope dealers, where teletypes chattered and mysterious machines spat out stinky-smelling wire photos. On either side of the wire room were the copy desks of the two papers, and then the desks of editors and reporters receded into the distance in both directions, until when you got to the corners where there was Royko at the *Daily News* and me at the *Sun-Times*.

I was in the far southwest corner of our newsroom. This was not a place of honor. It was simply the desk that was empty the day I went to work for *Midwest* magazine, which was the paper's rotogravure supplement. (Words like "rotogravure" summon up a whole lost world of journalism.) Our paper's stars were all right there in the same room. Eppie Lederer, who wrote the Ann Landers column, sat at the same kind of desk I had. I went to work for the paper in September of 1966, not long after Royko's column, which had appeared on an op-ed page, was moved to the page 3 position of honor.

Everybody talked about Royko. He was good. He was good in a way that other reporters knew was good. After work we gathered at the bar at Riccardo's, which was out the back door and down the street (a block from Billy Goat's), and if we hadn't already read the afternoon paper we read it now, reciting lines out loud. I knew him by sight. I'd see him at Ric's or the Goat's, lighting an unfiltered Pall Mall, holding court. I wasn't even full time yet (I was a graduate student at the University of Chicago) and hesitated to approach him.

He was in those years a young man, much younger than I am now. He never seemed like a young man. Like Robert Mitchum or Walter Matthau, he seemed born middle aged, with years of poker games and last calls in his background. He seemed more . . . authentic . . . than the other guys around. He came from different roots. We knew, because he wrote about it, that his father used to run a tavern, that he came from a tough neighborhood. When he wrote about Slats Grobnik, we knew that Slats was not a real person, but in a deeper sense we knew that Slats was more real than most of the businessmen, sports heroes, and politicians who filled up the paper. He was the distilled essence of the guys Mike grew up with, hung around with, fought with, palled around with, feared, kidded, pitied, and got in trouble with. He was real, and he was from Chicago, and when Mrs. Grobnik walked out on Slats' father and took the family to live above the war surplus store and told Slats, "you're the man of the family now," we knew we were hearing echoes of scenes that had shaped Royko and made him grow up quickly.

It was New Year's Day of 1967. Snow was falling—the curtain-raiser for the Great Snow of '67, which paralyzed the city. I was working late on a story. The city room was almost empty. The *Daily News* was emptier. It must have been a Saturday, with the paper not due to publish again until Monday. The ceiling light was on in Royko's corner. He was at work.

"Hi, kid." I looked up and it was Mike Royko. "You got a ride?"

I did not. He said he was driving a borrowed Checker with chains on the tires and would give me a lift. It was just as well. The snow was piling up. First he had to stop at the corner of North and Milwaukee, to pick up a prescription. His family had dealt with that drugstore since he was a kid. We drove through the silent streets. Chicago, having partied the night before, was laying low while the snow built up.

The prescription was not ready. "We'll wait in the eye-opener joint under the tracks," Mike told the druggist. He led the way to a bar so small the bartender could serve every customer without standing up from his stool next to the speed rack and the radio. Mike and I were both a little hung over, and Mike suggested blackberry brandy, a hair of the dog which would also settle the stomach.

Mike told me what an eye-opener was. "This place opens early. The working guys around here, they stop in for a quick shot on their way to the L." He told me that someday I should go next door to the Russian Baths on North Avenue, where, when he was growing up, kids went on

Saturdays with their fathers, since there were no bathtubs at home. This was a bathhouse, steam room, short-order grill, and shot-and-chaser bar that had operated since time immemorial. Mike said Irv, the manager, once interrupted two patrons who were engaging in an activity that became common in San Francisco bathhouses but was then little known on North Avenue. "Irv had an interesting way of putting it," Mike said. "He called it 'playing the piano without any keys.'"

The radio was tuned to the Chicago Blackhawks hockey game. I was from Downstate and had never seen a hockey game. The announcer breathlessly shouted about one goal after another. I started on my second blackberry brandy and my heart soared with the moment. I was under the tracks at North and Milwaukee in an eye-opener joint with Mike Royko, listening to the Blackhawks. I had at last penetrated to the authentic heart of Chicago.

"Jeez, they're scoring like crazy!" I said, after hearing the fourth goal in less than a minute.

"You jerk," said Royko, "that's the replay of the highlights."

Many years passed, but Mike never let me forget that moment. I would not have forgotten it anyway. Mike was the kind of guy that, when you were with him, you knew you ought to remember everything. You didn't wonder what it would have been like to hang out with Damon Runyon or H. L. Mencken, because if you hung out with Mike Royko, you knew you were in the same league.

There are so many Royko stories. I remember the time I went away to report for the draft. There was a farewell party at O'Rourke's. Everybody chipped in for the pizzas and beer. Mike wrote a check for $10—a good sum in 1969. I had rented my apartment, sold my car, and put my books in storage. The next day I left for Urbana to report for induction. They put me on the train back to Chicago, where I flunked the physical. I walked back into O'Rourke's that night. John McHugh from the *Daily News* was at the bar. He had organized the farewell party. "Royko heard you were coming back," he said, "and stopped payment on his check."

In the 1970s Mike wrote a lot of columns about the Fox, an antipollution guerrilla fighter who would race into the lobbies of giant corporations and toss around bags of vile-smelling substances that turned out to be what these corporations were dumping into our lakes and rivers. Mike was asked by CBS to write a Movie of the Week about the Fox, and he enlisted me as his co-writer, since he knew all about the Fox and I knew all about movies.

Our collaboration took place in Mike's corner of the *Daily News* and at Billy Goat's, where we would fill up yellow pads with scene ideas like:

EXT. (NIGHT)
A masked figure slips silently out of a rowboat and approaches a drainage pipe with a Baggie in his gloved hand . . .

The villain of the story was the public relations spokesman for a mega-corporation. Mike thought it would be funny if the villain knew the Fox but didn't know he was the Fox. "They play poker together every Friday night," he said. "That's why the Fox never strikes on Friday. We need a poker scene."

I had written most of the other scenes. Mike said he would write the poker scene. He went into the wire room and got an endless roll of paper from next to one of the AP machines. He put it on the floor behind his typewriter and threaded it through the roller.

"When you get to the end of a page," he said, "you have a temptation to stop. You light up, get a cup of coffee, something like that. This way I will never get to the end of a page."

His poker scene, by my estimation, would have occupied 40 minutes of screen time. It was not usable as a movie scene, but might have made a good one-act play, especially if the audience knew a lot about poker. Mike later used another endless roll of AP paper to write *Boss*, his classic book about Daley the First. He said he had heard that Jack Kerouac wrote *On the Road* the same way.

Mike was a complete columnist. You can see that with the pieces collected in this book. He could write funny and sad, truthful and whimsical, sentimental and nostalgic and angry. He understood local politics like nobody before or since and single-handedly turned the word "alderman" into a noun that was its own adjective. When there was a tragedy in the news, it was Mike's column that summed up how we felt. When politicians were running, they ran away from Mike, who mercilessly deconstructed the banalities of their acceptance speeches and campaign slogans.

Because Mike was Mike, he got stories nobody else got, because when a weird story came along, people just naturally called Mike about it. That explains one of my favorite columns from this book, about the strange men catching Grant Park pigeons for food. Readers would write Mike about these columns, usually indignant, and that would provide another column. (I am glad this book includes a selection of his exchanges with readers.)

Mike had a wonderful way of deflating pomposity. At a time when wine snobbery was at its peak, Mike supplied a helpful column advising readers what to do when the wine steward offers the cork for inspection: "Salt it lightly and eat it. This will cleanse the palate." Mike's ideas about cuisine were more basic and led to his famous barbeque competition, which inspired the Taste of Chicago. There was also his penny-pitching competition. With these events you got the sense of the grinning kid inside Mike Royko: the kid who says, come out and play with me and we'll get away with stuff.

When the *Daily News* folded, Mike's heart was broken. He wrote the headline story on the front page of the last edition. The *Sun-Times* spread out to occupy the entire fourth floor. Mike stayed in his cubicle for awhile, but with the extra space all the other columnists now got real offices. (Eppie left for hers kicking and screaming that she wanted to stay in the city room.) Mike finally took an office too, squirreled away on the side across from the IBM building. His decision to move to an office had more to do with being able to smoke than anything else. The paper's no-smoking rules, he explained, ended at his door. It was here that he acquired his own computer terminal, although for a long time he continued to type his columns on paper, assigning his Leg Persons to type them into the system. I am not sure I ever saw Mike actually typing on a computer, although I must have.

Mike worked at the *Sun-Times* until Rupert Murdoch bought the paper in late 1983. Mike had been involved in backstage negotiations which would have allowed James Hoge, the publisher of the *Daily News* and *Sun-Times*, to buy the paper. Marshall Field, who owned half the paper, said he was willing to sell to them, but Murdoch offered $10 million more than the Hoge group could raise, and Marshall's brother, Ted, insisted they take it.

This was a great blow to Mike. He went home and had a few drinks, and when the local TV stations brought their cameras into his den, he announced that a Murdoch paper was "not fit to wrap fish in."

The next afternoon I sat with him at Billy Goat's.

"I guess I resigned, huh?" he said, with that grin.

"I don't think Murdoch cares what you say about him," I said.

"It's not what I said about him," Mike said. "It's that after describing a Murdoch paper that way, how can I stay there?"

So he went across the street to the *Tribune*, which to my way of thinking was the wrong place for him. Mike was always happiest when he was working for a scrappy underdog. The *Daily News* and *Sun-Times* readers were his allies; the *Tribune*'s readers were his targets.

Whether at the *Tribune*, the *Sun-Times*, or the *Daily News*, Mike Royko wrote the best piece in town just about every day he wrote a column. How did Mike get up day after day, year after year, and create such wonderful prose, each sentence seemingly so simple, the final effect so subtle and funny—or profound? I don't know. But I know it took not only genius, but courage and determination. And a sense of humor.

To read these columns again is to have Mike back again, nudging, chuckling, wincing, deflating pomposity, sticking up for the little guy, defending good ideas against small-minded people. Most of them are timeless. I once suggested to the *Sun-Times* that since the paper owns the copyrights on a lot of this material, and since Murdoch and his fish-wrappers have long since departed the scene, the paper should just start reprinting Mike, one a day. That would be the first page I would turn to.

Roger Ebert

INTRODUCTION

The first book of Mike Royko's columns published after his death in 1997 was Mike's idea. He had asked his wife, Judy, to produce it in case he did not survive brain surgery. The result was *One More Time,* a collection of 110 columns culled from more than 7,000 that he wrote during his illustrious newspaper career. This second book sprang from the enthusiastic response to the first. Mike's fans—newcomers to the fold as well as his legions of longtime readers—told us, in effect: "For the love of Mike—we want more."

A group of Mike's close friends and his son David helped Judy compile *One More Time.* Rereading Royko was a joy for all of us who worked on that book. We heard his voice again, entertaining and dazzling us and provoking us to see and think in fresh ways. But the process was torturous, too. How could we pick only 110 columns from thousands of masterful little essays spanning 34 years and call them "the best"? Of course, we wound up with hundreds of others that just as easily fit that description. So, when readers of *One More Time* asked for more, we were ready to do it again.

We began with favorite columns that we couldn't squeeze into the first book. Then the three of us once again read all 7,000-plus, plucking gems that had slipped through the first time around. We also decided on a different organizational pattern. *One More Time* presented columns in chronological order, providing a panorama of America during the Royko decades—its political and social and cultural highs and lows, as interpreted by this unique Chicago-style genius. This new collection is built around Mike's favorite themes, topics he returned to again and again because they enraged him or touched him deeply. Or, in the case of the chapter we call "Brainstorms," simply because they inspired him to madcap flights of fancy.

One of Mike's favorite topics was Mike himself: his formidable nose, his graying hair, his aching back, his boyhood and his fatherhood. He seemed obsessed with revealing what he didn't like about himself—usually hilariously, but also with a touching melancholy. Thus the chapter "Here's Looking at Me, Kid."

And, naturally, we have Mike the long-suffering Cub fan. Mike the bemused observer of Chicago aldermen and other peculiar political creatures local, national, and international. Mike the quintessential hometown patriot. Typically, he did not express his love of Chicago by saying he loved Chicago, but by hurling the most dreadful insults at virtually every other part of the United States of America.

The familiar buddies that roamed Mike's mind through the decades also roam this book. There is his playmate and, later, his barmate Slats Grobnik. Dr. I. M. Kookie, the expert in lots of stuff. The eternally depressed Wally the Worrier. And the poet laureate of Roykodom, Willie Hyena. There is even a buddy who actually exists: Sam Sianis, owner of Billy Goat Tavern.

Mike Royko did not become the most honored columnist in the country simply by making people laugh, though he had no peers in that respect. It was his rage against injustice—as practiced by bigots of any shade, brainless bureaucrats, big shots lording over little guys, nation abusing nation—that built his reputation and kept it strong and honorable. These themes are represented in several chapters in this book, beginning with the voting rights struggle in the South in the mid-1960s to racial profiling in a tony Chicago suburb in the mid-1990s.

Mike had a penchant for spotting injustice where conventional wisdom missed it; thus our chapter "Now, Wait a Minute." He was so sensitive, in fact, that occasionally he found it in the most peculiar situations. How else can we explain his deep sympathy for short-legged boy dogs tripping through deep Chicago snow? Or his inordinate fury at people who put ketchup on hot dogs?

Mike's fans told us there was something they missed in *One More Time:* his periodic columns titled "Letters, Calls, Complaints, and Great Thoughts from Readers." He enjoyed printing the most venomous of these comments; kind words rarely appeared. And then he delighted in topping the put-downs. This time, we attached a number of reader reactions to the appropriate columns, insults outrageously intact.

We are grateful to the rest of the group who worked on *One More Time* for providing the foundation for this book: David Royko, Hanke Gratteau, Rick Soll, Pam Zekman, Ellen Warren, Wade Nelson, Morgan Powell,

James Warren, Janan Hanna, and Clarence Petersen. The idea of including excerpts under the heading "Hey, Mike, Whaddaya Think About . . ." came from Mike's friend Rick Kogan, who extracted many of them.

As with *One More Time*, we thank John Tryneski, executive editor at the University of Chicago Press, for his guidance and enthusiasm. And, once again, we are grateful to the *Chicago Sun-Times* for allowing us to reprint columns and photographs from 1965 through 1983, when Mike worked for the *Chicago Daily News* and the *Sun-Times*, and to the *Chicago Tribune* for permission to reprint columns and photographs beginning in 1984, when Mike joined the *Tribune*.

And a special thank you to the distinguished Chicago journalist M. W. Newman, whose work Mike greatly admired. It was Bill Newman who, upon hearing that we were preparing another Royko collection, gave us the title. So here, for the love of Mike, are more of Royko's best.

Judy Royko
Lois Wille
Wayne Wille

BRAINSTORMS

HEY, MIKE, WHADDAYA THINK ABOUT . . .

Teenagers?

The finest teenager I ever knew was Slats Grobnik, who devoted his formative years to useless activities. . . . He knew that in a few short years he would have to go out and get a job and begin doing something useful. And, on his 40th birthday, he did. As Slats always said about work: "If it's so good, how come they have to pay you to do it?"

—*Chicago Sun-Times,* February 7, 1982

Happiness?

Show me somebody who is always smiling, always cheerful, always optimistic, and I will show you somebody who hasn't the faintest idea what the heck is really going on.

—*Chicago Tribune,* March 17, 1987

How Slats Lost His Cymbals

Many people were shocked by the recent news report of the two base-ball players who swapped their wives, their children—*even their dogs*. They see it as still another example of our new, loose morality.

That may be. But it isn't the first time such a thing has happened.

I remember a slightly similar incident involving the Grobnik family, who used to live in my old neighborhood.

The cause of it all was Slats Grobnik, the eldest son.

One day he decided to join the alderman's marching boys band, which played in his parades and rallies and also threw stones at win-dows displaying pictures of his opponent.

The alderman had been Slats' hero ever since his father had said the man never worked a day in his life.

Because of his peculiar ear for music, Slats was given the cymbals to play. He rushed home and immediately began practicing. He hoped that if he did well, the alderman would let him play something else, such as the horses.

Mr. Grobnik was working nights at the time, so when Slats began marching through the flat, clanging the cymbals, he came roaring out of bed.

He hit Slats on the head with one of the cymbals, causing the boy's eyes to roll even more than they usually did.

This touched off a terrible row, with Mrs. Grobnik crying that her husband should not stifle Slats' musical development.

That was when Mr. Grobnik said he would like to swap his family.

"I would trade all of you for a little peace and quiet," he shouted, hit-ting Mrs. Grobnik with a cymbal, too.

"Ma, you can get alimony," Slats yelled. "I will be your witness."

Mrs. Grobnik gathered her clothes and children and said she was leaving and would not return until Mr. Grobnik apologized.

At first, Mr. Grobnik could not believe they were really gone. To make sure, he changed the locks. Then he want back to bed.

Mrs. Grobnik took the children and went around the corner to stay with her friend Ruby Peak, who had a nice apartment above the war-surplus store.

"Now you are the man of the family," Mrs. Grobnik tearfully told Slats. He turned pale, thinking that meant he might have to go to work.

Word of the breakup quickly spread through the neighborhood. Naturally, some of the unattached women set their caps for Mr. Grobnik. They didn't get anywhere with him, though, because he didn't like women who wore caps.

The shapely widow who ran the corner bakery hurried over with some fresh sweet rolls for him.

And as Mr. Grobnik ate them, she leaned forward and whispered huskily in his ear:

"Is there anything else you would like?"

"Yeah," he said, "next time bring a loaf of rye."

When Slats' teacher heard of the separation, she worried that he might suffer a trauma.

The next day he came to class with tears streaming down his face.

The teacher assumed it had something to do with his home life. Actually, somebody in the school yard had told a filthy joke, and Slats had laughed until he cried.

She put her arm around him and said: "There, there."

Slats said: "Where, where?" and gave her a pinch.

She ordered him from the room, which didn't bother Slats, as he figured he had learned enough for one day.

A few days after the separation, old Mrs. Novak asked Slats what his mother was doing.

"She is going to Reno," Slats said.

He didn't know what that meant, but he had heard someone say it in a movie.

Old Mrs. Novak didn't know what it meant either. She figured it must mean Mrs. Grobnik had run off with a man named Reno.

So she went to the grocery store and told all the other ladies about it.

"I'll bet he is a no-good gigolo," one of them said.

That afternoon, they all told their husbands that Mrs. Grobnik was carrying on with Mr. Reno, a notorious gigolo.

The husbands discussed it in the tavern. One of them said: "I think I know the guy. He lives over in the Italian neighborhood."

Another said: "I know the one. He has a mustache and hangs out in the pool hall."

When Mr. Grobnik stopped for a beer, they told him his wife was in love with a notorious pool shark and fortune hunter named Reno, who had a mustache and pointy shoes.

"Everybody in the neighborhood knows about it," the bartender said. "I hear she has even sold her wedding ring to give him money."

Enraged, Mr. Grobnik went to the pool hall and punched the first man he saw wearing a mustache. He turned out to be a jukebox distributor, and three of his boys beat Mr. Grobnik with pool cues.

When Mr. Grobnik came to in the hospital, his wife and children were at his bedside. Mrs. Grobnik said she would come back home and make Slats give up the cymbals.

"Will you stay away from Reno?" Mr. Grobnik said.

"But Reno is in Nevada," said Mrs. Grobnik.

Mr. Grobnik smiled. "Good. I must have really taught him a lesson."

MARCH 13, 1980

Vegas in Akron?

The political commercial has become the means by which most voters are exposed to candidates and their views.

Thus, the commercials and what they say have grown to major importance in modern American politics.

Today, someone like Abraham Lincoln could never get away with beginning his message: "Four score and seven years ago, our forefathers brought forth. . . ."

Instead, his TV advisers would insist that he stick to a slogan like: "A tall man for a tall job."

Because of their importance, throughout this election year I will be analyzing the TV commercials of the major candidates, unless they all lose in the primaries and drop out.

I'll begin by looking at George Bush's most widely shown commercial.

This is the one in which Bush, who is chasing the Republican nomination for president, is shown grabbing hands and saying, "We can turn this country around."

In analyzing this commercial, I've sought opinions from a panel of experts, including an engineer, a sociologist, an economist, and a political scientist.

First, the opinion of the engineer:

Is it possible to turn this country around?

"Sure. We have the technology, the know-how, but it would be an expensive job. Remember, this is a very big country—about 3,000 miles by 2,000 miles. And it's quite heavy, depending on how far down you want to go. So, it's not as simple as turning a piece of furniture around."

How would we go about it?

"We'd have to figure out a way to jack up the whole country, then slowly turn it like a Lazy Susan. It would be tricky business because you couldn't spin it too fast or everyone living along the edges would go flying right off into the oceans or Mexico and Canada."

Sounds difficult.

"Turning a country around would be difficult. Remember, some regions are heavier than others, such as the mountains, so you'd have to be careful not to let them tilt or you could have lakes spilling out and causing all kinds of a sloppy mess."

But it could be done?

"A country that can put a man on Mars can do anything."

But we haven't put a man on Mars.

"Whatever."

Next, we talked to the sociologist.

What would the impact be on people if we turned the country around?

"There would be a very great sociological upheaval. For example, take all those little old Jewish ladies living in Miami Beach. After we turned the country around, they'd be way up in the Pacific Northwest—possibly where Vancouver, Canada, is. One day they'd wake up and find themselves up to their behinds in snow, bears, and pine trees. Oh, that would shake them up, all right."

I would think so.

"Yes, and Southern California would be where New England is. You'd have thousands of unwary sun creatures going out surfing and freezing into tanned chunks of ice."

And New York?

"If we turned the country around, New York would be where California is. I imagine the trauma of being 'laid back' instead of manic-manic would cause mass trauma among the New Yorkers. They'd be confused. Wouldn't know whether to mug someone or offer him a bite of granola."

What about Chicago, Detroit, Milwaukee, and other northern industrial cities?

"It would be a dramatic change because these northern cities would become southern cities. Naturally, many of you would cease being northern ethnics and would become hillbillies, crackers, and cajuns. We'd have southerners named Bubba Bajonski, Billy Joe Caputo, and Joe Bob Weinstein."

A strange change, I reckon.

"Turning the country around would put Texas where Minnesota is, and that would be interesting because you would have Canadians instead of Mexicans sneaking across the Texas border."

Would we call them coldbacks?

"Maybe. And because Minnesota would be where Texas is, you'd have cowboys named Sven and Ole."

Then we talked to the economist.

George Bush wants to turn the country around. What would the economic impact be?

"Turning the country around would have great economic impact because we would have a new Sun Belt. People would be rushing to live in Newark, N.J., because it would be warm and semi-tropical, but San Diego would become a grimy, depressed northeastern city. Las Vegas would wind up being somewhere around Akron, and all those call girls and card dealers would have to be trained to make rubber tires."

What else?

"Turning the country around would mean that future Rose Bowl parades would be held in the Bronx, while gang-bangers would be running wild in Pasadena."

Finally, we questioned the political scientist.

Why do you think George Bush wants to turn the country around?

"Probably because he thinks he would have a better chance of winning the South if the South became the North. And he might do better in California if New York became California. On the other hand, Reagan would do poorly in New York, since it would become California. It's a very interesting strategy."

What long-range effect would it have on the country's politics?

"The most significant change of turning the country around would be that San Francisco would wind up being where Washington, D.C., is."

What would that mean?

"We'd probably have a gay president."

SEPTEMBER 24, 1980

Jay's Bottom Line

I don't understand why Jay McMullen, husband and press secretary to Mayor Jane Byrne, is so upset at being quoted about his wife's legs and behind.

He has been angrily sputtering—and nobody angrily sputters better than Jay—because *People* magazine said that he bragged that our mayor has "great legs and a great little ass."

"That quote was demeaning, vulgar, and false," says McMullen. And he vows that he is going to write to *People* and demand a complete retraction.

He also said the magazine was just trying to make him look like a "raffish character."

Well, maybe so. But what is wrong with looking like a raffish character? In trying to look like raffish characters, American men spend hundreds of millions of dollars a year on hairpieces, urban cowboy clothes, disco lessons, imported sports cars, aviator glasses, tailored jogging suits or jump suits, health club memberships, and sex manuals.

And after all that trouble and expense, most of them just look tired.

Rather than protesting, McMullen should be feeling proud of himself.

The fact is, one of the saddest developments in our modern society has been the deterioration of traditional family life.

There are many reasons for this, but the most important has been the high divorce rate.

And why do so many people get divorced?

Because not enough men say: "My wife has great legs and a great little ass."

It's strange, but men are always offering eloquent testimonials—in the form of leers, hoots, grunts, lip-smacking, and creatively obscene remarks—to the fine legs and bottoms of other men's wives, or those of airline stewardesses, secretaries, waitresses, females on the street, and ladies in TV pantyhose commercials.

Next to sports, the most common topics of conversation among married men are the legs, bottoms, tops, and other parts of females who aren't their wives.

But what do they say to each other about their own wives? They say: "I better get home or she'll be on my back."

And when talking to their wives, they limit themselves to such remarks as:

- "Shhhh. It's third and one for the Bears on the five-yard line. We can talk during half-time."
- "Shhhh. It's the half-time highlights. We can talk after the game."
- "You seen my blue shirt?"
- "Don't forget to take the car in for a tune-up."
- "Is my suit back from the cleaners?"
- "We're out of beer."
- "Where's the paper?"
- "While you're up, get me a beer."
- "While you're up, switch to channel 4."
- "While you're up, adjust the color."
- "Send out for pizza."
- "Set the clock."

It's little wonder that more and more married women are packing a bag and setting out to find their identities, independence, and a little whoopie.

But it wouldn't happen nearly so often if more married men were like McMullen and publicly praised their wives' shanks and bottoms.

If you are a married man, ask yourself what you say to your wife when you arrive home. Do you ever walk in the door, point a finger at her, and declare that she has a great set of legs and a great behind?

Probably not. If you are like most men, you say: "What's for supper?"

When you are sitting around at a party, and there is a lull in the conversation, do you ever nod in your wife's direction and say: "Have you folks ever noticed that my wife here has a great set of legs and a great little ass?"

Of course you don't. What you probably say is: "I'll just have one more for the road. You drive."

When you introduce your wife to some friends from work, or clients, or golf buddies, I don't suppose you ever say: "This is my wife. As you will probably notice, she has a great set of legs and a great little ass."

Probably not. Instead you say: "This is the wife. Why don't you get us a drink?"

Or have you ever, in a spontaneous moment of exuberance and pride, stood on your porch or leaned out of your window and shouted for every neighbor or passerby to hear: "Listen to me, everyone: My wife has a great set of legs and a nice little aaaassssss!"?

Believe me, she would be delighted. Or if not delighted, at least surprised.

We would have a much happier and stable society if more men did as McMullen denies doing.

And instead of denying the quote, McMullen should admit to it and maybe even make it part of city policy. They could draft a resolution declaring a "Tell Your Wife She Has Great Legs and Ass Week in Chicago."

Also, I would caution Jay against demanding a retraction from *People* magazine. If they give him a retraction, it will probably come out saying something like this:

"In our September 29 issue, Jay McMullen, husband and press secretary to Chicago Mayor Jane Byrne, was quoted as saying that his wife has great legs and a great little ass. Mr. McMullen denies making that statement."

Then some other magazine will notice that item and will carry a story of its own, saying: "Jay McMullen, husband and press secretary of Chicago Mayor Byrne, has emphatically stated that Mayor Byrne *does not* have great legs or a great little ass."

Then some gossip columnist will notice that and will run an item saying: "Why is Jay McMullen saying nasty things about Jane Byrne's figure?"

Then Jane Byrne will read it and say: "Jay, don't you love me anymore?"

And then she'll say the saddest thing a wife can say to her husband: "You're fired."

SEPTEMBER 30, 1980

Letters, Calls, Complaints, and Great Thoughts from Readers

NORMA SMITH, St. Joseph, Mich.: Regarding your column on Jay McMullen's remarks about Mayor Byrne's legs and bottom: Modern women crave comments on their intelligence and creative talents. I know I do.

I think anatomy compliments are just a touch old-fashioned.

COMMENT: You're probably right. So the next time I want to pay a compliment to a modern woman, I'll say: "Hi, doll—you got a nice set of frontal lobes."

THERESA NOVAK, Chicago: I was very disturbed to read your column about what Jay McMullen said about Mayor Byrne's figure. I was disturbed because you repeatedly used the word "ass," and my 10-year-old son read it. I heard him laughing and asked him what was so funny and he showed it to me.

I don't appreciate that kind of language being in the paper where a little boy can read it and start thinking that this is a proper way to talk.

Couldn't you have used a— instead of spelling the word out? I think that if you had used a— instead of the full word, everybody would have known what you meant, and it wouldn't have been as offensive.

Please, I don't like smut in my daily paper.

COMMENT: On the other hand, if I had used a—, some people might have thought McMullen had said that his wife "has a great little axe." And people are nervous enough as it is without thinking that they might be beheaded.

NOVEMBER 27, 1980

Pilgrims' Progress

A woman strolling through Grant Park on a recent Sunday was horrified to see two men stalking pigeons.

One man would throw some bread crumbs on the ground to lure the pigeons to him.

When the pigeons gathered, the other man would sneak up on them and slam a long-handled fishing net over one or two of them. Then he would stuff them into a canvas sack.

"They caught more than a dozen pigeons just while I was watching," the woman said.

She asked the men what they were doing. Neither man spoke much English and had difficulty understanding her. But finally one of them smiled happily, pointed at the sack, and said: "Eat, eat!"

"Can you imagine?" the woman said. "They were catching the pigeons to eat them. It's unbelievable."

Not really. People have been snatching pigeons out of the parks and eating them ever since there were pigeons in the parks.

The police say the practice has always been most popular among more recent European-born immigrants and some Asians who eat pigeons in their homeland.

When I told the woman that, she said: "Then it must be illegal. And isn't it unhealthy? I mean, they're such filthy little things."

No, it is not illegal to catch and eat a city pigeon unless it happens to be someone's trained homing pigeon. And in that case, it's doubtful that the owner would know you had eaten his trained homing pigeon. Besides, if the little bugger doesn't have enough sense to go home, then he has to face the consequences.

I asked the Chicago Park District's main office if there is any law against catching pigeons, and spokesman Ben Bentley said: "The pigeons go in the park, but we're not responsible for them. We have enough to worry about with muggers without trying to keep an eye on the pigeons."

As for their being unhealthy, that is not true. The city's health department says that there is nothing harmful about eating a city pigeon, so long as you remember to remove its feathers first. And don't swallow the bones. Or the beak.

"Oh, my God, that's terrible," said the squeamish woman who brought this matter to my attention. "They're like pets—little tame things. How can anyone eat something that's almost a pet?"

I'm sure many people share her feelings. And I find their attitude ridiculous. What's wrong with eating something that's like a pet? People do it all the time.

After all, many people keep tropical fish or goldfish in their homes. They feed them, make sure they have enough air bubbles in the tank, and change the water. These fish are treated as pets.

But those same people will go to a restaurant and eat fried smelts, although these little creatures are just as cute and wiggly as their tropical fish.

People eat ducks all the time, although the duck is, in my opinion, a far more likable bird than the city pigeon. All a duck wants to do is paddle happily around a lake, sticking its rear end up every so often, just like a tourist.

Yet, people who might cringe at the idea of eating a Grant Park pigeon will eagerly plunge their teeth into the dead body of a poor little ducky-wuck.

Or consider the lamb. You won't ever run into a more pleasant, even-tempered, friendly, pet-like beastie than a lamb. There is no record in all of history of a lamb ever attacking a human being. All they do is go baa. Lambs are quite decent.

Compare the temperament of the lamb to that of the cat. Cats are really vicious. They kill little birds, squirrels, tiny mice, and anything else that is defenseless. If a cat doesn't like your looks, he'll sink his claws into your arm. My elderly aunts all swore that if you dared sleep with a cat in the house, he would surely pluck out your jugular vein some dark night. Cats give people the evil eye.

Lambs never do any of those terrible things. But people are always eating lambs. They eat their ribs and shanks and all different parts of the little dears.

Yet, these same lamb-devouring people would turn green if you suggested that they eat a cat.

I don't see why. I've never eaten a cat. At least, not yet. But there are some parts of the world in which cats are eaten when they are available.

They're supposed to taste pretty good, if prepared properly, although I still haven't found a cookbook with a recipe for cats.

Don't misunderstand me. I'm not recommending that anybody go to Grant Park and catch themselves a Thanksgiving dinner, although there are many excellent recipes for pigeon—and I assume that you would cook up a city pigeon the same way as a commercial bird.

Nor do I recommend that anyone eat a cat—theirs or anyone else's. Whether one eats a cat or not is a personal choice, and I don't want to sway anyone one way or another.

But if you do, there is one obvious cooking tip: Always remember to remove the bell from the cat's collar before cooking. You don't want to make a tinkling noise every time you burp.

JUNE 3, 1981

Love Lost in Lingo

He was staring morosely into his beer and every so often he'd sigh deeply. The bartender was too smart to ask him what the problem was. But I wasn't.

What's bothering you? I asked.

He shook his head and said: "I just ended a . . . we just ended . . ." And his voice choked and cracked.

Ended what?

"We ended . . . a . . . relationship."

A relationship?

"Yeah. She broke off our . . . relationship."

I bought him a beer, advised him not to let life wear him down, and quickly moved on.

I'm not without sympathy, but I hate the word "relationship." If he had told me he had suffered a shattered romance or a broken love affair, I'd have stuck around and endured the boredom. But I refuse to listen to someone blubber about a "relationship."

What an awful word. It's the kind of sterile word used by lawyers and sociologists and other menaces.

Exactly when the word relationship began being used as a substitute for romance or love affair, I don't know. But that's the way people talk now.

And not only does it sound like something out of this impersonal, computerized, digital, credit card era, but what does it rhyme with?

That's the real question. Try to rhyme relationship with something. Battleship? Landing strip? Broken hip? Scholarship?

With words like that, how are we ever going to have schmaltzy poems and heart-plunking love songs? And with them, someday the ultimate romantic statement will be: "Your place or mine?" Maybe it is already.

Sure, you can string together a few words like relationship. But can you imagine anyone ever saying "They're playing our song" when they hear: "We started our relationship on a landing strip, while watching a Messerschmitt fly by"?

If the word relationship had been in use over the years, I hate to even think about the kind of popular love songs we would have been hearing.

How about this:

"I'm in the mood for a relationship, simply because you're near me."

Or: "You've got to give a little, take a little, and let your poor heart break a little: That's the story of, that's the glory of a relationship."

How about the classic "Star Dust"? "Tho' I dream in vain, in my heart it will remain: My star dust melody, the memory of relationship's refrain."

From the Beatles we would have: "Yesterday, relationship was such an easy game to play; now I need a place to hide away. Oh, I believe in yesterday." Or: "And I relate to her. . . . A relationship like ours could never die, as long as I have you near me."

I could go on and on. So I will:

- "Fish got to swim and birds got to fly, I got to have a relationship with one man till I die, can't help relatin' to that man of mine."

- "I can't give you anything but a relationship, baby, that's the only thing I've plenty of, baby."
- "Oh, how we danced on the night we were wed, we vowed our true relationship, though a word wasn't said."
- "You made me relate to you, I didn't want to do it, I didn't want to do it."
- "What the world needs now is relationship, sweet relationship. It's the only thing there's just too little of."
- "Relationship is a many-splendored thing."
- "When the moon hits your eye like a big pizza pie, that's a relationship. When the world seems to shine like you've had too much wine, that's a relationship."
- "On a day like today, we passed the time away writing relationship letters in the sand. Now my poor heart just aches, with every wave that breaks over relationship letters in the sand."

Then there's another phrase. "Significant Other." It is now used by many people to describe the other party in a relationship. It has become a substitute for words like girlfriend, boyfriend, etc.

You could really make some heart-tugging songs out of "significant other."

How about this? "Let me call you significant other, I'm relating to you. Let me hear you whisper that you're relating to me, too."

There's the oldie: "Five feet two, eyes of blue . . . but could she relate, could she woo, could she, could she, could she coo—has anybody seen my significant other?"

And there's the old juke box favorite: "You Are My Sunshine," which would sound like this: "You are my significant other, my only significant other, you make me happy when skies are gray. You'll never know, dear, how much I relate to you. Please don't take my significant other away."

One thing I forgot to ask the guy in the bar: When his significant other ended their relationship, did she at least osculate him goodbye?

FEBRUARY 20, 1987
A Devilish Night for Oral Roberts

I don't know how the Reverend Oral Roberts puts up with it. If it isn't one thing, it's another.

Just the other night, he was on TV describing a terrifying experience he had in his own bedroom.

"The devil came to my room," he said, "and I felt those hands on my throat, and he was choking the life out of me. I yelled to my wife, 'Honey, come.'"

His wife rushed into the room.

"She laid her hands on me and rebuked the devil," Roberts said, "and commanded the devil to get out of my room. I began to breathe and came out of my bed strong."

That shows how lucky a man is to have a wife with good hearing—especially one who can rebuke the devil and make the nasty bugger take a walk. Some lazy woman might have slept through the whole thing.

Roberts told this story to show how difficult his life has been since he revealed that God has been putting the arm on him to raise money.

As many of us know, some weeks ago the TV preacher revealed that God had warned him that if Roberts didn't raise $8 million for worthy causes by the end of March, he would die.

That kind of deadline can't be an easy thing to live with. It's one thing to get a computerized letter from American Express saying that you are a week overdue in paying for your high-living follies.

Or to have a bartender walk over and say: "I got these chits you signed the other night when you were in here and bought drinks for all those . . . uh . . . you remember. You wanna square it?"

But it's something else when God himself tells you to come up with eight really big ones *or else*.

Making it even worse were those who doubted Roberts. Other preachers said God is not an extortionist, God is not a terrorist, God doesn't tell TV preachers to raise money or die.

This led me to urge people to withhold their contributions. As much as I admire Roberts, I had to point out that if he fails to raise the money and drops dead on March 31, he will prove the skeptics wrong and cause a mass conversion of atheists, agnostics, and other wandering souls.

But now we have this new element: Roberts being choked in his bedroom by the devil.

How much, I ask, can a man be expected to tolerate?

On the one hand, he has God telling him to hustle his TV congregation for eight mill or be wafted off to heaven.

Now, $8 million isn't what it used to be, but it's still a tidy sum. And it's not like Roberts is Ivan Boesky and can run a scam on a bunch of

Wall Street chumps. He has to depend on the kindness of little old ladies watching TV in boardinghouses.

Many of them don't have checking accounts. They have to totter to the currency exchange to get money orders.

So there is poor Oral, counting up all these little money orders, with God peeking over his shoulder, poised to zap him.

That's pressure.

And after a hard day, what does he get? He goes home, eats dinner, tells his wife, "Don't worry, we've still got more than a month," and turns in for a good night's sleep.

Under these trying circumstances, that's the least a preacher is entitled to: a good night's sleep.

But, as John Belushi would have said: "Nooooooooo."

He wakes up in the middle of the night, and there is the devil squeezing his throat.

I could understand how someone with a weaker spirit might say: "Hey, I've had it with the preacher business. Starting tomorrow, I sell used cars."

And who could blame him? I've known corporate creatures who had nervous breakdowns because they weren't promoted from fourth vice president to third vice president.

Here we have a man who is being threatened by God with death—just when the golf season is starting—and along comes the devil choking him in his bedroom.

Roberts didn't say how he knew it was the devil. Assuming he doesn't use a night light, I would think that most furtive characters who choke you in your bed would look alike.

Maybe it was just a neighborhood mugger.

But I'll take his word that it was the devil. Maybe the guy's eyes glowed in the dark, which would be a tip-off.

I'm just glad that his wife was there to rebuke the devil. I just wish he had said what form the rebuke took.

Under the circumstances, does a wife say: "You nasty thing, you, take your hands off my husband's throat. Are you some kind of pervert?"

With five or six weeks before God's deadline, who knows what will happen next. Demons with pitchforks in the breakfast nook? Underworld fiends in the dining room?

It isn't easy being Oral Roberts or his wife.

Maybe they ought to buy a big mean dog.

Letters, Calls, Complaints, and Great Thoughts from Readers

HAL BERGEN, Longmont, Col.: In reference to your Oral Roberts columns. Are you aware of what God's word says will be done to a man who has done what you did when you wrote about this chosen vessel of the Lord?

Mark my word, I am not putting a jinx on you, but you are in for nothing but trouble unless you apologize and ask His forgiveness.

COMMENT: Roberts has said that God warned him that he'd expire by March 31 if he doesn't raise enough money, that a 900-foot Jesus appeared and talked to him, and that the devil popped up in his bedroom and was choking the life out of him until his wife came to his rescue. And you think I've got problems? He ought to find another line of work before he gets in real trouble.

MRS. E. J. HARWOOD, Winston-Salem, N.C.: Before you write another column about Oral Roberts, I want you to ask yourself this question:

If you were at the gates of Heaven and were asked why you should be allowed in, what would you say?

COMMENT: I haven't thought about it. But do you think if I said "Candy-gram," they might fall for it?

BRUCE SMITH, Fergus Falls, Mich.: I have been reading with mixed interest your recent comments concerning Oral Roberts' attempts to raise $8 million by March 31. You failed to mention that Oral Roberts built from nothing a fully accredited university and a major medical center.

How many people have you helped in your lifetime? It seems the only things you can write about with any expertise are drunks, whores, booze, pimps, crap games, and crooked politicians.

COMMENT: Hah! You left out grave robbers, so the laugh's on you.

A Word About Debate "Poopery"

Like many Chicagoans who watched the mayoral candidates debate, I was puzzled by a strange new word used by Mayor Harold Washington.

The word was "poopery." The mayor used it twice, referring to a poopery of tax proposals.

Because I had never heard the word "poopery" before, I looked in my dictionary to see what it meant. In fact, I looked in several dictionaries.

I was surprised to find that it was not listed. So I asked a co-worker, who has a degree in English, if he knew what "poopery" meant.

"Sounds to me like it might be some kind of fancy outhouse," he said. "You might ask somebody who lived on a farm."

I doubted that the mayor would be discussing outhouses during the debate, but in this campaign, you never know.

So I called an acquaintance who had been reared on a farm and asked him if they had referred to their outhouse as a poopery.

"First of all," he said, "we did not have an outhouse. And if we did, we would definitely not have called it a poopery. My guess is that a poopery is what they call a washroom in the gay bars."

Pursuing that suggestion, I called a gay publication. The young man who answered the phone said: "If that's some kind of April Fool joke, it isn't funny," and hung up.

Someone else suggested that it might be another word for a cat's litter box. Someone else said it might have something to do with a child's potty training.

None of that applied to anything I heard in the debate. On the other hand, maybe it did.

Anyway, I finally did what I should have done in the first place: I called an aide to the mayor and asked what a poopery was.

"A what?" he asked.

I repeated it.

"Is that something Vrdolyak or some other alderman called us?"

I explained that the mayor had used the word during the debate.

"He did? Poopery? How is that spelled?"

Just the way it sounds.

"Naw."

Yes, he did. I heard it twice, and I have it on tape. He said "poopery."

"Let me check and I'll call you back."

In a few minutes the phone rang and he said: "The word the mayor used was—I'll spell it—P-O-T-P-O-U-R-R-I. That's potpourri."

Aha! That explained it. The mayor had made the mistake of using one of those French words. And, as is often the case when Americans toss around French words to show how erudite they are, he screwed it up.

He had said poopery when he meant to say poe (as in toe) and pyu (as in pee-you) and ree (as in whee).

Poe-pyu-ree, not poopery.

At least, that's how a friend who took high school French explained it to me. But he cautioned: "It's very difficult to write something in French phonetically. The second syllable in that word is sort of between a long O and a U."

That's what I meant when I said that using French words in an American conversation can be disastrous. I don't know how to make a sound somewhere between an O and a U, and I wouldn't want to, unless I was snoring or sick to my stomach.

But the mayor, who loves flaunting his vocabulary, tried to slip a French word past us, and it came out as poopery. Serves him right. Mayor Daley would have fired anybody he suspected of even thinking in French. And if somebody had used the word "poopery" in the presence of ladies, Daley might have ordered his arrest.

After looking up potpourri in the dictionary, I assume that the mayor was using it to mean: "a miscellaneous collection."

So why didn't he just say: "A miscellaneous collection"? If he had, we would have understood what he meant. He could even have said: "A mixed bag," and we would have dug him.

Instead, he had to show off. And the result was that thousands of confused Chicagoans have been pondering the meaning of poopery.

However, since the mayor introduced this new word to the world, we might consider making it part of the vocabulary. It has a certain ring to it. It could be used in a conversation such as this:

"What did you think of the mayoral debate?"

"I thought some of it was pooporious, at times pooperific, and a few moments were pooperendous."

"And your overall reaction?"

"Overall? I'd say it was a lot of poopery."

APRIL 14, 1987

Letters, Calls, Complaints, and Great Thoughts from Readers

ELLA ROBINSON, Chicago: I did not appreciate your picking out one verbal mistake by Mayor Washington and poking fun at it. If there

was any "poopery" in that column, it was in your bad taste and obvious racism.

Members of the white press, such as yourself, should disqualify
yourself from criticizing him. Would you have treated a white mayor
with such disrespect by making fun of his speech?

COMMENT: Would I make fun of the way somebody such as, say,
Mayor Daley spoke? A man who once said that someone reached the
"pinochle of his career" and who never let five minutes pass without
uttering the phrase: "The wunnerful people of dis wunnerful city"?
Never. But if you're serious about my disqualifying myself from ever
criticizing Mayor Washington, I'll do it if you will agree to one thing.
You pay my real estate taxes. Do we have a deal?

MAY 15, 1989

A Smile a Day . . . Can Be Sickening

A clergyman has approached me with an idea he believes will make this
a happier and more peaceful society. He wants all of us to make a habit
of smiling at each other.

As Pastor T. L. Barrett Jr. put it, in his written proposal:

"The major objective of the 'Smile America' concept is to launch a
nationwide campaign, which will inspire, enlighten, and provide the in-
centive for the development of an inevitable consciousness of the ac-
knowledgment of mankind, through a natural, genuine smile."

To remind people to smile, he wants to see the "Smile America" slogan plastered over T-shirts, headbands, bumper stickers, coffee mugs,
and dozens of other products.

And when the nation is thoroughly inundated in "Smile America"
products, and we are all flashing our choppers at each other, he believes
we will all be nicer and the crime rate will go down and we will feel re-
laxed and experience good vibrations.

In sending me his proposal, he said: "I would like you to review it.
Your input would be helpful to me."

I'm afraid that the Reverend Barrett has come to the wrong person
for input on smiling.

As anyone who knows me is aware, I smile only when it is absolutely
necessary and unavoidable, which isn't very often. I have friends of
many years who can't say for certain that I have teeth.

There are many reasons I don't smile. For one thing, smiling is unnatural because it violates the laws of nature.

When you smile, your facial muscles resist gravity. It is far more natural for your face to let gravity do its thing and cause your face to droop. If nature intended us to be smiling all the time, we would have been made with our heads upside down.

So by defying gravity, smiling can be compared to bouncing up and down for no reason, or flapping our arms and trying to fly like a bird or bat. What kind of society would we be if everyone kept bouncing and flapping their arms? Pretty silly-looking, I say.

Also, consider which other earthly creatures smile to show friendliness and happiness, sincere or otherwise.

The answer is none. When a dog or cat or any other beastie pulls back its lips and shows its teeth—an act we call a smile—it means that it is about to chomp on you and you'd better take off.

Only humans show their teeth as an act of friendliness. And even then, you can't be sure of the motive.

Think about it. Which humans smile the most? Politicians, used-car salesmen, quiz-show hosts, and drunken conventioneers, that's who.

Is that who this Reverend Barrett wants the whole country to emulate? Car salesmen, politicians, quiz-show hosts, and drunken conventioneers?

Look through history books and see if you can find one picture of Abe Lincoln smiling. Of course you can't. He knew what was going on, and if you know what's going on, you don't smile much.

On the other hand, turn on your TV and watch David Letterman. He never stops smiling, even when there isn't anything to smile about, which on his show is just about all the time. If you stuck your thumb in Letterman's eye, he'd smile.

So ask yourself: Would you prefer a nation of Abe Lincolns or David Lettermans? (Please don't send me your choice. I'm sure the results would be depressing.)

It might be unfair, but I don't trust people who smile all the time. As Slats Grobnik put it: "Anybody who smiles all the time is hiding something, even if it is only sore feet."

And many scientific surveys have shown that people who are habitual smilers are more inclined to say: "Have a nice day."

This dumb phrase is one of the nation's leading causes of mental stress and depression, because most people will not have a nice day. So after someone tells them to have a nice day, and they have a bad day, they wonder if there is something wrong with them for not having a nice day.

And, of course, they shouldn't blame themselves. Most people get up in the morning and go to work or to school. They buck traffic or wait for a dawdling bus. They confront a demanding boss, a nasty customer, a crabby teacher. They get traffic tickets. They have headaches. They fear getting bald, fat, or wrinkled. They have debts. They see things in store windows that they can't afford. They lose a contact lens or suffer some other tragedy. They go home and find that the puppy has wet the rug.

With all this torment, how can they have a nice day? And why should they go around smiling or tolerating chronic smilers?

They shouldn't. They should do what comes naturally, which is to scowl. You can always trust a scowler. Have you ever walked into a car lot and been sold a lemon by a scowler?

Some sharp-eyed readers have probably noted that in my picture up above, I am smiling. It is a small smile, but a smile nevertheless.

So, you ask, if I am a scowler, why did I smile for the picture?

The photographer made me do it. He told me he had a terrible toothache.

FEBRUARY 16, 1990

There Go Another Wasted Three Pounds

The brain. What an amazing organ. Only three pounds or so in an adult, but containing millions of cells that create and transmit chemicals and electrical impulses controlling virtually everything we do. Every movement and thought. Every emotion. Our senses of hunger, thirst, smell, sight.

Think about that. It was that mere three pounds of gray and white matter in his skull that led Edison to create the phonograph, the light bulb, and thousands of other devices we now take for granted.

From Einstein's three pounds of brain came thoughts that brought about the Atomic Age and opened new concepts of the universe.

The brains of Mozart and Beethoven brought forth sounds that today, centuries after they have died, still move audiences to joy and tears.

The brain of Shakespeare probed man's capacity for good and evil. The brain of Leonardo da Vinci conceived of man flying four centuries before the brains of the Wright brothers made it reality.

Remarkable machines took men to the moon and sustained their lives. But three-pound brains created those machines. We have computers that, in a twinkling, solve mathematical problems that once took weeks, months, or years. But the human brain created the computers.

All around us are soaring skyscrapers, incredible ground and air vehicles, shelf upon shelf of great literature, electronic impulses sending sights and sounds around the world in an instant. Everything from the superconducting supercollider to the humble yet gratifying McDonald's french fry—the products of those three pounds of gray matter in the skull of man.

But how often do most of us think about the brain, except when we have a headache? Many scientists study it, and they've solved many of its mysteries. But still they know only a little of what there is to learn.

The rest of us? Depending on our age and gender, we give far more thought to our biceps, breasts, buttocks, scalps, facial skin, and reproductive organs.

Ask yourself: When was the last time you thought about your brain? Or anyone else's brain, for that matter? Not lately, I'll wager.

And I'm as guilty as anyone. But just the other night I found myself pondering the amazing workings of this most incredible of organs.

It was during Wednesday's blizzard. I was behind the wheel of my car, waiting for the light to turn from red to green, so I could continue my homeward journey.

As I waited, I saw a car creep into the intersection, then stop directly in my path. The female person driving that car stopped because traffic ahead of her was jammed for blocks. She should have known that would happen. But she moved into the intersection anyway, then just sat there.

The light changed. Now it was my turn to go forward. But I couldn't. The man next to me couldn't. The dozens of people behind us couldn't. We just sat because the woman and her car barred our way.

That's when I began thinking about the incredible human brain. Einstein's equation: Energy equals mass times the velocity of light squared. Edison searching the world for a filament that would light our homes and streets. Beethoven's Ninth Symphony, Popiel's Pocket Fisherman.

But there sat this creature, blessed with a three-pound brain mass and those millions of cells. Yet she was incapable of a simple thought: "If I put my foot on the gas and creep a few more yards, I'll stop and when the light changes those people on my left won't get past me." Or a simple question: "I'm not going anywhere anyway, so why should I block their way and make a bad situation even worse?"

The light changed again. And again. But she still couldn't move. That was her bad luck, but why should she make her bad luck my bad luck? And the bad luck of dozens behind me.

Then she glanced to her left and saw me glaring at her. She quickly looked away. I guess the sight of a stranger's bared fangs was unpleasant.

It occurred to me that her brain's problem might be a lack of information. Input, as the computer people call it. I decided to give her some input.

I stepped out of my car and bellowed: "Lady, you know what you are? You are a [*Tribune* editor's note: On rare occasions, Royko uses language that isn't appropriate for a family newspaper. In this case, it wouldn't be appropriate for an X-rated movie. So we have removed it. But you can use your imagination]."

"That's what you are, you stupid [*Tribune* editor's note: Same disclaimer]."

Because I have a loud voice, she heard every word. And her jaw dropped. A good sign. It meant the brain cells that receive and interpret crude, vile, obscene language were functioning. So were the brain cells that make jaws drop.

The driver on my right honked his horn. He waved and give me a thumbs-up gesture, an indication that his three-pound cerebral mass was in good working order.

For a moment I thought about asking him if he would care to join me in getting out our tire irons and smashing her headlights and windows. But a portion of my brain told me that while it would be an act of true justice, it would accomplish nothing more than to make me feel good.

Eventually, she moved on. And as her wheels spun, she turned and stuck out her tongue. How disappointing. It meant that my input had been rejected and, when the opportunity arose, she'd block another intersection.

Nevertheless, I'm still amazed at the workings of the human brain. And someday science will figure out why brains are wasted on so many damn fools.

MARCH 22, 1990

Letters, Calls, Complaints, and Great Thoughts from Readers

J. MAE POLAND, Chicago: It is marvelous to think of the brain, but it is even more marvelous to think of the soul. When was the last time you thought of your soul?

COMMENT: When I stopped in at Lou's Shoe Repair Shop. I thought of my heels, too.

JANUARY 24, 1996

Treatment of Crabs? Some of Us Don't Have a Leg to Stand On

I felt guilt pangs when I saw a TV news report about animal lovers who are trying to end the practice of boiling live lobsters.

A woman from People for the Ethical Treatment of Animals said: "No compassionate person would boil an animal alive."

That's something I hadn't thought about before because I have never boiled a lobster and hardly ever eat them.

Although they taste good, they look like giant insects. So do shrimp and crayfish, which I also avoid.

As I once told a Creole friend from New Orleans, where they love to chomp on crayfish and other crawly creatures: "You people eat things that we'd call the Orkin man for."

So why should I feel guilt about lobsters when I don't eat them?

Because it got me thinking about stone crab legs, which rank near the top of my favorite food list.

For years, I've taken vacations in Florida and almost always on the Gulf Coast. That coast not only has fewer New Yorkers, but the gulf is where the stone crab legs are harvested.

I don't eat them in restaurants because they cost too much, and it isn't as much fun.

Instead, I go to a small old-time Florida fishing village where local stone crab leg fishermen bring their catch.

I buy a huge sack of the legs, which have been cooked, and the whole family sits around that evening whacking the thick shells with hammers and gorging ourselves on the firm, sweet stone crab meat.

Besides being delicious, stone crab legs don't look at all like big insects. Maybe an entire stone crab does, but I don't know, because I've never seen one. Few people have.

That's because the people who put out the stone crab traps don't keep the entire creature.

What I'm going to say now is not for the faint of heart and the queasy of stomach.

The stone crab fishermen just break off one of the creature's legs and toss the rest of the crab back in the water.

Wait, please. While that might sound cruel and insensitive, it isn't as bad as you might think.

In a miracle of nature, the stone crab doesn't die. To the contrary, it lives on and eventually grows another leg to replace the one that was snapped off by the human creature in the boat.

So someday, that very same stone crab might be caught by the very same human creature and have that new leg snapped off. And again and again.

This means that a stone crab—unlike a lobster or most of the other things we pluck from the sea—can be caught and yet lead a long life.

Why, then, should I feel guilty for having eaten many hundreds of stone crab legs over the years?

Well, I have no idea what goes through the minds of stone crabs. But I have to guess that it must hurt like the dickens to have a leg popped off.

How would you feel?

And I would imagine that if I went to the bottom of the Gulf Coast and wandered around, I would see an awful lot of gimpy stone crabs.

The demand for them is enormous, not only in restaurants all over Florida, but in seafood joints throughout the country.

Every day, thousands of stone crab legs are served in Florida restaurants and shipped by air to restaurants in New York, Chicago, and other big cities.

So think about that. For every one of those thousands and thousands of crab legs that are being devoured each day, there is a newly disabled stone crab limping around the Florida Gulf Coast.

It must be a terrible sight down there—all those one-legged stone crabs trying to make their way in the ruthless, fish-eat-fish society of the sea.

I once asked an old wrinkle-faced, red-necked stone crab catcher how all the gimpy stone crabs manage to survive. Do they swim in circles? Hop along on one leg? Do they get any help from fortunate able-bodied stone crabs? How does it affect their sex lives? How do they find food?

The old-timer nodded silently as he listened to my questions. Then he said:

"How the heck do I know? I just catch 'em and take their legs. I don't socialize with 'em."

Obviously, he is not a prospective member of People for the Ethical Treatment of Animals.

Despite my feelings of guilt at contributing to such widespread misery and disability, I'll probably go on eating stone crab legs. But I wish there was some way we could reduce the pain, suffering, and inconvenience.

Maybe tiny canes?

CUB CAPERS . . . AND
GAMES WE PLAY

Picking a Super Bowl Team to Root For?

I never choose a team on the basis of its players. Instead, I consider the city they represent. . . . Neither Miami nor San Francisco is a real football city. In a true football championship, you would have Chicago playing Pittsburgh or Cleveland against Detroit. In other words, smokestack cities— cities of tattoos, broken noses, missing teeth, bottle scars, shots, beers, and soot-covered snow. A football game should be played in mud and snow, with a wind chill factor of 20 below, the blood freezing on the noses and lips of the combatants, and the fans staying alive through regular transfusions of Jim Beam.

—*Chicago Tribune,* January 18, 1985

Chicago Sports Teams?

As a Cub fan—and this could also apply to Sox, Bears, and Hawks fans—you should have known better. But you became a true believer. You forgot the one hard rule of being a Chicago sports fan: If anything bad can happen, it figures that it will happen to us.

—*Chicago Tribune,* February 8, 1996

"Ungreatful" Cub Fans

I can't help feeling resentful toward those young people of today who happen to be Cub fans.

With all the other benefits of this affluent society, they even have a winning team to cheer for.

Those under 30 probably don't appreciate it because they don't know how bad, how disgusting, the Cubs used to be.

There was an era about 20 years ago when being a Cub fan took great willpower.

It's hard to describe how bad those last-place teams were. Sitting in the stands, you always knew that the best athletes on the field were the other team. And the next-best athletes were in the ground crew.

Players who were so bad nobody else wanted them were always traded to the Cubs. Then a miraculous change would occur: They'd get worse.

The best way to explain it is to quote from my 1950 Cub Year Book.

The purpose of a team year book, sold by the management in the spring, was to get the fans excited and optimistic about the coming season.

But even the Cub Year Book was depressing. If a fan read it before the season began, he would become morose. By the time the first pitch was thrown, he might be sobbing.

Here are some quotes from the year book about the players of that year:

Every team is supposed to have an ace pitcher. The Cubs' ace was Johnny Schmitz, who had won 11 games the year before. "Johnny got off to a slow start last season," the book said, "and never seemed to recuperate from a sore arm."

The Cubs' other top pitcher was Bob Rush, who had won 10 games and lost only 18. "Bob might have won considerably more," the book explained, "but for a sore shoulder."

See what I mean? Looking for encouragement, you read that your two best pitchers already had sore arms.

You wondered, if their arms stayed sore, who would pitch?

Maybe Doyle Lade. "Doyle won 11 games in his freshman year, but fell off the last two summers, most of his troubles stemming from a sore arm." Good grief, did they all have sore arms? You read frantically.

Ah, there was pitcher Bob Chipman. He didn't have a sore arm, and he had won seven games in 1949. The book said enthusiastically: "What makes this record even more remarkable is that he has been a victim of undulant fever since 1939."

Sore arms. Fever. You knew things couldn't get worse—until you read about Monk Dubiel.

"Monk was rarely in shape last season, due to a recurrent side injury, an ear infection, and a multitude of other ailments."

Leaving the pitchers writhing in agony, you looked for hope in the other players. There were the catchers:

"Bob Scheffing appeared headed for his greatest year in baseball last season, until he broke the thumb on his throwing hand. The break didn't heal properly and had to be rebroken several times."

Backing him up was catcher Al Walker.

"Recognized as one of the brightest prospects in baseball, Al Walker broke his ankle early last season and is hitting the comeback trail."

Who else but the Cubs had bright prospects already making comebacks?

Of their third-string catcher, you read: "But for an accident that wrecked his right shoulder in the Army, Burgess today might be acclaimed as one of baseball's greatest catchers."

If, by then, you weren't sobbing, you learned about a young man named Bob Ramazzotti. The Cubs got him from Brooklyn. Why did Brooklyn give him to the Cubs?

"The young infielder was one of the most highly rated prospects in the Brooklyn organization until 1947, when he was hit in the head by a wild pitch."

And you read about Roy Smalley, who is a Cub legend today because of the way he used to snatch up ground balls and fling them at the sun.

"Just about any other Major League club would like to have Smalley on their roster since he is one of the slickest fielders in the game.

"Roy, incidentally, is playing with a deformed middle finger on his right hand."

At this point, anyone still reading was either a masochist or figured that the Cub manager died in the last chapter.

So they found out that the Cubs had obtained a feared slugger in a trade—Hank Edwards. But if he was a feared slugger, how come he was traded to the Cubs?

"Hank fractured his right collarbone. . . . Since that time, Edwards never was able to play at top speed, since the collarbone continually popped out of joint at the slightest provocation."

But there was hope. They had operated on him, the book said.

"If the operation on Edwards is successful—and the collarbone will not pop out again—Hank will again be one of the league's outstanding sluggers."

It popped. With those Cubs, it always did.

MARCH 23, 1976

At Long Last, the Cubs Again

During the long delay of baseball's spring training, many sports-weary cynics said they didn't care if it ever began.

I didn't feel that way. To me, spring does not arrive until the sports-writers' dispatches begin arriving from Arizona, telling of the high hopes of the Cubs for the new season.

That's what spring training is all about—a fresh day dawning, a putting aside of past failures, a symbolic rebirth of hopes and aspirations. Hey, hey!

And I was not disappointed by the very first report I read about the prospects of the Cubs. It had to do with Jose Cardenal, their tiny but speedy outfielder.

Cardenal has become my favorite Cub. With his huge puff of hair atop his slight frame, he looks like a swarthy dandelion.

And he has an instinct for the dramatic.

Remember last spring and the big news then? It was Jose's eyelid. He has two of them, but I'm not sure which one it was.

Anyway, a strange malady had afflicted the eyelid and it was stuck shut. Nobody knew why, and it was feared that it wouldn't open in time for Opening Day.

To be honest, I had hoped it wouldn't open, because that would have given the Cubs the distinction of having had baseball's only one-eyed Cuban outfielder. As it is, they are the last team to have had a 38-year-old Venezuelan rookie pitcher who wore a golden earring. Cub history is full of such marvels.

Anyway, the suspense mounted through spring training about Jose's sticky eyelid. He sat on the bench during the practice games and sadly stared out at half of his teammates. People were careful not to approach him from his blind side, for fear of being bitten.

Then, as if by a miracle, Jose's eyelid popped open in time for the season's opener. Some say that it happened when the fans stood and sang the National Anthem and Jose thought they were singing "Jose, can you see?"

The fans were delighted with his recovery, and after watching the Cubs for a few games, their eyelids dropped shut.

Now, in case you missed it, here is the first report we have received from the Cubs' training base:

"SCOTTSDALE, Ariz.—Jose Cardenal says there is a cricket in his room that keeps chirping every night. It is keeping him awake.

"He would like to kill the thing, but he can't find it."

Ah, the wonderful Cubs and the incomparable Jose.

Other teams begin spring training with talk of pennants, the World Series, and rookie phenoms who can throw with blazing fury, hit the ball beyond the horizon, and run with the speed of an Old Town mugger.

But we have a sleepy outfielder stalking an elusive cricket.

Moments like that are part of the Cub heritage. A few years ago, the Cubs had a rookie who created a sensation at spring training by marrying Mamie Van Doren. He, too, said he was not sleeping well, but he did not want to kill anybody.

Another spring, the Cubs decided they wouldn't have a manager—they would rotate the job among the pudgy coaches. Then the coaches all fired each other and one of the radio announcers took over. Everybody laughed, but they didn't do any worse than before.

Sometimes I feel sorry for cities that don't have a team with a tradition like that of our Cubs. You can't name one player in the brief history of the Oakland A's who is the equal of Roy Smalley.

I'm sure some young fans think I'm talking about a star infielder by that name who is currently playing. No, I mean his father, who was once a Cub.

The elder Smalley was the only shortstop in baseball who had a deformed finger on his throwing hand. Only the Cubs would seek out such a unique specimen.

When he was a rookie, some fans feared the finger would hamper his throwing. But it didn't. Deformed finger and all, he could still heave the ball completely over the first baseman's head and the dugout and into the upper deck. He loved to do that.

Smalley was the symbol of that long-past era, when the Cubs were really terrible. There were others who symbolized the later era, when they were also terrible.

Adolfo Phillips, remember him? There was a true Cub. He could run, hit, and throw, and everybody agreed that he would be a Cub star for many years. But the thought of being a Cub star for many years worried Adolfo so much that he got ulcers and went away.

The names of the greats trip across our memory, just as they tripped across their own feet: Steve Bilko, Dee Fondy, Pete Whisenant, Toby Atwell, Frank Ernaga, Dick Drott, Ed Bouchee, Moe Thacker, Merritt Ranew, Vic Roznovsky, Roberto Pena, Billy Faul, Ken Rudolph, Carmen Fanzone, Joe Pepitone.

What they achieved is the most awesome record in sports, and worth remembering as another season begins.

Thirty years ago, half the countries now in the United Nations didn't exist. Cars had running boards. The atom bomb was still our secret weapon. All airplanes had propellers. Movies cost 25 cents. Richard J. Daley was an obscure ward heeler. Chicago had streetcars. Stalin, Truman, and Churchill ran things.

And the Cubs began not winning pennants. They have not stopped not winning pennants since. No other team in all of professional athletics has not won a championship for as long.

Yet, we still love them. Which should be a good lesson to all of us. There are more important things in life than winning.

Like catching a cricket and getting a good night's sleep.

APRIL 20, 1980

A Farewell to Cubs

Most of my friends didn't believe me when I told them about my intentions.

"You can't mean it," one of them said. "It would be like switching citizenship."

Another argued: "This is more serious than a sex-change operation."

And a third said: "Give it more thought. It's comparable to changing religions."

I agreed. It's a serious step—one of the most serious that a person can take.

But I've done it. I have officially ceased being a Cub fan and have taken an oath as a follower of the White Sox.

As you can see from the picture in today's column, the oath was administered to me at Comiskey Park by Bill Veeck, boss of the Sox.

It was a solemn occasion. I placed my left hand upon Veeck's famous wooden leg and raised my right hand, and Veeck said:

"Repeat after me: I do solemnly swear to honor the memory of Luke Appling, Billy Pierce, Nellie Fox, Early Wynn, Minnie Minoso, Jungle Jim Rivera, and Fat Pat Seerey."

I repeated his words.

"I agree to attend White Sox games as often as possible and will learn to sing 'Na Na Na Na.'"

I agreed.

"I hereby declare you a Sox fan," Veeck said. "Now drink your beer like a good boy."

Thus ended more than 40 years of loyal servitude to the Cubs—years that had joyous moments (homers by Pafko, Sauer, Banks, Williams, or Moryn; fielding gems by Hack, Kessinger, Jeffcoat, Hubbs, or Waitkus) and moments of gloom (the mad, flailing bats of Serena, Terwilliger, Ramazzotti, and Chiti; the ground balls caroming off the foreheads of Merullo, Smalley, Madrid, or Miksis).

Unfortunately, there was more gloom than joy, since the Cubs have the most amazingly dismal record of failure in professional sports.

But that didn't matter. To the contrary, I always believed that being a Cub fan built strong character. It taught a person that if you try hard enough and long enough, you'll still lose. And that's the story of life.

And it really didn't matter if the Cubs won or lost. What really counted were the more subtle points of the game. For example, it was always exciting to see whether all three Cub outfielders would collide—on their way to the dugout.

In recent years, though, it has become more and more difficult to work up an enthusiastic case of the hey-heys.

My loyalty began to slide when the Cubs got rid of Leo Durocher, who could kick foul-line powder on an umpire's shoes better than any manager in their history.

Then they traded away Jose Cardenal, the tiny outfielder who was an inspiration to those of us who believe in sleeping late, walking slowly, and calling in sick at the office. It was the great Jose who could hardly play at all during one spring training because he said his eyelid was stuck shut. The next year, he couldn't play in spring training because a cricket in his motel room kept him awake all night.

And Jose's wife once beat up a Chicago cop. You just don't trade away that kind of star quality.

But what finally caused me to turn away from the Cubs forever was my own soft heart and kindly nature, for which I'm well known.

It has become more and more difficult for me to watch the Cubs, knowing what personal agonies those poor lads are going through.

When the star relief pitcher appeared, I would think about his loud cries of pain at having to accept a one-year contract for $700,000 a year.

When the center fielder came up, I would think about his public moans of misery at earning only $150,000 a year—after he hit a sensational .275 or so, which surely qualifies him for the Hall of Fame.

Their catcher is dissatisfied with the way he is treated. And so is the right fielder. The Cubs are just about the most unhappy group of young men I've ever heard about.

Being of a sensitive nature myself, I'd find myself sharing their misery, and instead of enjoying the ball game, I'd become depressed and big tears would run down my nose and into my beer.

It's no fun watching a ball game when, instead of shouting, "Hey hey," I would be on my feet crying: "Oh Lord, have mercy on these poor wretched, suffering souls. Give them more money."

On the other hand, the White Sox seem to be good-natured fellows. You have to scour the sports pages to find even a tidbit about a Sox player demanding to be traded unless he's given a lifetime $50 million contract.

And Bill Veeck himself has a happier nature while stumping around on one leg than most of the Cub players have on two healthy legs. He can run faster than some of them, too.

There was one other factor in my defection—the burden of the guilt I have been carrying.

Dave (Ding-Dong) Kingman, the Cub slugger and budding author, instructed his ghostwriter to say that I am one of the reasons the Cubs have been such failures.

I caused them to fail because I didn't write about how magnificent they are and show confidence in them. This made them brood and feel rejected. And the ball would pop out of their gloves, or roll through their legs, or sneak past their bats.

That's not an easy thing to live with. As a loyal Cub fan, my conscience was wracked by the knowledge that I caused them to lose. Not their weak arms, their weak bats, their slowness afoot, their bad hands. Me!

So I'm shedding my guilt by shedding the Cubs. Now they can go on to new successes, new heights—to greatness. Maybe they'll even win as many games as they lose.

And I'll go to Comiskey Park.

As Bill Veeck said when I asked him if I would have to feel guilty when the Sox lost:

"Not if you pay your way in and buy a beer."

Na Na Na Na, Na Na Na Na, hey, hey, hey, goodbye.

APRIL 29, 1980

Letters, Calls, Complaints, and Great Thoughts from Readers

K. S. STERBENC, Munster, Ind.: As a Cub fan, let me just say this:

A. They have enough trouble and they don't need you.

B. I hope you get mugged on the way to a Sox game.

C. Good riddance.

D. Up yours.

COMMENT: As a fan of a first-place team, I have no time to quibble with a fan of a second-place team. Na Na Na, Goodbye.

LINDA JOHNSON, Chicago: I'm not at all surprised that you have become a Sox fan, since you have obviously a Sox fan's character and personality and were out of place as a Cub fan.

You are a loud, rude, ignorant, obnoxious, ill-mannered, disgusting, macho pig.

I'm sure you will feel at home as you swill beer, belch, have a pot belly (which you will bare for your fellow slob fans), and will get into your share of brawls.

Tell me, do you also pick your nose in public?

COMMENT: No, I don't. But nobody's perfect.

APRIL 9, 1981

When Ya Gotta Go

It's like being the fat guy on a strict diet who stares at the piece of pizza. Or the drinker on the wagon who eyes the martini. Strength, oh give me strength.

For days it's been going on—the temptation. Friends of mine have been tantalizingly saying: "Say, we have tickets for the Cub opener. Why don't you come?"

I plead that I can't. And they know it. Last season, after a long lifetime as an obsessive Cub addict, I quit them cold turkey.

And I did it publicly in order to set an example of courage for other addicts who might think it's impossible to shake the habit.

From that moment on, I didn't go to another Cub game. I didn't even watch them on TV. I intentionally let barroom friends beat me in Cub trivia quizzes. Not once did I take my Cub bubble gum card collection from the drawer or wear my Cub cap.

When the season ended, I was sure I had the habit licked. At least until the past few days, with the balmy spring weather and the approach of the opener.

But you never are *completely* cured. Somewhere, inside a dark corner of your brain, there is always that insidious little voice whispering to you. I've been hearing it lately, wheedling, tempting, rationalizing:

Oh, come on, what's one little opening game? You can handle just one. Just one teensy Opening Day game. If you don't like it, you can walk away from it. C'mon, just this one.

No, I can't. If I have one, that will just lead to another. And another. And then I'm on the road to degradation—listening to Jack Brickhouse's hey-heys, studying the box scores, poring over the batting averages. Caring! Caring whether some $200,000-a-year mumblemouth trips over his glove. I won't do it. I've shaken the habit. I'm clean. Leave me alone!

Don't get excited. I just thought for old times' sake you might want to go. To help you remember those good old days. Remember when you were a kid, you'd go there real early so you could set up the folding chairs in the box seats and earn a free pass? The long ride on the streetcars? Remember the 1945 opener?

Yeah, our last pennant winner. A bunch of wartime 4-Fs. But at least we had the best 4-Fs.

Sure, and remember that Opening Day lineup? You were there! Stan Hack and Lennie Merullo, Andy Pafko and Don Johnson, Mickey Livingston and Phil Cavarretta, Bill Nicholson and Hank Sauer.

Not Hank Sauer, dummy. It was Ed Sauer. He played left field that game because Peanuts Lowrey was still in the Army. Hank Sauer came to the Cubs later. Everybody knows that.

See? You know things like that. You probably remember how that opening game came out.

Of course I do. Big Paul Derringer spun a seven-hitter, while Bill (Swish) Nicholson smashed a towering four-bagger, and Don Johnson lashed a single to drive in the winning tally in the ninth, as the Cubs won a 3-2 thriller over the St. Louis Cards. We used to talk that way in those days.

How can you let this vast knowledge go to waste? A lifetime of dedicated study, a baseball scholar's mind. And you won't even go to Opening Day. At least think of how the hot dogs will taste.

The hot dogs taste lousy. The best thing to do is buy your hot dog before you go in at one of the stands outside the park.

The hot dog doesn't matter anyway. It's the history, the tradition. Think of Roy Smalley and Moose Moryn and Don Cardwell's no-hitter, and Sad Sam (Toothpick) Jones and his no-hitter, and the great Hack Wilson.

Yeah, Hack Wilson. He was always drunk or hung over. He came to the ballpark so smashed once that they had to soak him in ice for an hour before the game. Then he hit three homers. He was my first childhood hero.

Right. And remember Chuck Connors, the Cub first baseman who became "The Rifleman" on TV, and Rube Walker, the rookie who threw up in his first Cub game, and Dim-Dom Dallessandro, who was so tiny he had to be lifted out of the dugout, and Lane Tech's own Phil Cavarretta.

Yeah, Phil Cavarretta. He came to my school once to make an inspirational talk to us kids. He started his speech: "Shut up, you noisy little [bleeps]." He was my second childhood hero.

And don't forget the great Cubs of 1969. Ron Santo and Billy Williams, Ernie Banks and Glenn Beckert, Don Kessinger and Randy Hundley, Kenny Holtzman and Fergie Jenkins. Why, almost every guy in the lineup made the All-Star team that year.

Yeah, the greatest Cub team in the last 40 years. And they finished second.

But winning isn't everything. That's why you were a Cub fan. So you could develop character and wisdom and strength through suffering and misery and self-punishment and deprivation.

Yeah. Like belonging to a religious order.

Of course. Remember what you once said: Being a Cub fan prepares you for life because everyone in life winds up a loser. Just check the cemetery.

That's true. And we're the best prepared losers in America.

Then go out there. Just for the opener. You'll like it.

I can't. I took my vow. I swore off. Besides, I can't stand those guys. That's why I quit. I never minded losers—but I absolutely cannot stand losers who are whining that they aren't paid enough for losing.

But the whiners are gone! You haven't been paying attention to spring training. They got rid of all the real whiners. Now they have players who hustle and pull for each other and pat each other on the bottom, and they really come to play. Believe me, you'll love this Cub team.

I will? Why?

Because it is a classic Cub team. They'll hustle, they'll try, they'll "come to play." But they won't be very good.

That's a Cub team in the finest tradition.

Right. And they all love being Cubs. Hardly any of them want to be traded.

That's true. It is a tradition for Cubs to love the team and not ask to be traded because they know that no other team wants them.

So face it—you've got to go.

Yeah, I suppose that when you've got to go, you've got to go, which sounds like it could be a Cub slogan.

Then you're a Cub fan again?

Does the fish swim? Does the bird fly? Does the skunk stink? Does the pig burp, does the nose pick, does the toilet flush? I'm a Cub fan.

APRIL 14, 1981

Letters, Calls, Complaints, and Great Thoughts from Readers

SID CURTIS, Chicago: I am demanding accuracy in journalism.

On Opening Day, I read your column about returning to the Cubs and how you remembered great moments in Cubs history, such as when coach Rube Walker made his first appearance in the big leagues as a rookie catcher and threw up.

Then, later in the day I heard Jack Brickhouse say on TV that Rube Walker denied that he threw up during his first appearance and that Walker was trying to contact you so you would make a correction.

Who is right? You or Walker?

COMMENT: I'm not sure. I could have sworn that Walker threw up during his first appearance with the Cubs. But thinking back on it, maybe it was me who threw up. And I've been doing that at Cubs games ever since.

MIKE RILEY, Chicago: You are not a man of honor. Only a year ago, you placed your hand on Bill Veeck's wooden leg and swore allegiance to the White Sox.

But I notice that you did not take any kind of sacred oath when you returned to the Cubs. So it seems to me that unless you do, you are still bound to the White Sox and you have a chance to change your mind.

COMMENT: I will take a sacred oath to the Cubs as soon as owner William Wrigley lets me put my hand on his wooden head.

APRIL 8, 1986

For It's 1, 2, 3 Maalox at the . . .

I didn't need a calendar to know it was Opening Day. All I had to hear was Wally the Worrier telling the bartender to put two Maalox pills in his martini.

When he saw me, he posed the question that is tormenting all Cub fans. It is being asked in the home, the work place, the school, the bars, the sports pages, and, for all I know, from the pulpit.

"Do you think," Wally said in a somber voice, "that Ron Cey is too old?"

I told him that only Mrs. Cey could answer that question.

"That's not what I mean," said Wally. "Can he still hit the ball?"

Only time will tell, I said, quoting any number of profound TV commentators. It's a long season. When it is over, we will have the answer.

Wally moaned. "By then it will be too late."

Too late for what?

"I don't know. Just too late."

Look, why don't you relax and enjoy the grand spectacle of it all. The crack of the bat against the old horsehide, the diving catches, the mad dash toward home plate, the chant of the crowd for a strikeout, the roar for a home run, the pudgy coaches mouthing obscenities at umpires, the batters spitting and adjusting their athletic supporters for the cameras. Relax. It is but a game.

"How can I relax? What about Matthews? Do you think the Sarge is too old?"

If he is too old, we'll soon see the telltale signs. His hair and teeth will fall out, he'll snore with his mouth open, and he'll cackle and offer candy to girls in the stands. Until then, don't worry.

"Don't worry? We need healthy pitchers. What about Sanderson's aching back?"

What about my aching back?

"Who cares about your back?"

Well, I do. I'll bet my back is in worse shape than Sanderson's back. It's in worse shape than Quasimodo's.

"Who's he with?"

Used to be with Notre Dame.

"Never mind that. What about the kid at shortstop, Dunston? He looked good at the end of last year, but the pressure was off by then. Do you think he's for real?"

What is reality? What is truth or beauty? What is the meaning of life? As that Greek philosopher, Hophead Gus, once said: You gotta go with the flow.

"Well, if Dunston can't handle shortstop, we're in real trouble."

I'm not in any trouble. I've paid my taxes and parking tickets. They don't have a thing on me, see.

"And I worry about Bull Durham, too. He's always getting hurt."

Then don't worry about him. The Tribune Company has excellent medical benefits. He and his loved ones will be well taken care of.

"But there are so many question marks on that team."

Life is a big question mark. And the answer is often written on the page that has been torn out.

"What does that mean?"

I'm not sure. But it's something to think about.

"Well, I'm thinking that we've got to have big years out of Dernier and the Zonk and Jody."

The bigger the year, the better, I always say.

"That's right. Remember, as great as he is, Ryno can't do it all by himself."

No man is an island. No woman is an island, either. For that matter, no island is a man or a woman.

"Yeah, but what about our middle relief? Oh, what a headache that is. We got starters, if they stay healthy. And we got a stopper in big Lee. But what do we do about the middle?"

I hear sit-ups are good for the middle, if you can stand the pain and don't have a hernia.

"Well, one thing I'm sure of is that this year the Cubs got a great bench."

As well as an excellent water cooler, a more-than-adequate latrine, and hot water in the showers. Who could ask for anything more?

"But I worry about the weather. What if the wind blows in a lot this year? Does it help us or hurt us?"

It depends on which way you're facing.

"Sometimes I think it's not worth it all, being a fan I mean. The season lasts so long. There's so much pain. Even if they have a great year, they lose a third of their games and I have to suffer every time. Sometimes I wish I could just go to sleep after Opening Day and wake up for the last game."

That's possible. Bartender, another martini.

"Dry. With a triple Maalox."

MARCH 12, 1987

[Editors' note: The Chicago Cubs led the National League Eastern Division by 9½ games in mid-August 1969. Pennant fever infected the city. Four weeks and one Cub collapse later, the upstart New York Mets led. They went on to win the World Series.]

Read On, Gluttons for Punishment

A New York publishing house has sent me a copy of a new paperback book it has just brought out.

With it came a note that said: "We take pleasure in presenting you with this review copy and ask that you please send two copies of your notices to our offices."

I seldom review books in my column. But in this case, I'm going to make an exception. This book is called "If At First . . ." with a subtitle that says "With the exclusive inside story of the 1986 Championship Season."

The author is Keith Hernandez, who is the first baseman on the New York Mets baseball team. Actually, he didn't write it—some professional ghostwriter did. But the words and story originated with Hernandez.

I will begin my review by saying that this is a very solid book. The moment I opened the package and saw what it was about, I threw it against my office wall as hard as I could. Then I slammed it to the floor and jumped up and down on it. I beat on it with a chair for several minutes until I slumped onto my couch, emotionally and physically spent.

Although slightly scuffed, the book was still intact.

It is also a book that can cause excitement. I dropped it on the desk of a friend who has had weekend season tickets at Wrigley Field for the past 10 years. It immediately stirred him to emotional heights. He shouted:

"Why are you showing me that piece of [deleted]? I say [deleted] Hernandez and [deleted] the Mets and [deleted] the whole [deleted] City of New York. And [deleted] you too."

Then he flung it against a wall and gave it a kick. It still remained intact. I told you it was a solid book.

It's a book that can move a sensitive reader to tears, as I discovered when I showed it to a man who has been going to Cub games since 1946, a year that is known as The Beginning of Darkness.

When he looked at the cover, he choked back a sob, a tear trickled down his cheek, and he said: "Why them? Why not us? What was our sin? How can we atone for it? You know, I asked my clergyman that, and he said he wishes he knew, because he lost $50 betting against them."

And it's a powerful book. As reviewers like to say: It can hit you right in the guts. This was confirmed when I showed it to a Wrigley Field bleacherite who said:

"Excuse me. I am going to throw up."

But enough of generalities. Let us consider the contents of this book.

On the very first page, Hernandez and his ghostwriter say:

"ad made the second out on a long the Mets were through for 1986: o out, nobody on, two runs down, ox already leading the World series en our scoreboard operator at"

And on page 81, Hernandez says: "round during infield practice, I draw a line nan and myself and call our manager over. Avy? I ask. He laughs."

Moving to page 125, we find: "Oh, sweet bird of youth, however, were a different story. It's diffquietly as I work my way out of a bad me to listen to his judgments. I wrong with my swing. I know hot to th hardheaded. Dand and I have had"

I know, it sounds kind of garbled, incomprehensible. But that's the way a story reads when you rip the pages of a book in half, one by one, as I've been doing.

Don't misunderstand me. I'm not doing that out of spite. I'm a good sport, a cheerful loser. Why, in the past two years, I don't think I've watched my video of the movie *Fail Safe,* in which New York City gets nuked, more than 30 or 40 times.

The fact is, I have found this to be a useful book.

I have been tearing out the pages and crumpling them into little wads.

When I have about 30 or 40 of these wads, I put them in my fireplace under the kindling and light them. They're excellent for getting a fire started.

Then I pour myself a drink, lower the lights, sit back, and stare at the crackling flame.

And I pretend that I'm looking at Shea Stadium.

Cub Fans, Let's Be Careful Out There

As fans of old horror movies know, when the sun goes down and the moon comes out, spooky things can happen.

Bela Lugosi used to rise from his coffin, a gleam in his eye, and go into the night to give young ladies some really unsightly hickies.

And when the moon was full, Lon Chaney Jr., a nice fellow during the day, would sprout fur on his face and feet, let out a howl, and chew the first rustic he met.

It was always after dark that Jack the Ripper, blade in hand, prowled foggy London in search of a helpless doxy.

In fact and fiction, night is scarier than day. Things go bump in the dark. Shadows take on strange shapes. Who knows what menace lurks in those dark corners?

That's why ancient tribes huddled near their fires. And modern tribes huddle near their Mitsubishis.

As T. B. Aldrich wrote: "Night is a stealthy, evil raven, wrapt to the eyes in his black wings."

And tonight in Chicago we're going to begin finding the answer to a fascinating psychological question that concerns the debilitating effect of night on the human mind:

Does the coming of darkness cause otherwise decent, polite, hygienic Cub fans to have a fiendish compulsion to make wee-wee on a stranger's lawn?

This, of course, is a specter that has haunted many North Side Chicagoans since it was decided that night games would be played in Wrigley Field. They have visions of beer-bloated Cub fans rushing from the ballpark to the nearest patch of yuppie-owned grass.

Then jostling each other for space while shouting: "Lemme through, I get first shot at that lawn."

"Okay, then I get the tulips."

"What about me?"

"You can take the hedge."

And other cries of: "Downwind, you fool, always aim downwind."

The coming of night baseball has created a few lesser issues, too. Parking, traffic congestion, and noise. And a magazine even raised the frightening prospect of Cub fans, depressed by defeat or high on victory, storming into nearby gay bars to harm winsome young men.

But the single greatest fear I've heard expressed has been from those who have said: "I know it's going to happen. Somebody's going to do it on my lawn."

I've heard it so often that I'm starting to have my own visions of people in the Wrigleyville neighborhood rowing boats down their flooded streets. And National Guard troops stacking sandbags along Waveland Avenue.

I can see TV news anchor Bill Kurtis in hip boots, standing on Waveland Avenue and saying to the camera: "I'm here with Nadine Yuppwife, whose home is one of those that have been flooded by the bladders of Cub fans. Mrs. Yuppwife, what is the extent of the damage to your property?"

"We lost everything. Even our beloved BMW has floated away with my husband in it."

Should this happen, there is a price the city will pay beyond the abused lawns, the splattered porches, the soaked sidewalks.

Because the eyes of the nation will be on us, the entire city will be humiliated. Most of America will be laughing at us.

That's because hundreds of reporters, TV crews, and other professional gawkers have flocked to Chicago for the novelty of our first Cubs night game. You would think Tom Edison himself was going to pull the light switch.

And if the fears of the neighborhood are realized, we will turn on our TV sets and hear David Letterman singing: "Chicago, Chicago, that tinkling town."

On the other hand, the presence of so many media creatures might have a beneficial effect. Besides the newspeople, there will be almost 200 cops. And there will be the residents of the neighborhood out in force, once they've finished covering their homes and loved ones with plastic sheeting.

There will be so many watchful eyes that if anyone reaches for a zipper or even hitches up his trousers, he'll promptly be surrounded by all three networks, CNN, *USA Today,* and three members of the police department's Special Wee-Wee Strike Force.

This alone should discourage any wanton spraying of lawns, gardens, or small individuals.

And if that isn't enough, then as an elder Cub fan I am making a personal plea to my fellow Cub fans:

Don't give the Wrigleyville yuppies a chance to say: "I told you so." Conduct yourselves properly. Don't give in to the temptation presented by that patch of grass. Let us all try to project an image of decency and propriety.

In other words, be a gentleman. Do it in the alley.

AUGUST 25, 1989

Rose Can Count On the Memories

Every time I drive past the park I look at the spot. It is near the field house, exactly 381 feet from home plate. I know, because I paced it off.

Years ago, scouts from the St. Louis Cardinals held an open tryout camp in that park. A buddy and I showed up with our gloves, bats, and spikes.

We and dozens of others ran, shagged fly balls, fielded grounders, and threw.

Then a game was played, with players being shuttled in and out so the scouts could take a look at all of us.

When I came to bat, the pitcher was a tall, gangly guy with a high kick and a fast ball.

He threw it down the middle, waist high, and I hit it as hard as I could. It landed at the spot near the field house, and I trotted around the bases.

I had one more time at bat and I lined a single to left.

When the camp ended, one of the scouts talked to me. He said I had a good swing, which was true. I had always been able to hit.

But he also said I was slow, which was true, had a weak arm, which was true, had bad hands, which was true, and there was absolutely no chance of my being anything more than a Class D minor league player.

In those days, that meant about $20 a week in Piddlepool, Alabama.

So my buddy and I got back on the streetcar and went home. End of dream of being the next Joe DiMaggio.

Which means I have something in common with millions of men, ranging in age from teenagers to geriatrics. Some of us could hit well, some could run fast, some could throw hard, some could scoop up ground balls.

Some were good enough to play on their high school teams. Others made it into college lineups and even the minor leagues. There were fine sandlot players and semipros.

But of the millions and millions of young guys who played the game at one level or another, only an incredibly small percentage had the talent to get to the majors.

Since they started keeping records, there have been only about 13,000 who have made it to The Bigs, including those who were in and out after only a few swings or pitches.

And of those, only 168 have been good enough to be voted into the Hall of Fame.

This popped into my head when I heard a radio babbler use the phrase "American tragedy" while talking about the Pete Rose case. I snorted and jabbed a button for another station.

A tragedy? Here is a man who, by all accounts, was a lousy husband, an indifferent father, a poor judge of friends, and a liar.

Of course, that doesn't make him any different than a few million other guys.

But what sets him apart was that he was born with exceptional hand-eye coordination and athletic ability. That, plus total determination, made it possible for him to play major league baseball for 24 years, to come to bat more than 14,000 times in 3,562 games, and to get 4,256 hits.

Oh, to have spent 24 years enduring such tragedy. Or would you settle for a month, a week, even a day? You bet you would. It beats sitting at that desk, trying to sell that customer, driving that truck, or drilling that tooth.

So now Rose is out, banned from the game because he knew the rules but chose to ignore the rules. Justice at its simplest.

But what difference does it make? He was no longer playing anyway. And the way his team was going, he probably wouldn't have been managing much longer.

What matters is that he had those 24 wonderful summers and those 3,562 games. And whatever kind of jerk he may have been in his private life, it was obvious that when he stepped out onto the field he loved every moment of it. How many people can say that about 24 years in the same job?

It may be that his gambling habit has left him broke. But a lot of people are broke or close to it. He can find work, which is what most people do when they need money.

There's silly jabber about whether he will or won't be in the Baseball Hall of Fame. What's the difference? It's just a plaque on a wall. What counts is that he played the games, got the hits, and had the magic moments. That was the reality, not some plaque.

Besides, there are no halls of fame for those who do things that are far more useful than hitting a baseball. The paramedics who give mouth-to-mouth to strangers; cops who walk into dark gangways; men who spend their lives emptying garbage cans. Or even women who put up with husbands like Pete Rose.

It's not a tragedy. It isn't even sad, as the baseball commissioner put it. Tragedy is a kid getting hit by a car. Sad is being old, alone, and lonely.

Rose had the life that almost every American boy has dreamed of. He played The Game and was paid and cheered for it.

Now it's time for him to become a grownup. The game is over.

But he'll have the memories, and that has to help.

I know. As I said, the ball landed exactly 381 feet from home plate. Of course, the wind was blowing out.

OCTOBER 5, 1993

Three Ex-Cubs Assure Spurning of Atlanta

The experts have spoken. The Atlanta Braves are the best of the playoff teams. The bookies have made them the favorites to get to the World Series and win it. Some sports pundits already talk of them as one of the great teams of all time.

The experts just never learn.

As always, they ignore that strange, mysterious, and almost-always fatal malady known as the Ex-Cubs Factor.

Regular readers of this column know about the Ex-Cubs Factor. But bear with me as I explain it to newcomers.

Twelve years ago, a Chicago sports nut named Ron Berler stumbled across an amazing statistic.

Since 1946, 13 teams had entered the World Series with three or more ex-Cubs on their roster.

Twelve of these 13 teams lost.

Berler theorized that it was a virus. Three or more ex-Cubs could infect an entire team with the will to lose, no matter how skillful that team might appear.

When Berler revealed his findings, the sports experts sneered and scoffed. Stupid and meaningless, they snickered. No scientific basis, they hooted.

Then came 1990, and they were still sneering, scoffing, and making their mindless predictions.

That was the year about 99 percent of the experts declared that the Oakland A's could not possibly lose the World Series.

Even before the games began, they hailed the A's as one of the greatest teams—maybe the greatest—in the history of the game.

As the *Washington Post*'s resident baseball genius put it: "Let's make this short and sweet. The baseball season is over. Nobody's going to beat the Oakland A's."

As Ben Bentley, the Chicago sports savant, said: "Could the Oakland Athletics be the greatest in baseball history?"

Yes, cried the experts: the greatest, a dynasty, a team of immortals. They could win while yawning.

But out there were two lonely voices: Berler and this writer.

We warned of the Ex-Cubs Factor. We pointed out that the A's had foolishly defied the terrible virus by signing a third ex-Cub. And before that World Series began, Berler publicly stated: "As good as they are, they will lose. And they can blame their own arrogance for ignoring history."

So what happened? Not only did the A's lose, it was world-class humiliation. Four straight defeats. One of sports' all-time flopperoos.

That made it 13 out of 14 teams with three or more ex-Cubs to collapse in the World Series since World War II.

The A's haven't been the same since. Once it struck, the ex-Cub virus burrowed into the fiber of the franchise. In only three years they have gone from a dynasty to limping mediocrity. Sources say their hot dogs don't even taste as good as they once did.

Have the experts learned anything? Of course not. As the late Mayor Richard J. Daley once said: "Duh experts—what do dey know?"

The sports experts are now hailing the Atlanta Braves as the super-team of this era.

On Sunday, Dave Kindred, columnist for the *Sporting News,* wrote: ". . . Atlanta has become baseball's best team since the Yankees of Mickey Mantle and Yogi Berra . . . the NL's best team since the Brooklyn Dodgers of Duke Snider, Gil Hodges, and Pee Wee Reese."

He may be right. They have thunderous hitters, overwhelming pitchers, and a seamless defense.

But they also have the dreaded virus. Of the four teams in the playoffs, only the Braves are afflicted by the Ex-Cubs Factor. Only the Braves have three former Cubs.

They are Greg Maddux, the superb pitcher, Damon Berryhill, the reliable catcher, and . . .

Even a bleacher creature would be hard-pressed to name the third ex-Cub.

But Berler, the virus discoverer, knows. "I have it all in my computer," he says.

A relief pitcher named Jay Howell. Although he has been in the major leagues for 14 years, he's not a big name, not a big star, no flashy stats. A solid journeyman. Probably good to his family, a nice neighbor, a patriot; and he doesn't kick little dogs.

But he is one of the three skeletons in the Atlanta closet. He has a sordid past.

For a brief time in 1981, when he was a mere lad, he was a Cub. He pitched in only 10 games, a total of 22 innings, and wasn't very good.

But as Berler says: "That is all it takes. He is a genuine, bona fide, star-crossed ex-Cub, the poor guy. He is a carrier. It always comes back to your roots. Once a Cub, always a Cub."

Berler, who is a free-lance writer and teacher, recently interviewed Maddux, who chose to become an Atlanta Brave multimillionaire, rather than a Chicago Cubs multimillionaire, because he wanted to play on a winning team.

"I told him: 'You think you're leaving a loser? Ha! You are a loser. And you're going to infect your 24 teammates.'"

He explained the Ex-Cubs Factor to Maddux. And the star pitcher responded by shouting: "I don't believe it, I don't believe it, I don't believe it!"

So if the Braves defeat the Phillies and make it to the World Series, bet on the Braves at your own peril.

But this puts a Chicagoan such as myself—a devout Cubs fan—in a difficult position.

Those who are true fans of the White Sox or Cubs loathe the other team. This crosstown rivalry takes precedent over city pride. So if the Sox play the Braves, I must root for the Braves. It is the only decent thing a Cubs fan can do. Sox fans, being dedicated haters, will understand.

It will be the first time I will be cheering for a virus.

[Editors' note: The Philadelphia Phillies and the virus beat the Braves, four games to two, in the playoffs.]

JUNE 8, 1995

Yes, Golf Tantrums Are for Males Only

It pains me to report that this paper recently printed a blatantly sexist item that insulted countless female persons.

This was brought to my attention by the sharp-eyed blond with whom I live, when she stormed into the room while waving the sports section and said:

"Have you ever seen a woman golfer throw a club when she makes a bad shot?"

I have no such memory.

"Have you ever seen a woman golfer slam a club into the ground or throw it into a pond?"

Never.

"And have you ever heard a woman scream filthy four-letter words on a golf course?"

No, not even a "damn" or a "hell."

"Then tell me why your paper would print something as insulting and demeaning to women as this?"

And she read from Wednesday's special golf page. It was an article giving advice to the growing number of women who have taken up the game.

The advice included this tip: "No temper tantrums—even if you miss your first shot."

"Has your paper ever told male golfers that they should not have temper tantrums?"

Of course not.

"Why?"

Because everybody knows that emotional outbursts are part of the male golf tradition.

When a man botches an important shot, or even a trivial one, he is expected to cry out as if undergoing abdominal surgery without an anesthetic.

As his ball sails toward a pond, he might scream: "Turn, turn, you lousy [bleep]."

And when it splashes toward the depths, he might turn his frustration on himself, shouting: "What a [bleeping] [bleep]head I am."

Or he might direct his fury at the world in general, braying as many four-letter words, or combinations thereof, as he can think of. As in: "Oh, [bleep, bleep, bleep], why the [bleep] did I ever take up such a [bleeping] stupid game? [Bleep] it forever."

Different men have different styles of expressing their agony. A friend of mine named Jim unfailingly follows a botched shot by emitting an ear-splitting: "Jimmy . . . Jiimmmyyyy . . . JIMMMMYYYYY . . . YEEEEEEE!"

Another turns his rage on outside forces of evil. "Those stinking birds," he'll shout, "they start chirping in the middle of my backswing. Why are birds allowed on a golf course? And those church bells ringing in my follow through. Why can't they bury someone without clanging bells? Show some respect for the living, for Pete's sake."

It is a reasonable guess that golf courses are the scene of more male temper tantrums that any other place in our society, with the possible exception of the goofs on the Internet.

But the blond is right. Male golfers are never told to avoid acting like a kid denied a visit to Chuck E. Cheese.

Only women. And why? Because temper outbursts are part of the female stereotype. In movies, a macho guy will say to an angry woman: "Has anyone ever told you that you're beautiful when you're mad?" But a woman never says: "Has anyone ever told you that you're handsome when your eyes are bulging, your teeth are grinding, and you are shouting obscenities?"

I will probably be condemned by many men for saying this, but it is my observation that on a golf course men are a far greater nuisance than women. And women can be more civilized golf companions, especially those who look good in tight shorts.

The greatest of golf sins are (1) slow play, (2) cheating and lying, and (3) telling really bad dirty jokes.

The fastest players are women and real old guys because they don't waste a lot of time twisting themselves into what they believe is a classic stance, when they look more like constipated hunchbacks.

And the slowest of all male players are yuppies, strutting and posing as in Dockers commercials. Or trying to dazzle each other with wisdom nuggets they learned while getting their MBAs.

The law should prohibit any yuppie from being on a golf course until he has become fat and bald like a decent guy.

Women don't hesitate letting faster players pass them. They believe that as lesser creatures they must stand aside. But most men act as if waving someone through would leave them impotent for life.

Women count all their shots and sink even the shortest of putts. But the average male hacker acts as if a curving three-foot putt is not worthy of his incredible skills.

I have never heard a woman tell a dirty joke on a golf course, or even a clean one. But in every male foursome there is a guy who mistakenly believes that he is the second coming of Henny Youngman.

So to paraphrase Professor Henry Higgins: Why can't a man be more like a woman on the golf course?

However, I must point out something that the blond, in her anger (she looks awful when she's mad), happened to overlook.

The offensive phrase in this paper was written by one Patricia Baldwin, editor-in-chief of *Golf for Women* magazine.

Tsk, tsk. I guess some of us are just more sensitive than others.

AND JUSTICE FOR ALL

the Reception a Black Family Got When It Moved to a White Suburb?

Whoever threw the bricks and fire bomb came sneaking around at night, which shows that they were sufficiently ashamed not to do it in broad daylight. I consider that real progress. By Chicago standards, it is almost brotherly. Maybe in 25 more years, there will be no more fire bombs. Only bricks. But, then, I'm a born optimist.

—*Chicago Sun-Times,* June 1, 1978

Bureaucrats?

They create a dizzying paper-work world of regulations, or-dinances, rules, codes, forms, and applications. And they ex-pertly maneuver these elements so that they are always right, even when they are obviously wrong. And they are never wrong, even when they clearly are. It must have been a coin-flipping bureaucrat who was the first to say: "Heads I win; tails you lose."

—*Chicago Sun-Times,* July 9, 1980

The "Truth" in Selma

SELMA, Ala.—The biggest complaint heard in Selma today is not about Martin Luther King Jr. and the horde of civil rights demonstrators who are disturbing the tranquillity of this city.

White residents complain most bitterly about what they consider to be a huge conspiracy to give Selma a bad name. All across the nation, they say, a completely false picture of Selma is being painted.

It is not clear how they know this, since out-of-state newspapers are not to be found here. But almost to a man, they ask the same question:

"Why don't you tell the truth?"

Certain "truths" have become the rage in Selma this week.

It is true that the death of the white minister was tragic. But it is also true that he barged in here, where he wasn't invited.

It is also true that he was killed by hotheads—not by the majority of decent, law-abiding citizens. And the hotheads were agitated by agitators.

Therefore, if we follow the truth closely, it appears that the outside minister's death was caused by the outside civil rights demonstrators.

(Just in case, though, defense-fund collection boxes for the four accused slayers can be found in many places.)

More Selma truths:

- Negroes and whites live together in great contentment.
- Negroes are happy with what they have, and they do not want anything more.

But the greatest Selma truth of them all is that peace and other benefits would return if outsiders would go away.

A sad-eyed blond young man elaborated on some of these points as he sat in a motel lobby.

"You see, it ain't our local niggers that is stirring up all this trouble. It's the troublemakers like Luther King, just trying to make some money.

"We get along fine with the colored folks here. You talk about integration? It's nothing for me to be walking downtown and have some colored boy I know come up and say, 'Mister Jack, can you let me have a couple of dollars for a couple of days?'

"I'll give him the money even though I know he's going to drink it up. And he don't have to call me Mister. I never told him to. He does it on his own.

"I'll tell you, I like a lot of niggers. There's some I trust more than some white people I know. Hell, we got a colored woman is just about raising our baby boy for us.

"I know a rich woman had an old colored gal working for her. That old woman got sick and for three days there was a Cadillac parked out in front of her house. That rich woman was inside helping tend her.

"These niggers is like children. They need someone to take care of them. They can't take care of themselves.

"Now you take Sheriff Clark. I know him real well. He's a good man but he doesn't look that way on television. He's the one who's kept this from getting worse.

"When this whole thing started, he was smart enough to round up some of the toughest hotheads in town and make them his deputies. He figured he could keep his eye on them this way."

A middle-aged salesman sat in a bar and gave his version of Selma truth.

"These people are crazy. I never heard of nothing so crazy as talking about walking all the way to Montgomery. They can't walk no 50 miles on that highway.

"They're complaining about Lowndes County [halfway to Montgomery] not having no niggers voting. You got to understand the people who live over in that county.

"Chances are, a farmer there has land that his folks have had for a couple of hundred years. They don't like outsiders. All those people like are farming and hunting.

"I wouldn't be surprised if there are some of them just waiting there in the woods and in swamps by the road if those demonstrators come through. They do a lot of hunting up there."

A sturdy 30-year-old Negro gave his version of Selma truth as he sat on the steps of his house in the big Negro shantytown area. His boots were caked with reddish mud, from walking rutted clay streets that run through the Negro sections.

"This is a nasty place. I've lived here on and off all my life. It's nasty.

"Those men in that sheriff's posse, they're just dirt farmers. They had no education. They don't know how to read a book. A man shouldn't have a job he can't do, and they can't do this job.

"I seen them kind of people all my life, but I still don't understand them. They let us tend their children and cook the food they eat.

"And they hate us. How can they let us do those things and hate us? I don't know why I stay here. I got my wife nearly talked into leaving. She's never been outside Selma in her life.

"Sure, I'm going to march today. If we get the vote, we can get Sheriff Clark out of there, and people like him.

"When you're gone they're going to try and get even. It's going to be harder than it is now. And we're going to have to be careful.

"But the younger ones won't forget this. They learned something."

A Negro bellhop, bringing a drink to a room, was asked for his version of the truth. He looked frightened and anxious to leave.

"I'm sort of busy, sir, I've got work to do. I don't have time for marching and those things. I've got lots of work to do."

But as he closed the door, he said softly:

"You see, the people around here just want to vote. I think every man should vote, don't you, sir?"

MARCH 19, 1965

The "Truth" in Chicago

MONTGOMERY, Ala.—A Chicagoan in the Deep South is often called upon to defend his city's reputation.

Many people here have a distorted picture of Chicago's racial matters. They even think we have problems.

It has been my civic duty to explain things as they really are. Among the most often heard falsehoods about Chicago are these:

"I hear that up in Chicago the Negroes and the whites aren't any friendlier than they are down here."

"That is not true. We haven't had a race riot since way back in the year 1964. And that one wasn't even in Chicago, it was in Dixmoor, a suburb."

"Yep. I read about that one. They were protesting against discrimination, just like here, weren't they?"

"Not really. It was outside agitators that came in and stirred up a few hotheads. That's what the police said."

"But what about integration? I've been told you don't have any more white people and Negroes living in the same neighborhoods than we do because the white folks don't like them."

"What a foul rumor. Why, if just one Negro family buys into a white neighborhood, all the other white people get so excited at the prospect of integration that they rush out and want to sell their homes, too. And they even sell for less money."

"But what about that stuff I read last fall about a Negro trying to move into your own mayor's neighborhood and not being welcome? That seems kind of funny for the liberal North."

"That only shows how a story can get distorted. Actually, there was a huge welcome for the Negro. The whole neighborhood turned out to meet him. The streets were jammed with people all through the night. They shouted greetings at him and showered him with things. They even gave him all sorts of nicknames. They got so enthusiastic that the police department had to come out and calm them down."

"My, my. Then how come he didn't stay in the apartment too long? That's what I read."

"Well, he was kind of a shy young man. He got embarrassed at all the attention he was getting and so he moved the very same week."

"Don't the white neighborhoods ever try to keep Negroes from moving in, like I've heard?"

"Just the opposite. When a neighborhood gets word that a Negro is going to move into a building, they sometimes get together and plan a surprise—sort of a midnight house warming. Even the fire department gets invited."

"How about all them fancy suburbs of yours? I hear that they don't integrate either."

"I don't know how that story got started. The fact is, when a Negro plans on moving into a suburb, a committee is formed to rush out and spread the happy news. It is usually composed of a priest, a minister, a rabbi, and maybe the mayor of the town. They go from door to door for weeks in advance, letting the people know so that they can control their enthusiasm. If they didn't do this, the residents might get all emotional, or maybe even hysterical."

"But I keep seeing stories about pickets, and demonstrations, marches, and sit-ins, just like we have down here. And it says that police in Chicago arrest them."

"That is blown up out of proportion, of course, by the hostile Southern press. The only time they are arrested is when they block traffic or disrupt governmental business."

"But they block traffic here in Montgomery every day."

"Well, we have far more traffic to worry about than you do."

"What about that school superintendent of yours? I hear the Chicago Negroes figure he is against school integration and that he ought to be run out of town. Why isn't he fired, since they are always demonstrating against him?"

"Well, in the North, unlike the South, there are two sides to every story. The mayor can't fire him just because some people take their protests into the streets. You can't have government by pressure in Chicago. After all, a lot of white people happen to like the school superintendent. A decision like that has to be thought out calmly and not in the heat of emotionalism."

"But I don't seem to understand."

"That's the idea."

MAY 28, 1968

Fascism Isn't Accidental

It was a pleasant, sunny day. Jim Trattner had a couple of hours to kill. His motorcycle was being tuned up and he was waiting for it.

The repair shop was near Lane Tech High, on the Northwest Side. Lane has pretty, grassy grounds. So Trattner and a friend got a couple of sandwiches, sat on a bench, ate, and talked.

That's no big deal, two guys sitting on a bench eating sandwiches. People do it all the time—workmen, secretaries. I can look out my office window at lunch time and see them in the building's plaza. A fine way to have lunch.

But it became a big deal because Trattner is different. He has long hair, a mustache, off-beat clothing, the entire hippie bit.

That's all right, too. It's his business what he wears. Or it should be. He's 29, married, and is close to a doctorate in psychology at Northwestern University. If he wants to wear his hair long, it is no more foolish or vain than middle-aged men paying $7 for a razor-cut with bush sideburns.

This being the United States of America, the land of freedom, a guy should be able to sit on a bench and consume a sandwich in peace.

Before he finished his meal, Trattner says, he was surrounded by Lane students, maybe 100 of them. Some were in ROTC uniforms, incidentally, or not so incidentally.

They were very angry at Trattner and his friend. They were offended because Trattner was sitting there with long hair, a mustache, and offbeat clothes, eating a sandwich in broad daylight.

"They started jeering at us, shouting obscenities," he related. "One said: 'You [bleeping] hippies better get outta here. We don't want weirdos around here.'

"Before we could go, they formed kind of a semicircle around us. There was more name-calling. Then somebody came up with a couple of pairs of scissors.

"One of them said they were going to cut all the hair off our heads. I was scared because I thought maybe we'd get stabbed with the scissors.

"Then I was hit by something—I didn't see what it was—in the back of the head. We were both pulled from the bench and kicked and punched. I guess it lasted a couple of minutes.

"There were some bystanders, adults. I think some were teachers. They just stood there and watched.

"It was a very helpless feeling to lay there and take the kicking and see that there was no one in the area who felt like helping a hippie-looking man."

Then, says Trattner, it occurred: that moment when the bugles blow and the cavalry arrives on the scene.

"A gang of black kids came out of the school. They waded right in and surrounded us to protect us. They picked us up, dusted us off, and called us 'soul brothers.' And they stuck with us until we were safe and could go back and pick up our cycle.

"The irony of having these black kids come in at the risk of their own safety and save us from more kicking is something. One said they did it because hippies aren't racists."

When his bruises heal, Trattner can mark off his experience as being educationally enriching, as the educators say.

He found out, in a few minutes and with a few kicks, what the national sentiment is. Not just toward hippies, but toward anyone who is rocking the boat.

As a relative of mine, not known for his civil libertarian instincts, raged one night: "I'm sick of seeing people protesting on the 10 o'clock news."

He wasn't at all sick of the problems that have brought about protests; he never gives them a thought. But his color TV is cluttered with antiwar protesters, the marching poor, the explosive ghetto-dwellers, the activist college students. His solution: Split their heads.

That's the spirit that moved the Lane students into action. Trattner was everything they dislike and fear. The solution? Hit him on the head.

We are becoming more and more tolerant of intolerance. It has become the official mood. The mayor was angry because only 11 people were killed last month in the riots on the West Side after the murder of Martin Luther King Jr. Daley bawled out the police for not plugging more.

So the police went out a week later and busted heads of peaceful marchers at the Civic Center. Not a murmur of protest from society. The news media, a good barometer, were almost silent.

Anyone who is different today faces harassment, whether it is in the way he dresses, or in the position he takes on important issues.

And when the price of being different is a cold fear, with good reason, then freedom as we peddle it in our international publicity releases is gone.

If and when it disappears, it won't be stolen by big government, the tax collector, or the Supreme Court. Fascism will be the people's choice. It usually is. We've managed to avoid it so far only because nobody nutty enough to give the people what they want has come along. Yet.

DECEMBER 24, 1968

For Too Many, There's No Joy

A year ago on Christmas morning, Darlene Hon was in Englewood Hospital, recovering from pneumonia.

It was the first time in 10 years of marriage that she and her husband, John, hadn't spent Christmas in their flat in Chicago's Bridgeport neighborhood.

But right after the nurse brought breakfast, John showed up with the three kids and an armload of gifts, and they celebrated Christmas there.

She gave him a velvet vest and a blue sweater. He gave her a waffle iron and a flat iron.

Mrs. Hon got well and came home. That was last Christmas. Things have changed since then.

On April 1, Mr. Hon, 31, a truck driver, was called up by the Army Reserve. He had already done a hitch, years earlier.

Six weeks later, he was shot in the head and died during combat in South Vietnam.

This Christmas season at Mrs. Hon's home, things look the same as before. There is a tree, and gifts, the children, and the fat dog.

"I'm trying to keep everything the same this year, like it isn't any different. But it is different, of course.

"It was always his job to put up the tree. This year, Cathy went in the other room until the tree was finished. She couldn't help."

And in Paris the diplomats ponder and debate the size and the shape of the peace table.

A year ago on Christmas morning, Martin Luther King was in Jamaica, writing and relaxing for the first time since he was an unknown minister in Alabama.

Four months later he was murdered while trying to help garbage men in Memphis get wages of more than $1.25 an hour.

On this Christmas morning, his widow and children will go to church. So will millions of other Americans. But most of them will feel the same about each other as they did a year ago.

A year ago on Christmas morning, Senator Robert F. Kennedy was in the mountains at Sun Valley, Idaho, relaxing and skiing with his wife and army of kids. Young Joe fell down and broke his leg and everybody got to sign the cast. John Glenn, the astronaut, was there, and some other friends, too.

This Christmas, Senator Kennedy has another child, a daughter he will never see. And the things he found wrong with this country, and talked about so stirringly, are still here.

Last Christmas morning, Delbert Simmons, 31, a bridgetender, gave his year-old son, Dwight, a little rubber dog that squeaked when you squeezed it. A squeaky dog.

"It was a good Christmas," Simmons said. "We had plenty of toys for the kids."

Sometime later, Dwight put his finger in a tiny hole in a wall, then in his mouth. Most of the walls in the flat on the West Side are covered with inexpensive but nice wood paneling. Mr. Simmons installed it when he moved in. But there were a few tiny spots where the soft, crumbly plaster was exposed.

In August, Dwight died of lead poisoning, one of 15 Chicago children to die of it in the past year or so.

When he died, the City Council was still drifting and dreaming of pleasanter things than dead ghetto babies or new laws requiring city building inspectors to check for lead-soaked plaster. They had the support of strong public apathy.

This Christmas, Mr. Simmons doesn't have to worry about crumbling plaster, because he doesn't have a son young enough to poke his finger in the wall. Or one young enough to laugh at a squeaky dog.

But somewhere there's another baby and another crumbling ghetto wall.

We really should try a lot harder between December 25ths.

One Word Tells All: Outrageous

SEPT. 9, 1966: Lucius Wright, a soldier in Vietnam for nine months, is on another combat patrol. His foot comes down on a hidden mine. The blast flings him like a rag doll. He is unconscious for 10 days while the doctors piece him together. The worst damage is to his head. When he opens his eyes, he can't talk and understands little.

JAN. 20, 1970: Lucius Wright, 25, went into the El station at Bryn Mawr Avenue and stood by the radiator. It was a cold day.

He had just finished his daily visit to a vocational training center on the North Side. They are trying to teach him to work with duplicating machines.

Now he was waiting for his girl, who works in a North Side factory. They sometimes meet at the station and ride back to the South Side together.

She was late, having missed a bus, and Wright stood in the station about 20 minutes, while people came and went.

Suddenly several policemen walked in. They surrounded Wright.

"What are you doing way up here on the North Side?" one of them asked Wright, who is black.

Wright hesitated before answering. Then he spoke very slowly. He always speaks slowly because he has aphasia, the result of the brain damage in Vietnam. He sometimes has trouble grasping the words of others and getting his own thoughts out. After Vietnam, it had taken six months of therapy in Walter Reed Army Medical Center before he was able to return to civilian life and a $400-a-month veteran's disability check.

"I'm waiting for my girl," Wright finally said.

The policemen turned him around and had him put his hands on the wall, in the classic "frisk" stance. They went through his pockets. One of them withdrew a vial of pills.

"Do you sell these?" Wright says they asked.

"I take them," he answered.

Once a week, Wright goes to the Veterans Administration Hospital on the West Side for treatment and medication. He is given three kinds of pills: a sedative, a tranquilizer, and a pill that wards off paralytic seizures.

The police put Wright's hands behind his back, snapped on the cuffs, put him in a car, and took him to the Foster Avenue police station.

On the way, he says, a policeman asked:

"Where do you get your pills?"

"Veterans Hospital. I was wounded in Vietnam. I need them for my seizures."

Wright says the policeman answered: "You don't get seizures from being wounded."

At the station he showed them his plastic VA patient's card and asked them to call his doctors or his VA counselor. It was a few minutes after 4 p.m., and if they called before 4:30, somebody would explain that he was a disabled vet and needed his pills.

They told Wright to keep quiet while they made out his arrest papers.

They put him in a room and a detective questioned him about the pills. Wright tried to explain about the mine and his head. Then, he says, he noticed something strange about the pill vial.

The VA hospital always puts on a label. The label shows where the pills come from and how often they should be taken. The label was there, he says, when they arrested him. Now, while he was being questioned, it was gone.

Wright was taken from the room. "Can I go now?" he asked a policeman. "No, you're going in a cell."

They booked him for illegal possession of dangerous drugs, a serious charge for which a man can be imprisoned.

They let Wright make a phone call and several hours later his sister raised bond money and went to the North Side to get him out. He was very nervous when she took him home. He says he had cried in his cell, partly out of confusion, partly out of anger.

He began crying, in fact, when he told me his story. Then he stopped crying and his mind seemed to drift, and he shook his head as if confused by it all.

"Maybe somebody saw me in the El station and thought something was wrong with me waiting there and called the police. I don't know. But I showed them my card. They could have called the VA, couldn't they? They'd have told how I had to have those pills."

An official at the Veterans Administration who is familiar with Wright's military and medical history was furious.

"There's nothing we can do, but it is an outrage. If they had any questions about those pills, a simple phone call to us could have cleared it up. Don't they try to determine the facts? We have many men walking around with metal plates in their heads and other problems. My God, it is conceivable that somebody could die in a cell without his medication."

A simple phone call could have told them a lot about Wright besides his injury, his Purple Heart, and his other military citations. They would have learned that he is a high school graduate, worked for a mail order house until drafted, has never been in trouble, and is trying hard to over-come the war injury he suffered.

The police would not discuss the arrest.

Wright goes to Narcotics Court on February 11. Presumably, the po-lice will discuss there and then why it is illegal for a black handicapped veteran to carry drugs prescribed by a veterans hospital. That appears to be the mystery in this case.

[Editors' note: On February 11, Wright was found not guilty. But, as Mike wrote in a fol-low-up column: "Like the Purple Heart, he'll have the police record the rest of his life."]

JULY 22, 1970

Bureaucracy—a Nightmare

People sometimes wonder if writing about problems ever gets results.

It does. And here is an example.

A few weeks ago, I wrote about a bureaucratic blunder that almost cost a baby its life.

The facts were fairly simple, once you got by the gobbledygook of the welfare world.

A caseworker for the Illinois Public Aid Department, Mrs. Gretchen Krueger, was convinced that a young welfare mother was mentally un-balanced and her 11-month-old child was in danger.

The woman did all sorts of strange things. She drank milk from the baby's bottle, while feeding the child candy. When her own mother tried to examine the baby, the young woman became violent.

She was separated from her husband, who had a drug problem, and was living with an older man. They sometimes left the child alone for hours.

A doctor who made post-natal examinations of the woman and child told the caseworker that he, too, thought the woman was mentally ill.

The woman's relatives were convinced that she was unbalanced and tried to petition Cook County Family Court to place the baby in a foster home. But because the woman was on welfare, the request had to come from welfare officials.

Finally, the woman disappeared from her flat with the baby and aim-lessly wandered the streets until a kindly landlord took her in.

That's when Mrs. Krueger wisely took action.

She drew up papers recommending that Family Court hold a hearing and decide whether the child would be safer in a foster home. She even lined up prospective foster parents.

She put it all in the report—the physician's fears, the woman's strange behavior, the wandering in the streets, and so on.

Then she sent it along through channels. The welfare system is nothing but a series of channels that lead from one desk to another desk.

Somewhere along the bureaucratic chain of command, someone arbitrarily decided that the child wasn't in any danger. There would be no court hearing. The child would remain with its mother. The matter was closed.

A short time later, the mother put the baby in a bathtub full of scalding water. Luckily, the landlord heard the child's screams and saved its life. But it suffered first-, second-, and third-degree burns.

Only then, after the damage was done, did the channels become unclogged.

The mother was examined and found to be schizophrenic, psychotic, suicidal, and homicidal, and she was committed to a mental hospital.

The child was assigned to a foster home, once it recovered.

And Mrs. Krueger was angry because that's what she had recommended in the first place.

So I wrote the story to show how cumbersome, inefficient, and harmful the bureaucratic welfare system is.

Now I can report that the column got fast action.

Mrs. Krueger has been punished by her superiors.

That's right. Mrs. Krueger, the only person who seemed to have enough sense to know the child was in danger, and the only person who tried to do something about it, has received a slap on the wrist.

Her superiors have issued a formal "warning notice" to her. It means she will have to shape up, and it goes into her personnel file as sort of a black mark.

Mrs. Krueger, the "warning notice" states, committed two sins.

First, there is some double-talk that I refuse to repeat, about ignoring "agency policy and procedures." Apparently she didn't make enough carbon copies, or use the right stapler, or some such nonsense.

Then we get to the real sin in the "warning notice":

"Mrs. Krueger . . . violated confidentiality of the record information by submitting the 'case data' to Mr. Mike Royko, a columnist for the *Daily News*—an outside source."

There is no "warning notice" for the higher-ups who sat behind a desk and made a stupid decision.

There's no questioning of a welfare system that allows such stupid things to occur.

But Mrs. Krueger rocked the boat, and that is unthinkable.

This is bureaucracy at its finest.

FEBRUARY 17, 1976

For Metcalfe, a 1936 Replay

After 40 years, Ralph Metcalfe still remembers the man's name and the words he spoke, even though they were in German.

"Hans Mueller was his name," Metcalfe says, a touch of distaste in his sonorous voice. "He was the starter in that race."

The race was the 100-meter dash. The event was the Olympic Games of 1936. The place was a huge stadium in Berlin.

Ah, what a television sports spectacular it would have made. The announcers would have been hysterical.

In the stands were thousands of proud Germans. And watching from his private box was Adolf Hitler, who had told them that just about everyone else in the world was inferior.

On the field were the black-skinned American sprinters, and you couldn't get much more inferior than that in 1936. Even back home, a lot of their countrymen thought they were pretty low.

But Ralph Metcalfe wasn't thinking about Hitler or crazy genetic theories. He was trying to get off to a good start, and Hans Mueller wasn't helping.

The start is important for any runner and it was even more critical for Metcalfe, who was heavier-muscled than most sprinters and usually came off the blocks a little behind.

But once he stretched out, he had tremendous speed and an amazing closing kick. Thus, slow starts and all, he had set three world records while in college five years earlier, when he had been called "the world's fastest human."

In Berlin, however, he was slightly past his peak and hadn't competed much for a couple of years. And Mueller, whose motives were definitely suspect, was making him edgy.

"A starter shouldn't create long delays," Metcalfe says of that race. "But Mueller did. He said: 'Auf die Plätze!' meaning we should get in place. Then he paused a long time. Then he said, 'Achtung, fertig,' meaning we should get set. He paused a long time again.

"It was then that I shifted my weight, just for an instant. At that moment the gun went off. And because of his lousy start I was the last one out and way behind.

"Half way to the finish, I was behind everybody in the race."

But Metcalfe still had the kick, and it must have been something to see in those few seconds. He shot past runners as if they were standing still. As he neared the tape, no question about it, he was moving faster than anybody on that track.

It would have made a great finish and a great story. But the kick wasn't quite enough. Jesse Owens reached the tape a hair before Metcalfe. Owens got the gold medal, Metcalfe settled for silver.

So the 1936 games will always be remembered as Owens' Olympics. He won three gold medals outright and shared another in the team relays, and the black Americans sent Hitler stalking from the stadium, twitching with rage.

Metcalfe has a slice of that Olympics, too, with his share of the relay's gold, and his silver for second in the 100-meter dash. (A few weeks later, he beat Owens in another competition. In fact, he beat him in about half the races they shared.)

But if it hadn't been for Hans Mueller, the too-deliberate starter, Metcalfe might have had an even bigger share of those Olympic memories.

"It really was," Metcalfe still says, "a lousy start."

Now, after all those years, Metcalfe has encountered another Hans Mueller.

His name is Richard J. Daley, and he is the starter for most political races around here.

And when Metcalfe speaks Daley's name, it is with even greater distaste than the memory of Mueller can provoke.

"He is the only enemy I've ever had in politics," Metcalfe says.

Well, if you have Mayor Daley as an enemy, you really don't need any others.

They weren't always enemies. There was a time when they might have been considered friendly equals. On paper, at least.

That was in 1952, when both were Chicago ward committeemen. Daley, however, was from the politically potent Bridgeport neighborhood. So he was a little more equal.

After Daley became Big Boss, they got along. Metcalfe became alderman, then U.S. congressman and the city's leading black politician.

They'd still be getting along OK, but a few years ago Metcalfe tried to convince Daley that there was such a thing as police brutality against blacks. Daley told him, in effect, to shut up and mind his own business.

Metcalfe didn't shut up. Whatever it was that drove a young black man, born in 1910, to become a track star, get through college, become an officer in World War II, and push his way into Chicago politics wasn't dead. Dormant, maybe, but still there. And since Daley's insult, Metcalfe has been his own man.

Now Daley wants to crush him completely. Boss has moved one of his flunkies into Metcalfe's district with orders to beat him in next month's primary election. And Daley has told Metcalfe's oldest political friends to help with the job or be crushed themselves.

It's Machine politics at its most basic and brutal. And if Metcalfe survives, it will be one of the bigger upsets in years.

Jesse Owens said something interesting about Metcalfe. He said Metcalfe was the fiercest competitor he had ever seen.

"You knew when he was behind you that he would come thundering up near the finish," Owens said.

Metcalfe helped make one dictator unhappy with that fierce drive. It would be fun if he could do it to another.

[Editors' note: Metcalfe won the primary in a landslide and kept his seat in Congress.]

NOVEMBER 18, 1979
Wrong Mom? Tough!

Mrs. Fran Lasota is in real trouble. She has been formally accused of abandoning her own baby. And she has received a summons, ordering her to appear in court and to bring the neglected baby with her.

Fran's friends and neighbors in the town of Marengo will probably be shocked and dismayed to read that Fran would abandon her baby in Chicago. Especially since Fran is in her 40s and hasn't had a baby for many years.

It came as a shock to Fran, too, when her phone rang a few weeks ago and a bureaucrat from the Illinois Department of Children and Family Services asked her why she had abandoned her baby.

"My what?" asked Fran.

"Your baby," the bureaucrat said.

"What are you talking about?"

The man told her that a week-old boy had been brought to a Chicago hospital to be treated for a rash.

The hospital cured the rash, but the mother never came back for the baby.

"Why do you think it is my baby?" Fran asked.

"Is your name Frances Lasota?"

"Yes."

"Well, that's the name of the mother," the bureaucrat said.

Fran told the man that he had the wrong Fran Lasota. And she asked him how she had been chosen as the errant mother.

From what he said, she gathered that he had just looked in phone books for people named Lasota until he found one named Fran.

"Well, you'll have to keep looking," she said, "because it's not my kid."

She thought that would be the end of it. But recently she received a registered letter.

It was the summons, telling her she had to appear in court on a neglect charge. And it said she should bring the baby with her.

Naturally, she was flustered. She called the Cook County state's attorney's office, which prosecutes neglectful parents, and explained her problem.

"He told me I had better show up in court," she said.

She called a lawyer in Marengo and asked him what to do.

"He told me I should get a Chicago lawyer to defend me."

She called the Marengo Police Department to see if it had any advice.

"They told me that I should probably go to court. If I didn't, I might be held in contempt of court for not showing up with the baby I don't have."

She called the Department of Children and Family Services and tried to explain her problem.

"They didn't seem to understand what I was talking about."

Now she doesn't know what to do. It's a long trip from Marengo to Chicago, and Fran doesn't see why she should have to come all that way for something she hasn't anything to do with. Nor does she want to spend money on a lawyer.

But she is afraid if she doesn't show up, she will be held in contempt and will be in even worse trouble.

So she sought my advice, which was a wise thing for her to do, since I've had a lot of experience in dealing with bureaucrats.

Over the years, I've dealt with people who have received letters from Social Security bureaucrats telling them their benefits were being cut off because they had died.

Some readers might also remember the man who came home one day and found his house knocked down. "Ooops," the bureaucrats said, "wrong address."

Then there was the man who lost most of his face in Vietnam, then received a letter from the VA saying that it couldn't pay his medical bills because his injury wasn't service-related.

So my advice to Fran is that she had better go to court.

And she had better take a baby with her.

Believe me, if you show up without a baby, they'll just get suspicious. They'll think you dropped the kid on his head and don't want to admit it, and you'll be in deeper trouble.

So borrow one. Somebody must have a baby you can use for a day. Go in there, show them the kid is healthy and happy, and maybe they'll let you off with just a stern warning.

On the other hand, they might decide you are unfit and take the baby away from you. Then you'd have to go back to your friend and say: "Sorry, but your kid's in a foster home. But thanks for trying to help."

That wouldn't be good because your friend would probably be miffed. So I'll have to come up with another plan.

OK, here's what you do. Go rent a monkey. There are places you can get them.

Put the monkey in baby clothes and take it to court and say to the judge:

"OK, Your Honor, I admit it. I abandoned my baby. But look at this kid. He looks like a monkey. It's from his father's side. If you had a kid this ugly, Your Honor, wouldn't you abandon him? I mean, he's got hair on his feet."

Chances are, the judge will be sympathetic and let you go, especially if the monkey bites him.

The worst that can happen is that they will declare you an unfit mother and take the monkey away from you and put it in a foster home.

You'll be out one monkey and the Department of Children and Family Services will be stuck with a foster baby that bites, climbs the drapes, and has hair on its feet.

And who knows—someday you might be proud. The kid could grow up to be an alderman.

MARCH 11, 1981

He Deserved It

The small crowd that gathered outside the prison to protest the execution of Steve Judy softly sang "We Shall Overcome." I guess that was supposed to pluck our heartstrings. Mine remained unplucked.

I don't know why they chose that song, which became an anthem of the civil rights movement during the 1960s.

Back then it was sung by people who were struggling, and in several cases dying, in the cause of bringing fundament rights to those who had been deprived of them for centuries.

I heard it sung, and I sometimes joined in, at battlegrounds like Selma and Montgomery and Chicago's Marquette Park, and it never failed to move me.

But it didn't seem quite the same, hearing it sung out of concern for someone who, upon finding a woman with a flat tire, raped and murdered her, then drowned her three small children. And then said that he hadn't been "losing any sleep" over his crimes.

Well, if a person doesn't lose any sleep over the memory of what it felt like when he held the heads of tiny, struggling children under water, then there can't be much humanity left in him.

So I can't share in the horror that these softly singing people felt because Steve Judy, with the aid of a jolt of electricity, was going to catch up on his sleeping time.

The people who protested Judy's execution probably shared Will Rogers' sentiment: "I never met a man I didn't like."

But I share the sentiment of a sad old cop who once said to me: "I never met a child-killer I liked."

At one time, I was against capital punishment. That was when racist judges and juries routinely applied separate standards for black and white killers. And I still oppose it except in cases where there are absolutely no mitigating circumstances.

By mitigation, I mean crimes of passion, in which husbands or wives or friends go berserk and turn on one another. Or people who are so squeezed by social conditions that just once in their lives they explode.

But two things changed my mind.

First, there were the many families of murder victims I met as part of my job.

It's one thing to read or hear the impersonal news account of a murder: "The body of a 26-year-old woman was found Tuesday in a forest preserve. . . ."

It's another thing to talk to the young husband or the mother or father of the murder victim and to see the undeserved life sentence of grief they have received.

I remember the grocer's wife. She was a plump, happy woman who enjoyed the long workday she shared with her husband in their ma-and-pa store. One evening, two young men came in and showed guns, and the grocer gave them everything in the cash register.

For no reason—almost as an afterthought—one of the men shot the grocer in the face. The woman stood only a few feet from her husband when he was turned into a dead, bloody mess.

She was about 50 when it happened. In a few years her mind was almost gone and she looked 80. They might as well have killed her, too.

Then there was the woman I got to know after her daughter was killed by a wolf-pack gang during a motoring trip. The mother called me every so often, but nothing I said could ease her torment. It ended when she took her own life.

A couple of years ago, I spent a long evening with the husband, sister, and parents of a fine young woman who had been forced into the trunk of a car in a hospital parking lot. The degenerate who kidnapped her kept her in the trunk, like an ant in a jar, until he tired of the game. Then he killed her.

I defy anybody to convince me that this man shouldn't be executed.

Those who oppose the death penalty say that nothing is gained by killing a killer, that the victim can't be brought back, so why should society share in the taking of life?

I think something *is* gained. Revenge. And if the act of revenge brings even the tiniest sense of relief and comfort to the families of the victims, then it is well worth taking the life of the killer.

Something else is gained. It is that society is saying it respects human life and that it cannot overlook the monstrous acts of someone like Judy. When it executes him, it is recognizing the worth of the lives of that woman and her three children.

The other event that changed my thinking on the death penalty was the trial in Israel of Adolf Eichmann, the Nazi bureaucrat who ordered so many of the death-camp killings during World War II.

There was never any doubt in my mind that Eichmann and other Nazi killers should be executed. What they did was not an act of war, but an act of murder.

So how could I believe that Eichmann should die for the cold, unemotional murders of helpless women and children, but that somebody like Judy should not be executed for the cold, unemotional murder of a helpless woman and her children.

Like Judy, Eichmann didn't lose any sleep over his crimes.

So the next time those kindhearted people gather outside a prison to mourn the execution of a killer, I suggest that they look for another song to sing.

There's an old spiritual that includes the words "All my trials, Lord, soon be over."

Those words could now apply to Judy. But I doubt that the father of those three murdered children can ever say that.

Baseball's Black Eye

When I was a kid, I knew who all the great ones of the past had been: Ruth, Cobb, Hornsby, Gehrig, Wagner, Alexander, Johnson, Dean, and dozens more. Even though I hadn't seen them play, I knew their names and what they looked like and could recite their awesome statistics from memory.

And the great players of my boyhood—DiMaggio, Williams, Musial, Mize, Greenberg, Blackwell—I saw them all. There wasn't a star player I didn't know about.

I should say "we." We, the kids in the neighborhood, would talk and argue about them for hours. Who was the more powerful hitter? Who had the most blinding fastball? Who could run down a deep fly ball fastest? Did they really all eat Wheaties?

We might not have agreed on any of these earth-shaking issues, but we knew *who* we were talking about. We might flounder through geography and sleep through geometry. But all of us could have pulled an "A" in Baseball History and Statistics.

Except that none of us had ever heard of Josh Gibson.

If someone had barged into one of our schoolyard debates and said that somebody named Josh Gibson was the greatest hitter there ever was, we would have gone home and said a crazy was loose in the neighborhood.

There was no great player named Josh Gibson. At least in our world there wasn't. And, sadly, our world was the one that counted.

But, of course, there really was a Josh Gibson. But we didn't know it. Hardly anyone knew it.

And he probably was the best hitter who ever played—better than Ruth, Hornsby, Williams, Aaron, and all the others. They say he could hit a baseball harder and farther than anyone who ever played the game. And he hit it often. They also say that no catcher ever snapped a harder throw to second.

But we didn't know it then, and few baseball fans know it now, because Josh Gibson was black and he died in 1947—the first year black men were permitted to play major league baseball.

Every time I think of that racial barrier, I find it amazing. And disgusting.

And I'm thinking about it again because Satchel Paige, probably the best pitcher there ever was, died a couple of days ago.

It was only 35 years ago that there still existed a baseball policy, an agreement, or whatever you want to call it, that a black American citizen could not play major league baseball.

It didn't matter that everyone in professional baseball, including the players, knew that Josh Gibson was the best hitter in the world, or that Cool Papa Bell was the fastest player, or that Satchel Paige was the best pitcher.

The baseball people knew that the segregated Negro League had teams that were as good as or better than the best in the major leagues.

They knew there were blacks playing in dusty southern rural ballparks, picking up pocket money in semipro games, who should have been playing in the World Series.

There couldn't have been a more dramatic example of the kind of stifling, vicious racism that existed in this country than the segregation of baseball—which was then the only truly national professional team sport.

Yet, almost nothing was said. This segregation was taken for granted. I don't recall the subject ever coming up for discussion among the old baseball fans in my neighborhood and family. Most fans probably didn't even know these black players existed.

But the team owners, to their shame, knew it. They were just too cowardly and profit-conscious to do anything about it until Branch Rickey, followed by Bill Veeck, decided it was time for a big step forward. The rest of them were afraid that the sight of a Josh Gibson hitting 600-foot home runs might drive away their white paying customers.

And, to its shame, the press knew it. At least those who put out the sports pages. But their business was selling entertaining reading. And they didn't think their readers would be entertained by being told that it was a disgrace that blacks were barred from playing an interracial game of bat and ball.

Even now, when someone like Satchel Paige dies, the stories about him really don't describe the significance of his life and career.

Actually, Paige did better than most men of his race. He did achieve some recognition, although it was late in life. And Josh Gibson earned a decent living all those years he played black baseball, although he was said to have died at 35 because he drank too much out of frustration at his talent being unrecognized.

What should be remembered about men like Paige and Gibson is that it was only 35 years ago that this barrier was lifted.

What should be asked, when we think of Paige and Gibson, is this: If, until only 35 years ago, these two enormously gifted men could be barred from playing bat and ball, how many other talented black people were stifled in other pursuits during all those years after they were allegedly freed?

This part of our history should be remembered whenever somebody says: "Hey, they've got all their rights. What's stopping those people from being as successful as me?"

Now, by law, nothing is stopping them. But think back to the way things were only 35 years ago in baseball. Consider the way things must have been in the rest of our society. And you get the answer: Yes, they're in the game now, but it was the late innings before anybody told them: "Play ball."

OCTOBER 21, 1983

Helms' Ranting Reminds Us How Far We've Come

I'm surprised at how upset so many people are by the way Senator Jesse Helms has been bad-mouthing Martin Luther King Jr.

Apparently they don't appreciate the essential role that Helms, an embarrassment from North Carolina, has played in the debate over a national holiday honoring King.

Twenty years ago, when King was approaching the peak of his influence, it wouldn't have been hard to find prominent public figures who maligned him. They were everywhere, blinking at the frightening specter of civil rights.

Senators from both parties did it. Governors and mayors did it. So did writers of editorials, disc jockeys, and anybody else who had the public's ear.

King was a troublemaker. He was rocking the boat. He was threatening national security, tranquillity, and the right of Americans to life, liberty, and the pursuit of happiness—if they happened to be born white.

Today most sensible people agree that King was, at the least, a force for needed social change in his time. And, more realistically, a genuinely great American.

So it's not easy to find someone prominent to say the nasty things about him that used to be so common. Especially with so many blacks now registered to vote.

That's where Helms comes in, bless his tiny brain.

It's as if somebody called the actors union and asked for someone to play the role of a thick-headed, small-minded, ignorant, bigoted, racist bumpkin.

Helms has been perfect. Of course, he should be. He's been rehearsing for the role most of his life.

How else could we appreciate King's memory and the things he accomplished if we didn't have Helms around to remind us of what King— and all other American blacks—were up against.

When I hear Helms talk, it's like turning the clock back to those frightening but inspirational days . . .

It was spring of 1965, and I was in Selma, Alabama. The scent of newly blossoming flowers was in the air. So was the scent of fear.

King had been leading civil rights marches there. He was after something revolutionary—at least in the minds of the South's political leaders. He wanted blacks to have the right to vote.

The marches were actually very tiny. A few dozen people walking down a small-town street, singing "We Shall Overcome."

But that caused bigots to froth.

During a lull in the confrontations, I walked across the bridge on which the world had seen marchers being whipped and clubbed and run down by cops on horses.

Then I went into a nearby diner. Some sheriff's deputies were having coffee. One of them—a ranking officer—said something to his companion so chilling I've never forgotten it.

He casually said: "Kill a few coons and this [bleep] will stop."

Well, they killed a few. Blacks. Whites. A clergyman. An Italian-American housewife from Detroit. In only a few months, they killed several from ambush and with clubs to the head.

But it didn't stop King or his movement.

And there was the day on the Southwest Side of Chicago, where King—in one of his more naïve moments—thought he could bring his message of brotherhood, justice, and equality.

The answer was a brick to his head.

In a way, it was an even more vicious act than those that happened in the deep South.

At least the white Southerner had his heritage and history as a rationalization—the Civil War, Marching Through Georgia, and all the things his grandpa told him about.

But the rock-throwers in Chicago had none of that. They were bigots in their purest form. Their parents got off the boat, but they were already throwing rocks at Americans with much deeper roots than they had.

And everywhere there were people who sounded like Helms sounded this week.

They didn't have to be Southern politicians. We quickly discovered how unifying a force racism was.

I remember a foreign-born Chicago politician, speaking in broken English: "Why dees black guy make so much trouble, huh?"

And there was the pillar of American law and order, J. Edgar Hoover, a born hotel gumshoe who overachieved his way to the top job in the FBI.

I always had suspected that Hoover was kind of a creep. I mean, he spent most of his life vicariously peeping through keyholes and hanging around with old bachelor buddies.

But I didn't know how creepy he was until I was approached by one of his Chicago pals, who offered to play tapes that would prove to me that King had a weakness for a good-looking woman.

It turned out that Hoover, a member of the President's administration, was peddling these tapes to newsmen all over the country. All the tapes proved was that King—like many great and ordinary men—had weaknesses of the flesh. But Hoover's problems were such that he should have talked to a shrink.

Now, like Hoover, the bigots of the '60s are gone. Or, like George Wallace, they've changed their tunes.

If it hadn't been for Helms, I might have forgotten the way things were.

So thank you, Senator Helms, you wonderful boob you, for reminding us of what we used to be.

And how far we've come.

SEPTEMBER 21, 1990

Where Good Sense Is in the Minority

You play the jury and decide. Does Mike Welbel discriminate in his hiring practices?

Welbel owns a small business, the Daniel Lamp Company, on Chicago's Cermak Road.

He buys lamp parts that are made elsewhere, and his workers assemble them in his plant. The lamps are shipped to furniture stores.

He has 26 employees. The jobs require little skill or education so the pay is low. But a job is a job. Welbel says that of his 26 workers, 21 are Hispanic and five are black.

At this point, some of you might say: Yes, Welbel discriminates because he doesn't have any non-Hispanic white employees.

Overruled. Welbel's business is in the heart of the Southwest Side's Hispanic community. So most of the people he hires are from the neighborhood. It's doubtful that anyone would want to travel a considerable distance to work in the lamp shop.

But yes, Welbel does discriminate. You might not think so, and I don't think so. That doesn't matter. Federal bureaucrats say he does. And so he's up to his ears in trouble.

It seems that a black woman applied for a job about 18 months ago. She wasn't hired. Welbel says he doesn't know why.

"I didn't interview her. Maybe the plant supervisor did. He's not here anymore. I don't know why she wasn't hired. Maybe we didn't need anyone. I just don't know."

But he does know that the woman filed a complaint with the Chicago office of the Equal Employment Opportunity Commission, the federal agency that is supposed to guard against discriminatory hiring practices. She complained that she wasn't hired because she is black.

And one spring day last year, two investigators came to his plant.

"I told them, 'Here's the records. Help yourselves. You can see everything.' What did I have to hide? I figured that if everybody who works for me is Hispanic or black, how could I be discriminating?

"You see, when I started the business nine years ago, I used to deal with the state Department of Labor or place help-wanted ads.

"Then I got to know these Hispanic organizations—the Spanish Coalition and Latino Youth in Chicago—and we could call and say we needed a couple of people, and they'd say 'no problem,' and send someone in.

"So that's how I've done most of my hiring the last few years. When there's an opening, I call them and they refer people and we hire the ones who are best suited for the work."

That's why Welbel wasn't concerned when the federal bureaucrats came snooping. With an all-minority work force, why should he worry? "I didn't even get a lawyer."

Now he knows why he should have worried. "Dealing with those government people is frightening. They do all the talking. They tell you how it's going to be. You just sit and listen. I've never even met the woman who filed the complaint."

The bureaucrats have told him how it is going to be.

First, they say he must pay the woman $340.01 in wages she lost by not being hired.

Welbel says: "Fine. I'll be glad to pay her that just to get rid of the headache."

But that's just for starters. Sort of a small ante in the pot.

The bureaucrats have also demanded that Welbel pay $123,991 in back pay.

Back pay to whom? Good question. The money is to be divvied up by six other blacks who weren't hired and whose names were found in Welbel's files. And by any other blacks who might have applied in 1988 and 1989.

And who are these others? Welbel doesn't know. Nor do the bureaucrats.

So the feds want Welbel to spend about $10,000 on newspaper advertising to find black people who say they applied and weren't hired. Then they can come in and get their share of the $123,991.

"They told me that I should have had 8.45 black employees in 1988 and 1989. They said that within a three-mile radius of my plant, companies that have 100 workers or more average 31.1 percent black. So I should have a 31.3 percent black work force. And that's how they came up with what I owe people who didn't work for me.

"And they want me to spend $10,000 on advertising to find people who didn't work for me so I can pay them $123,991 for not working for me."

Is Welbel going to do it?

"I can't. I don't have the money. To tell the truth, the whole company isn't worth that much. That's why I came in this neighborhood. I got the building cheap. Nobody wanted it. I have a non-skilled labor pool nearby.

"No, I can't pay that money. I'll have to close down, go out of business.

"This is incredible. I'm a small operation. I've got 26 minority people working for me. And here's this federal agency on my back with some mathematical formula that I never heard of before."

I called the EEOC for their side of it, but they wouldn't discuss the case. I can understand that. If I did something that loony, I wouldn't want to talk about it either.

So if the EEOC doesn't back off, Welbel might have to go out of business. And that will eliminate 26 jobs held by minorities. They won't have incomes, they won't pay taxes, and maybe some of them will have to go on welfare, which means someone else's taxes will be used to support them.

I wonder: Considering all the things the Japanese are acquiring in this country, do you think they might want to buy the EEOC?

[Editors' note: After a year of negotiating with EEOC officials, Mike Welbel finally settled for $25,000, plus lawyers' fees. "It was the best deal I could get," he said.]

APRIL 4, 1991

This Story May Not Have Happy Ending

I don't know if James Heyda snores. But in the telling of this story, let's assume he does. And that he snores loud and with some regularity.

Now, let's have Heyda sleeping soundly in his bed. It's the middle of the night, and he is snoring up a storm.

He's snoring so loudly that the sound carries into the next apartment. And there, lying awake, getting angrier and angrier at the ear-splitting noise, is his neighbor.

Finally the neighbor yells, "I can't take it anymore," leaps out of bed, dashes down the hall, kicks in Heyda's door, and bursts into the bedroom.

In our imaginary story, this neighbor is a very big, strong young guy.

"I'll teach you not to snore anymore," he shouts, grabbing the groggy Heyda's ear and yanking it so hard that almost two inches of the ear is torn loose from Heyda's head.

That causes Heyda to scream. And the loud sound makes the neighbor even angrier. So he starts beating on Heyda with his fists.

When he finishes, Heyda is a real mess. He has seven broken ribs on the right side, 12 broken ribs on the left side, a broken thigh bone, and two fractures near the right ankle and two near the right knees.

But, thank goodness, he recovers. And the short-fused neighbor is arrested, admits his crime, and is charged with aggravated battery.

Naturally, they go before a judge. And I would assume that Heyda would want to see justice done and the violent neighbor punished for almost yanking his ear off and busting up his bones.

But, in our story, the judge calls the prosecutor and the neighbor's lawyer into his chambers and has a meeting. He says that if the man pleads guilty, he will not send him to prison. Instead, he will give him probation. After all, the man has no record of ever beating up Heyda before. And it's unlikely that he'll do it again. So why not give him a break?

How would Heyda feel about this? I don't know. But I have to assume that he'd be a bit miffed. Wouldn't you?

As I said, none of these things happened, although James Heyda is a real person. In fact, he is a Cook County Circuit Court judge assigned to the Criminal Courts.

And this morning, he is going to be hearing a real case that has some similarities to the fictional story.

In the real story, it wasn't somebody snoring. It was a six-week-old baby crying during the night.

And it wasn't a neighbor who became angry; it was the baby's father, one Albert Valentine, 21, who is 6 feet 3 inches tall and weighs about 230 pounds.

Valentine lives with his girlfriend, the baby's mother. Those who have spoken to them say they aren't likely candidates for admission to Harvard or Yale.

According to police and hospital reports, the parents took the baby to Cook County Hospital with a torn ear. When a baby has an unusual injury, the doctors become suspicious. So they gave the infant a thorough examination. X-rays showed the injuries I mentioned above, plus others: broken ribs, thigh, legs, a total of 26 fractures.

The police were called and Valentine was questioned. The officers say he finally admitted that he had lost his temper because the baby was crying during the night. So, while changing a wet diaper, he yanked the infant's ear and gave him a few hard shakes. The shakes must have been vigorous to pop that many bones. Of course, a six-week-old baby has fragile little bones.

The prosecutors believe they have enough evidence to justify a conviction and a prison sentence.

However, sources tell me that the judge recently had a conference with the prosecution and defense. This is called plea bargaining. The judge told them, the sources say, that in exchange for a guilty plea, he is inclined to give Valentine probation. And the judge didn't seem to be impressed by the protests of the state's attorney's office, which wants Valentine sent to prison.

Now, I would not try to influence a judge's thinking. If it turns out that Judge Heyda thinks that probation is suitable punishment for almost yanking an infant's ear off and smashing his bones, that's what we pay the judge for: his wisdom and judgment.

On the other hand, the judge might consider how he would feel if it had happened to him. At least, he could try to defend himself. And he could speak for himself and demand justice.

But a baby is defenseless. A baby can't go to court and speak in his own behalf. So who goes to bat for the abused children? Not their parents. In this case, as in so many, one of them is accused of doing the abusing. So that leaves the representatives of society—the cops, the medical people, the prosecutor, and, finally, the judge.

And if any of them say, "Well, he is the father, after all, and a crying baby can fray the nerves, and he promises never to do it again, and the baby's broken bones and torn ear have mended, and the prisons are overcrowded, and we can avoid a time-consuming trial and make all of our jobs easier, so why not let him cop a plea and give him probation . . . ?"

If any of them say that, it's the same as saying that it's open season on defenseless kids. And we provide greater protection than that for wild geese.

JUNE 23, 1994

Lincolnshire Makes Lunch a Real Hassle

Kevin Perkins, 28, is starting to feel like one of those characters featured on TV shows about America's most-wanted fugitives.

The first time it happened was last summer. He took his lunch break at his technician's job at MDA Scientific, Inc., which is in the prosperous northwest Chicago suburb of Lincolnshire.

"I went over to the bank to use the cash station. I got some money, and as I walked out of the bank a police car pulled up.

"The officer told me to step over to his vehicle. He had his arms at his side like he was ready to draw his gun.

"I asked him, 'What's the problem, officer?' He said: 'The bank called and said there was a suspicious character.'

"That shocked me because I had been going to the bank for more than a year and the tellers all know me."

Even so, Perkins said, the Lincolnshire cop put him in the back seat of the squad car, radioed in his name and other personal information, discovered Perkins was not a wanted felon, and let him go.

Then it was January. Once again, Perkins took his lunch break, walked to the bank, and a Lincolnshire cop yelled: "Can I help you?"

"I ignored him and went in the bank. He followed me through the door and said: 'Can I help you?' I said: 'Can you help me with what?' He asked me if maybe I needed a ride somewhere. I told him, no, I didn't. Then he asked to see some ID. So I gave him my driver's license.

"Then another policeman came through the door. And they took my driver's license and read stuff off of it into their radio. And they again offered me a ride. I told him, no, I don't need your help. So I left and went back to my job."

Now it was last Thursday, and again lunch time.

"I'm walking to Italian Connection, a fast-food restaurant. About a half mile from where I work.

"All of a sudden a police car pulls up and the officer says: 'Where are you going?'

"I said: 'Why do you want to know?'

"He said: 'Perhaps I can take you there.'

"So I told him I didn't need him to take me nowhere. And he gets out of the car and tells me to put my hands on the car and to 'spread 'em.'

"I asked him: 'What did I do?' He pushed me against the car. He asked me for my name and my driver's license, but I told him I wasn't going to tell him anything until he told me why he was doing what he was doing.

"So he put handcuffs on me and put me in the back of his squad car and asked if I had any warrants or felonies he should know about.

"I told him I wasn't going to tell him anything until he told me what I had done wrong.

"So we exchanged some words. He said I was 'copping an attitude.' And I told him, yes, I was having an attitude because I was tired of being stopped by the police for no reason.

"Then he radioed in and the dispatcher told him: 'He works for MDA. You have to let him go.'

"So he let me out of the squad car and took the handcuffs off. Then two plainclothes detectives pulled up and he talked to them and they started hassling me for having used obscenities to an officer. I guess I did say something about this being a lot of bull[bleep].

"So we exchanged words and I told them that if they were going to arrest me, do it. Or else I was going to have lunch and go back to my job.

"When I got back to work, I was kind of steaming and I told our personnel department. And the next thing I knew, the president of the company heard what happened. And he went to the police station with me to make an official complaint. I couldn't believe it. The president of the company doing that for me.

"When we got there, the desk sergeant who took the complaint said to me: 'Hey, don't you remember me? I stopped you too.'"

The president of MDA, which services toxic-gas detectors, confirmed Perkins' story. John McAlear described Perkins as a model employee—well educated, dedicated to his job, with a fine work ethic. "You give him the work, he gets it done. What else can you ask for?"

He's so dedicated, in fact, that he commutes by public transportation more than two hours each way from his Chicago home.

"I have people who live two minutes away, and Kevin is at work before they are," said his supervisor, Frank Gambino.

So why is he always being arrested by the Lincolnshire cops? At this point, he has already been questioned by about one-third of the town's entire police department.

Seeking an answer, we called the police chief, but he was on vacation. An assistant said the matter was being reviewed and he had no comment.

Then we called the village manager and asked if he had any idea why Perkins had so much difficulty in going to lunch without being stopped by the Lincolnshire police.

The village manager said he didn't know, but the matter was being investigated.

"Could the fact that Mr. Perkins is black have anything to do with it?" we asked.

The village manager said he could not comment on that.

Well, even if he can't comment, he might think about it. It's what you call a clue.

CHASING THE
CHANGING SCENE

HEY, MIKE, WHADDAYA THINK ABOUT . . .

the Military Draft?

By eliminating the draft, we have eliminated one of the purest sources of misery for young men. As a result, we are producing one generation after another of middle-class young people who don't know what real misery is. Therefore, they aren't prepared for the realities of adulthood, which is 98 percent misery and even worse when things get rough.

—*Chicago Sun-Times,* August 22, 1979

Nachos?

Everyone to their own, but I've had nachos and melted cheese only once, and I'm convinced that those brave men died at the Alamo to prevent this dish from entering the United States.

—*Chicago Tribune,* October 30, 1989

the Title "Alderman"?

For the sake of political correctness, maybe the Chicago City Council should give thought to officially changing their title from the gender-offensive "alderman" to the gender-neutral "aldercreature." On the other hand, some of them might not want to be known as aldercreatures. One must think of the wife and children. "What does your husband do?" "He is an aldercreature." "Oh, my goodness, is there any treatment for it?"

—*Chicago Tribune,* December 15, 1992

High-Rise Lobby: The Old People Just Don't Fit In

The manager of a high-rise building on Lake Shore Drive recently sent this letter to his tenants:

> *Dear Tenant:*
>
> We have been receiving numerous complaints on the misuse of the lobbies by adults as well as children.
>
> We must ask, therefore, that "Lobby Sitting" be discontinued.
>
> Please note under Rules and Regulations:
>
> Children shall not be permitted to loiter or play on the stairways, halls, porches, or court areas or in public places generally used by the public or other tenants.
>
> The sidewalks, entryways, passages, vestibules, halls, and stairways outside of the several apartments shall not be used for any other purpose than ingress and egress to and from the respective rooms or apartments.
>
> We have been asked by many why we have sofas and chairs in the lobby if we do not permit their use.
>
> It is the intention of the owners that seating be available for the FEW MINUTES that a guest may be waiting for a tenant, or that a tenant and guest be waiting for a taxi or driver to pick them up, and to enhance our lobby.
>
> We are sure you will agree that we are constantly extending efforts to maintain our lobbies and public areas in a manner that will be pleasing to you and reflect the prestige of our building. It is our sincere hope that you will cooperate with us.

The letter angered a lady who lives in the building. She said it was directed at the elderly people who, during this winter's great blizzard, had no place to go. So they sat in the lobby just to get out of their apartments for a few hours.

The lady sent it to me because she felt I would share her anger.

I can't get angry about the letter because I think I understand the feelings of the building manager and the people who complained to him about all those old people hanging around the lobby.

Life just happens to be different in a high-rise than, say, in a bungalow or three-flat neighborhood.

And High-Rise Man sees things—himself included—in a different way.

High-Rise Man is like his building—soaring, lean, modern, gracious, cool, handsome, push-button, and filter-tipped, a symbol of today and today's young, calorie-free living.

In the morning, he can leap out of bed and stand there in his shorts, looking out of his sweeping glass window at the sun rising over Lake Michigan.

At night, with the lights dimmed, he might stand there sipping something-on-the-rocks, listening to something tasteful on his stereo, and gazing down at the twinkling lights on Lake Shore Drive. With a slight smile, he thinks:

"This is it. And I have made it."

Contrast him with Bungalow Man and Three-Flat Man. We think of ourselves as kind of squat, pot-bellied, ordinary, bricks-and-mortar, sidewalks-by-WPA—just like the real estate.

The sight of old people is not offensive to Three-Flat Man or Bungalow man because even when he is young, he thinks he is getting old.

Besides, old people are part of Three-Flat Man's world. They're always there, sitting on the front steps, watering a lawn, watering a dog, taking a walk for the paper, complaining about somebody's punk kids.

But when High-Rise Man and his High-Rise Mate step out of the cab, nod to the doorman's respectful greeting, and stride through their lobby, it can be jarring—shocking—to see a bunch of old people sitting around, dozing, knitting, cackling, or even, heaven forbid, coughing.

Not in their lean, young, soaring world.

Children are just as distasteful. When you see a child, you think of runny noses, scabby knees, diapers, boisterous behavior—none of which belongs in the world of muted tones, indirect lighting, thick-rugged hallways, and gleaming lobbies.

This is a problem, of course, because old people do live in those buildings.

And a few children, too.

And it seems somewhat harsh to bar them from the lobbies entirely.

Possibly the building managers could work out some sort of schedule as second lieutenants used to do with the day rooms in the military service.

They might tell them something like this:

Dear Tenant:

It has come to our attention that due to the cold weather, some of our elderly tenants would like to leave their apartments and sit in the lobby.

Therefore, we have amended our rules to permit "Limited Lobby Sitting."

No more than six (6) elderly people will be permitted to sit in the lobby at one time.

They will space themselves and will use those chairs that are arranged to face AWAY from the main entrance.

Lobby Sitting will not be permitted during morning hours when tenants are leaving for their offices or during the evening hours when dinner guests might be arriving.

It is NOT allowed on Friday and Saturday nights.

Lobby Sitting privileges will be revoked, of course, for violations of the above or for repeated complaints of cackling, knitting, dozing, coughing, or cracking sounds from joints.

Regarding children: We suggest that tenants who possess them consider giving them away.

AUGUST 10, 1970

Skirt the Issue and Live Longer

One of the biggest controversies going today is the length of women's skirts. But I am staying out of it because it is too dangerous a subject.

If I wrote that I want women to go on wearing short skirts, I would have to give my reasons.

And the only honest reason any man can offer is that he enjoys looking at females' thighs.

Over the years I have written many strange things, but I have never sat down and deliberately typed something like "I enjoy looking at females' thighs." If my boss wanted that kind of writing, he would do the job himself.

After work, somebody in the bar might ask me what I wrote about that day. I'd have to say:

"Today I wrote that I enjoy looking at females' thighs."

They would ask me if I actually got paid for writing something like that. The next morning they'd all be up here, telling my editor about their dreams and hidden thoughts, and applying for my job.

Or when I got home, my kids would ask me, as they often do, what I had written that day, and I'd have to tell them:

"Today I wrote that I enjoy looking at females' thighs." Then one of my children would tell the neighbors' children that "my daddy enjoys looking at females' thighs."

You know how kids are. Proud of their dad.

A neighbor's kid would probably go home and say: "Mommy, Mr. Royko says he likes looking at your thighs."

Her husband would say, "What?" And they'd have a terrible fight.

Then he would be pounding on my door, yelling that he knows what's been going on and that I'd better leave his wife alone.

The neighbors would hear it and they'd be running around telling each other: "Fighting over Charlie's wife . . . always knew he was that kind . . . walked right in on them . . . who would have thought . . . sneaky type . . . running away together, I hear . . . alienation suit . . . saw them together once in the A&P. . . ."

Naturally, I'd have to clarify the matter, so I'd explain that I hadn't been talking specifically about his wife, and that what I meant was "I enjoy looking at females' thighs" in general.

Then Charlie would tell the other neighbors. "He says he has got this thing about looking at their thighs."

"He admitted it?"

"So help me."

"Good grief, what else is he up to?"

When I walked the dog at night, they'd be pulling down their shades. When I got home from work, they'd start yelling for their kids to come inside. Squad cars would be coming by every 10 minutes, looking in all the gangways. It would be the last time I could ever take out my telescope and look at moon craters.

Of course, the alternative—to write that I am in favor of the long skirts—would be safer. But once again I would have to give reasons. You can't just write that women should wear longer skirts and let it go at that. You have to give a good reason, and the only one I can think of that would sound at all honest would be: "I do not enjoy looking at females' thighs."

So if I stopped in the bar after work, and somebody asked me what I wrote that day, I would have to say:

"Today I wrote that I do not enjoy looking at females' thighs."

They would all get up and move down to the other end of the bar. And if they didn't, I would.

Lib Gawkers Tiresome Talkers

I hate to admit it, but the conduct of my fellow male chauvinist pigs at the Civic Center rally was embarrassing.

The crowd was just beginning to trickle in at about 11:30 a.m. when a pudgy man asked several of us in general: "Did you hear about a bunch of them planning to take off their bras right here?"

I stepped back to avoid having saliva drip on my shoes and said: "Did I what?"

Excitedly, he said, "I hear a bunch of them are going to take off their bras right here."

When I told him the program would consist of nothing but speeches, he frowned. "I don't know, I heard that a bunch of them are planning . . ."

He had to be 40 years old. Presumably, most men who get to be 40 are, in one way or another, exposed to the sight of that which a bra contains. All he has to do is go to the Art Institute. Yet he was standing in a very hot sun, waiting, almost trembling, at the thought of seeing two or four mammaries.

He wasn't the only one. As the crowd began to build, several men staked out spots by the plaza pool. "I figure some of them are going to take off their clothes and jump in," one of them said, "and I want to see it."

Just for a moment, try to imagine that the rally wasn't for Women's Lib. Instead, it was an outdoor meeting of a labor union, and speeches about getting better working conditions, salaries, and so on were to be made by a bunch of men.

Then imagine you are standing there, waiting to hear the speeches, and a pudgy middle-aged woman says to you: "I hear some of them are going to unzip their flies," and another one says, "Yes, I am here because I hear some of them are going to expose themselves."

Most women would find such a woman to be strange. Yet, men who were panting around and saying basically the same things were considered normal.

By noon the speeches began and by 12:30 the plaza was jammed. Surprisingly, almost half of the people there were men. Most of them had drifted over in pairs from the office buildings on their lunch break.

A bra-less girl walked by, a certain amount of bounce in her blouse, and one fully grown man leaped about excitedly, waving his arms and saying to his office buddy, "Did you see that? Did you see that?"

Since his buddy's glazed eyes were bulging out to the tip of his nose, it was evident he had shared in the wondrous sight of a female's breast doing exactly what they have done for thousands of years when not contained by an arrangement of elastic and cloth.

The speeches, meanwhile, were good. Those were bright people doing the talking. They weren't saying anything about bras or nudity—they were talking about jobs, laws, politics, religion, and other issues.

The women were listening, but the men were gawking, their eyes darting from thigh to buttock, buttock to chest. There was more male giggling than at an old-time stag show, and more hee-hawing than at a mule farm.

Once again, try to imagine a rally being held by a crowd of serious men to air their grievances and muster support.

And imagine that all over the place there are women, some of them grandmotherly, and they are giggling as they point at various parts of the men's bodies that one doesn't normally point at, while they cackle: "Boy, I'll bet that he . . ." Or something like that.

That, you must admit, would be strange. It wouldn't? Well, you know your grandmother better than I do.

Even the quality of the male heckling wasn't much. There was the standard line from one hulking goof who bellowed at a speaker: "Yeah, well how are you going to have babies without us?"

He puffed out his chest and looked pleased with his flashing wit until a woman turned and said to him: "And can you have one on your own? I suppose you have tried."

It ended almost three hours after it began, with not one bra being shed or one skinny-dip in the reflecting pool. This probably led to the frustration on the part of the man who got angry when a female speaker said:

"You came here to see if we were freaks . . . but now you know that we are your wives, your girlfriends, your sisters."

The man looked furious, and he yelled: "My wife isn't here." Then he paused and added: "And neither is my girlfriend."

MARCH 31, 1976

Mary Pickford's Old "Error"

I didn't think it was possible, but Mary Pickford, the one-time screen darling of America, has managed to offend lots of people. She did it by growing old.

Actually, that's not entirely accurate. Growing old in itself was not Miss Pickford's error. It was in letting the Academy Awards TV audience see that she had grown old.

The gossip columnists seem to agree that her taped appearance for a special Oscar was, as one of them put it, "in bad taste."

And if the calls to the popular Wally Phillips morning radio show are any barometer of public opinion, and I think they are, then many people share the view that the TV audience should not have been subjected to Miss Pickford's appearance.

They were on the phone to Phillips as early as 5:30 a.m. the morning after the Oscar presentations to express their displeasure.

The producer of the Phillips show said:

"They thought in general that it was in poor taste to have that segment on the program. They felt that perhaps it destroyed an image of her that they had held.

"They would have preferred to never have known how she didn't measure up to the questions that were asked her, and seemed like a lady of 82.

"They knew her as a star of an era and instead saw a doddering, sickly old lady."

Imagine that! A doddering old lady in the midst of all those sleek, nubile young actresses and those handsome, broad-shouldered, virile actors. Eeek!

Well, maybe I'm not normal, or have weird taste, but I watched the show and saw the presentation to Mary Pickford and it didn't bother me.

One reason might be that I'm not surprised to discover that somebody might be wrinkled, frail, weak-voiced, and maybe a bit senile when they get to be 82. That happens to people who get to be 82. They sometimes get old, old, old.

The word doesn't bother me, either. Old. Oollllllldddd. I prefer it to "senior citizen." Or "twilight years." Old. Say it. Go on, your teeth won't fall out.

Or how about "wrinkled" or "sagging" or "liver spots"? Or "varicose veins"? These words don't offend me either.

But if they offend you, if you turn your head away from Mary Pickford and find it all so distasteful, then there's something wrong with you, kid, because it's perfectly normal. It happens to all of us, unless we croak first. We get old.

Take Margaux Hemingway, the tall stunner who was on the show. One of these days she's going to wrinkle up, and maybe her teeth will fall out, maybe even her hair, and her knee joints will go crackety-crack.

Is that too terrible to face—Margaux Hemingway's knee joints going crackety-crack?

For some reason, it doesn't bother people nearly as much when an elderly actress has her breasts propped up like the bow of a ship, her facial skin stretched out like a drumhead, her siliconed body girdled and buttressed into preposterous curves and lumps, and an inch of pink mortar stuck on her face.

Then the gossip columnists marvel at how young she looks, and the audience cheers. They cheer the illusion of Zsa Zsa, but they flinch at the reality of Mary Pickford.

What's wrong with looking old age in the face? Afraid? You bet.

Better to slap a hairpiece on that wrinkled pate, slip into a leisure suit, and scuttle across the dance floor like a spastic and fur-topped prune.

And better to slip Granny and Gramps, and all the grannies and grampses, into hideaways where we don't have to see their gums, hear their wheezes, and be reminded of what the future holds.

Many of those who saw Mary Pickford said they would rather remember her as she once was.

Why? She's not dead. She may be old, but she is a loving, breathing human being. She has thoughts, emotions, and, I'm sure, experiences happiness.

That's what I think I saw on my TV. When her brief segment ended, the camera came in close. And there was a tiny teardrop in her eye.

And when the audience was shown applauding, I saw her husband, Buddy Rogers, no kid himself, looking at her with love and pride, looking like he was almost crying himself from these feelings.

I thought that was very, very nice. Maybe because I'm not easily offended.

MAY 2, 1978

It's Love at First Click

A young man I know told me he was thinking seriously of getting married. He was married once before, to a woman who had strong limbs and good teeth, but an evil disposition.

Since his divorce, he had appeared happy and contented. At least he was happier than most of my other friends who aren't divorced.

So I was surprised when he told me he was once again going to take a step that could lead to so much heartache, misery, remorse, and lawyers' fees.

He said: "This time I'm almost sure it will work out."

"But are you absolutely sure? Remember, right now she is a pretty young thing. In 50 years, she will be a wrinkled old crone of 78, with one tooth, when you are still a vigorous, youthful buck of only 80. Do you want to be stuck with someone like that?"

He said he was not completely certain, so he was going to put himself and his lady friend to a test.

They are going off to a secluded little resort on the seashore together for a few days, maybe even a week.

"If we click, I'll be able to tell," he said.

I told him he was an idiot.

There is no worse way to determine if two people "click," whatever that means, than by going off together to some secluded resort on the seashore.

What will happen is that she will take his hand and they will run on the beach, her long legs flashing in the sun, her hair bouncing on her shoulders, probably in slow motion.

His mind will start going "click, click, click, boyohboyohboy!"

There will be dinner by candlelight on a terrace overlooking the sea. Fine wine. Her white teeth nibbling on lightly sautéed scallops. Click, click, click. More wine. Click, click, click, boyohboyohboy!

Then, after a slow, aimless moonlit walk on the beach . . .

Clickclickclickclickclick.

. . . In the misty morning, a sleepy breakfast of eggs Benedict in bed. Strawberries dipped in champagne. A Jacuzzi bath. She in her filmy robe, standing on the balcony and stretching like a cat. Click click, clickity, clickity, click.

And another sun-drenched, windswept day of hand-in-hand running on the beach. More hair bouncing in slow motion.

Of course it will click, you mope. In that kind of setup, it would click if you were there with your favorite toy rubber duck.

That is not the way to test yourself and her. If you want to know if it will click, spend a few days together and make some of these sure-fire tests:

- Instead of going to a seaside resort, go to the A&P on a Saturday afternoon to buy groceries. When unloading the basket at the car, see if she can handle any of the heavy bags or if she sticks you with them.
- When changing clothes, throw your underwear in one corner, your socks on a lamp, your shirt on the windowsill, and your pants on the stereo. See if she picks them up.

- Borrow or rent some small whiny children with runny noses and a tendency toward car sickness. Put them in the back seat and go for a drive to the Wisconsin Dells on a hot weekend. Pretend the air conditioner is broken and turn it off.
- Tell her you're going out to play a fast game of softball. Say you won't be gone long. Wander in at about 2 a.m. with a dozen teammates and sit in the kitchen drinking beer, swearing, and loudly telling stories about lewd women you have all known. Ask her to whip up some sandwiches for you and all your buddies. See if she appears visibly happy to have the opportunity to be hostess to your friends.
- Get a really bad cold. Spend a weekend lying around on the couch, watching ball games, wheezing, sneezing, coughing, complaining that you are miserable, asking her to bring you aspirin, soup, or orange juice, or to scratch your back, dry your brow, and change channels on the TV. If she moves slowly, yell at her to snap it up. Watch closely to see if she appears grateful for the opportunity to take care of you.
- Let her invite all of her closest friends over for a party. Let them know that you think most of them are a bunch of jerks. See if she appreciates your frankness and honesty.

After I suggested these simple click tests to the young man, he gasped: "If I ever did that before we got married, she'd never talk to me again."

Which just proves my point. She would be revealing that she isn't sincere and is probably the flighty sort. Would he want to spend the rest of his days with someone who can run on the beach but is of little use when you have a cold?

He thanked me for my mature advice and said he would give my plan some serious thought, and I hope he does. To be fair to himself, he has to give divorce a chance to work.

Because there are many young men with problems of this kind—love, marriage, lust, and so on—those of us who are experienced should try to help them muddle through.

Therefore, I plan to make this service a recurring feature of this column. If anyone has any problems that require experienced counseling, just write.

If I can't solve your problem, the least I will do is give you some new ones to think about.

Survival of the Fairest

As you trade in your big gas-eater for a tiny car, or stuff newspapers around your leaky windows, or squirt heat-saving gunk between your walls, don't feel alone. Those rich pleasure-lovers known as "The Beautiful People" also are doing their part to conserve the nation's energy resources.

As my authority, I cite *W,* the New York-based fashion newspaper put out by the *Women's Wear Daily* people that devotes much of its coverage to the goings and comings and doings of those it calls "The BP." (That means Beautiful People, you homely dummy.)

In a recent issue, *W* interviewed a couple of dozen of the beautiful ones about how they are going to cope with the more frugal times that are expected during the energy crisis in the '80s.

To be honest, I don't know who most of these Beautiful People are, since we don't hang around the same polo clubs, international casinos, yacht basins, or Milwaukee Avenue saloons.

And *W* does not identify them beyond their names. Presumably, those who are in the know are aware of who they are. So we can safely assume that if *W* says they are Beautiful People, they are, even if a few of them do sag.

Anyway, here is what they say they will do to conserve energy. You might pick up some helpful tips.

"Recently I visited my brother's 20-room mansion," said a BP named Beverly Johnson. "I spent a lot of time switching off the lights and turning down the heat."

What a fine idea. I think the rest of us, when visiting our brothers' 20-room mansions, should do the same.

Harriet Deutsch, a blond Beautiful Person whose photo shows what appear to be two diamond chandeliers dangling from her ears, says:

"I prefer to entertain in our own home and, in doing so, we actively make efforts to conserve energy and use everything economically. We are fortunate to have a marvelous chef who guides us along those lines."

That's something for the rest of us to think about. When hiring a chef, we should think beyond the texture of his salmon mousse and ask whether he knows how to roast a quail with solar energy.

Françoise de la Renta (Why don't Beautiful People ever have names like Myrtle or Gert?) is doing her part. She said:

"When we go to the country, we have only wood fires; they're better than heating with oil. And I open my window in the summer instead of turning on the air conditioner. I live with the natural elements."

Fancy that. Opening one's window in the summertime. Françoise, with the help of people like you, we'll get the price of oil down to 40 cents a barrel yet.

Then there is Nan Kempner, who said: "Less is more." (I'll bet she doesn't say that to her stockbroker.) Her idea for energy conservation:

"I now wear long underwear, and not just for skiing."

What a coincidence, Nan. My grandfather used to wear long underwear, too—and when he wasn't skiing. He used to tell us: "Always wear long underwear day and night, winter and summer, because if there is a fire and you have to run outside without your pants, you won't be embarrassed in front of the neighbors." It never occurred to me that his philosophy could have made him one of the Beautiful People.

Susan Mary Alsop seems to have a pessimistic view of the '80s. She said:

"People will have less and less staff. And practically no one will be having live-in servants. Instead, we'll have to be more self-reliant and use more caterers, which is dreary."

I know how you feel, Susan. The day I let my live-in butler and chef go, I felt lost. That night I phoned a caterer and asked him to make me a salami sandwich as a bedtime snack, and it just wasn't the same. It was a dreary, dreary, dreary salami sandwich. Care to join me in a suicide pact, kid?

There is more to Susan's dreary view of the future. She said: "As for vacation houses, people will have to choose between traveling abroad or keeping up a vacation home. I'll not be taking trips abroad and keeping my house in Maine."

Me either. I'll probably flip a coin to see if I go to the Wisconsin Dells or stay in town and bicycle around Goose Island factories.

Pat Buckley, who is pictured with a neck full of mink, has come eyeball-to-eyeball with the energy crunch. She says:

"As far as conservation goes, the real change in my life is the moped, which I ride to the fish store."

I kind of like the idea of Mrs. Buckley setting out from her estate on her moped to buy a fish.

"Where are you going, my dear?"

"I am going on my moped to buy a fish."

"But Charles will drive you."

"No, no, no. We must conserve. Charles can drive me to the furrier, or the jeweler. But when I buy a fish, it's by moped."

"God Bless America, my dear."

And finally there is Betsy Bloomingdale, who is doing her part to fight OPEC this way:

"One of the ways I save energy is by asking my servants not to turn on the self-cleaning oven until after 7 in the evening. We all must do little things and big things to conserve energy."

Indeed we must, Betsy, and my hat is off to you and your servants and your self-cleaning oven.

But I wonder: If Susan Mary Alsop is right, and hardly anyone will have live-in servants anymore, who will Betsy Bloomingdale get to turn on her self-cleaning oven after 7 p.m.?

Are there caterers—dreary as they might be—who will come out and turn on Betsy Bloomingdale's self-cleaning oven?

Or will her oven just get dirtier and dirtier?

Oh, the 1980s frighten me.

MARCH 20, 1989

Something's Fishy at the Old Ballpark

In a couple of hundred years, when historians study the decline and fall of the once-great nation known as the United States, they will pinpoint April 1989 as being the beginning of the end.

No, it won't be because of a nuclear disaster, the rise of Japan's economic strength, the free flow of drugs and guns, the flood of illegal immigrants, the communist menace, the "greenhouse effect," or even Dan Quayle's IQ.

They will find that the fall began with the deterioration of traditional values, the rejection of our heritage, the plunge into cultural decadence and effeteness.

And they will be able to look to Southern California to see where it began. More precisely, to San Diego. And even more specifically, to Jack Murphy Stadium, where the San Diego Padres play baseball.

They will find that in April 1989, the San Diego Padres became the first major league franchise in the long history of America's great national pastime to sell—brace yourselves—sushi to the fans.

Yes, sushi in the ballpark. Strips of raw or marinated fish, wrapped around a ball of rice with maybe a dab of fish eggs on top: the preferred snack of the yuppiest of yuppies.

What will San Diego fans be singing?

Take me out to the ball game
Take me out to the crowd
Buy me some sushi and I'll feel fine
I might wash it down with a glass of white wine

I should be surprised, but I'm not. It was inevitable. Years ago, when the Brooklyn Dodgers moved to Los Angeles, I told my friend Slats Grobnik:

"This is a bad thing for the country. Some day they will be selling sushi in ballparks."

He said: "What's sushi?"

I said: "I don't know. But mark my words, it will happen."

And now it has. And, as I feared, if it happened anywhere, it would be in California, where they have no respect for tradition.

For almost a century, a hot dog was good enough for baseball fans in New York and Chicago, Cleveland and St. Louis, Cincinnati and Pittsburgh, Brooklyn and Boston. A hot dog, peanuts, and beer. It wasn't merely good enough. It was baseball food, just as turkey and dressing is Thanksgiving food. Would you serve Peking duck on Thanksgiving? Maybe, in California.

Don't dismiss the terrible significance of what's happening. This season, there will be fathers in San Diego who will take their five- or six-year-old sons to the ballpark for the first time, as fathers have been doing for generations. Assuming the surf isn't up, which takes priority in that strange land.

And 20 years from now, when they have grown to what passes for manhood in that sun-kissed place, these young men will recall:

"Yes, I remember the first time my dad took me out to the old ballpark. I remember the smell of the suntan lotion, the nubile young things in their halters. But most of all, I remember my dad buying me my first sushi and Perrier. It was tuna with a dollop of caviar. And soon I will take my son, Lance, to the ballpark and do the same for him. However, I'll recommend he try the shrimp sushi, too."

A few years ago, I happened to mention that San Diego was not deserving of a championship because (a) the fans had not yet suffered enough, except when they forgot to put on suntan lotion and (b) they were beach bums, quiche eaters, and wine sippers.

They were outraged. Many wept openly. And some wrote letters defending their manhood. As one of them said: "I happen to be very macho, and you are nothing but a puddle of poodle wee-wee, so there."

Now they have sushi in the ballpark. So much for their wet-eyed protests.

Baseball lore tells us that the most famous stomachache in sports history was suffered by Babe Ruth, also known to baseball scholars as the Bambino or the Sultan of Swat.

He got the stomachache after eating a snack of 20 hot dogs. The Babe did not do things in a small way.

It made headlines all over the country. And the national reaction to this heroic gluttony was:

"What a guy!"

I can't imagine any such excitement if a San Diego Padre ever eats 20 pieces of sushi. If it ever happens, the response will be:

"What? A guy?"

APRIL 11, 1991

It's Same Old Song Sung with a Twist

Let's test your knowledge of music. Tell me what song these lyrics are from:

1. Oh dah-lah-hah la-hah-haha-eee-hee-hah-aaaand-uh uvva-uvva fruh-heee-heeeeee.
2. Anna homma-duh homma-du-du-du hom-maaaaaaaaaa.
3. Dee-uh-dee-hah-hah-hah buh-huh-eee-buh-huhe-eee-eee-eee-ray-have.

You say you don't recognize it? Nonsense. Of course you do. It's likely that you've heard and sung it dozens or hundreds of times, depending on your age. Your parents sang it. And probably your grandparents, too.

You still don't know it? All right, I'll throw out a few hints.

It's a very old song. The words were written more than 150 years ago. The melody is even older than that.

You still don't know? Then you don't go to many Opening Days at baseball parks.

Of course, when Francis Scott Key wrote that line, as well as the others that precede and follow it, he kept the lyrics much simpler for the human brain to comprehend: "O'er the land of the free and the home of the brave." And for many years, that's the way it was sung.

But it's no longer done that way. In recent times, there has developed a sort of informal competition among singers at ballparks, hockey rinks, basketball stadiums, and other patriotic gathering places to see who can best turn "The Star-Spangled Banner" into something most resembling the howls of a maniac locked in the asylum tower.

I'm not sure when and where these free-form interpretations began, although I vaguely remember a guy named Jose creating a stir a few years ago by opening a World Series with a rendition that sounded like the Star-Spangled Cha-Cha-Cha.

Since then, I have heard the anthem performed as the Star-Spangled

Rock, the Star-Spangled Disco, the Star-Spangled Gospel, the Star-Spangled Blues, the Star-Spangled Hootenanny, the Star-Spangled Barbershop Quartet, and the Star-Spangled Scalded Cat.

A few weeks ago, a woman who sang it before a Chicago Bulls game is believed to have set a record by using a variety of prolonged howls, shrieks, warbles, screams, and other vocal acrobatics to drag it out to more than five minutes.

A man who was there told me: "I couldn't understand one word. And, I swear, if I were a Chicago policeman driving on a street in my squad car and I heard those sounds coming from a building, I would radio for backup, then draw my gun and go crashing into the place on the assumption that a woman was being brutally attacked by a gang of fiends."

I think it is time to draw the line. After all, it is our national anthem. As such, it should be performed with some dignity, rather than sounding like the singer has been bitten in the rear by a pit bull.

It's doubtful that anyone would stand in central court at Wimbledon and sing: "Ga-hah say-hey-he-hey-iv ow-ow-owah guh-ray-hey-hey-hey-hey shush Qwa-hey-qua-hey-heee-eeeen." (That's "God save our gracious queen," ballpark style.) The English would say more than tut-tut, I'm sure.

Nor would they be impressed north of the border if someone gave them: "Oh-hoooo, Cay-hey-cay-neee-dah! Owah, yes, owah ahooooma, ahoooma and ney-yeh-ney-yey-tivuh-tivuh-baby-baby-light my-uh fuya lah-hah-hee-huh-ay-and." ("O Canada! Our home and native land!")

If Mr. Key could return and be transported to an athletic arena to hear a modern interpretation, he'd recognize the tune, but he'd probably say: "Ah, English is no longer the native tongue?"

And think of the children. Generation after generation of parents take their children to ballparks to introduce them to the national pastime. Do we want these children later standing up in assembly hall and saying: "No, teacher, it starts like this: 'Oh-hoh-hey cah-han-you-uh-see-uh by-the daw-haw-hawns err-uh-err-ee-uh-lee-lah-lite'"?

Even worse, these wild-eyed renditions of the Sta-hah-stah-hah-span-uh-gulled bayuh-bayuh-ner-her-hers encourage the more excitable, beer-soaked, rock-oriented members of the audience to leap up and clap their hands above their heads and shout, "Wow . . . hey . . . yeah . . . go . . . baby . . . go. . . ."

That isn't what Francis Scott Key had in mind.

On the other hand, some musicologists say that the melody can be traced back to England, where it had different lyrics and was a drinking song.

So maybe it's not totally inappropriate for today's singers to sound as if they had just downed a quart of Southern Comfort.

NOVEMBER 1, 1994

Happiness Floats in a Bowl of Misery

Various polls show that the overwhelming majority of Americans are glum. They dislike the national decline in everybody's morality, meddling government, doublespeak politicians, arrogant media, highly paid athletes, sports strikes, and many other annoyances.

The question is why are people so unhappy when times are relatively good, the economy seems perky, and it's unlikely that Judge Ito will totally ban TV coverage in the O. J. Simpson trial?

To get answers, I arranged for an exclusive interview with Dr. I. M. Kookie, the internationally renowned expert on lots of stuff.

Dr. Kookie has been studying the droopy American spirit at the think tank he founded: The Institute to Determine What's Up. Here are some of his findings:

"People are unhappy for one very simple reason. They are not unhappy enough."

But that doesn't make sense. How can they be unhappy because they are not unhappy when it is clear that they are indeed unhappy?

"That is a very good question. Actually, it is a stupid question, but I will try to be polite. So I will answer it anyway. OK, when you are real thirsty, what makes you feel better?"

Having something to drink.

"Right. And when you are real hungry, what makes you feel good?"

Obviously, having something to eat.

"Very good. Now do you understand?"

I'm afraid not.

"Misery. We need more misery. Until we get more misery, people will be miserable. Now you got it?"

We need more misery to be happy?

"Exactly. We got it too good. When was the last time you had to call your brother-in-law to bring over his jumper cables because the cold weather killed your car battery?"

It has been so long, I don't remember.

"See? It used to be that when we got a cold snap, every brother-in-law was out with his jumper cables. But now they make better cars and batteries that almost always start. So how can you feel good when your engine starts if you weren't miserable because it didn't start in the first place?"

So we need dead batteries to be happy?

"More than that. In the Great Depression, what made people miserable?"

That's easy. Being out of work, not having food or a roof over their heads.

"Right. So what made them happy?"

A job, food on the table, and a warm place to sleep.

"You got it. Any kind of job made a person happy. The job didn't have to fulfill them or be on the fast track, as long as it provided a paycheck. Food was pretty good haute cuisine if it filled the belly. And nobody complained about not having as nice a house as their parents had, because most parents were lucky to have clean linoleum and a toilet that flushed."

So you are saying that in order to appreciate what you have, you have to have been deprived.

"It helps. But now we got every kind of machine we need to keep us cool when it's hot, warm when it's cold, entertained with movies or sports or games or music when we're bored. To make our coffee and cook our food real fast. To cut our grass, throw our snow, wash our dishes, clean our clothes, exercise our legs, check our blood pressure, count our calories, and do our arithmetic. Fifty years ago, the world's richest people didn't have the luxuries that the average guy—even some low-income guys—take for granted today."

But if we have it so good, why are the majority of Americans unhappy?

"Because they want more, and there ain't no more, but people think there is. That's why millions of them are running out and buying themselves or their kids computers with a CD-ROM. A few years ago, they would have thought that CD-ROM was a mantra: See-Dee Romm-Romm, See-Dee Romm-Romm, hey, hey, hey, goodbye. Now they think a CD-ROM will bring them happiness. But it won't. All that will happen is that it will keep popping out and goofy messages will come on the computer screen saying, 'Insert Disk,' 'Remove Disk,' 'Take Disk and Shove It.' Then they will tell a pollster that life is doo-doo."

So you seem to be saying that to be happy, you must know some misery first. Only then can you enjoy the simple pleasures.

"Well, I would not put it in such a sappy way, but that's part of it. See, what we really need is for government to say that we are going to be hit by a giant meteor."

A giant meteor from outer space?

"Right. They should announce that it is going to crash into this planet in 30 days and kill everything except the cockroaches. And so in a few million years, the cockroaches will evolve into sharpies like us and will be unhappy with their CD-ROMs. Yes, we need an end-of-the-world meteor alert."

But are we in danger?

"Of course not. But if it was announced, it would scare everybody out of their wits for a few days and there would be mass hysteria. Then the government could announce that it was a mistake and that we aren't all going to die after all, and everybody would be relieved and happy to be alive."

Then people would appreciate what they have and be happy?

"Maybe. Or they'd be unhappy and would impeach the president. Either way, it's worth a try."

Thank you.

"Don't worry, be happy."

SEPTEMBER 13, 1996

Where Have All the Protesters Gone Concerning Iraq?

As many of us recall, back in the 1960s we were involved in a war in which young Americans were being killed and maimed each day.

But the collective conscience of those who took part in the anti-war movement was so strong that when they marched and protested in the streets, they hailed the name of Ho Chi Minh. And they hurled obscenities at President Lyndon Johnson.

To many Americans, this didn't make sense since we were fighting against communism, a totalitarian ideology that enslaved entire nations.

And those in the streets who chanted "Ho, Ho, Ho Chi Minh" appeared to be not only backing forces that were killing brave young American soldiers, but also supporting that totalitarian ideology.

It was not exactly a new conflict. In the early 1950s, about 36,500 Americans had died fighting communist China and North Korea. The deaths in Vietnam ran the body bag total close to about 94,500—making the war against communism one of the costliest in our history.

These were important wars—Korea and Vietnam—because they made clear to the Soviet Union and China and Cambodia and the other communist butchers that if they were going to dominate the minds of the world, they'd have to shoot their way to power.

But to much of this country's population, it wasn't quite as simple as American democracy against communist totalitarianism.

It was a question of humanity, conscience, goodness, decency, right, wrong, and not dropping bombs on innocent non-combatants. Or even ferocious combatants.

And as we are frequently reminded, taking a stand against one's own country took considerable courage.

Jane Fonda, for example. Had she been stricken with sagging breasts and a large butt, her anti-war rhetoric might have ended her showbiz career.

And the college-kid revolutionaries who rampaged down Clark Street in Chicago during their so-called Days of Rage, caving in the windows of barbers and other small businessmen, now boast about how they showed more true courage than the sheep-like working-class dum-dums who accepted being drafted into the Army and taught how to kill innocent foreigners.

But how quickly this anti-war conscience and sentiment has dried up.

It is a safe guess that the majority of those who now hold jobs in the Clinton White House were part of the anti-war movement. A draft-age Clinton sure was. So were many of his aides whose social consciences twitch as much today as they did when the body bags were being shipped back here.

But now acts of war by the big, bad, mean, capitalistic U.S. of A. are OK.

Here we have a president who doesn't think he has to tell the Congress of the United States: "Excuse me, but I'm going to shoot missiles at the nation of Iraq." Our system of government requires that a president check with Congress before we go to war.

But he doesn't bother with this constitutional nicety since the United Nations has said we should be rent-a-cops aiding the Kurds in northern Iraq.

Of course, the UN hasn't told us to shoot missiles at Iraq.

So all of this shooting is happening without the approval of the Congress of the United States or the United Nations.

But is there even one mild peep from those who used to call themselves "anti-war"?

Where are the voices of those in government and journalism and academia who wailed so loudly when we were fighting communism in Vietnam?

Is it less immoral to shoot missiles at the Muslim followers of Saddam Hussein than at the communist followers of Ho Chi Minh?

If we drop bombs on Iraq and kill a few civilians or even military guys who have wives and children, are their lives more expendable than those of the Viet Cong?

Or the question might be put this way: When you are anti-war, are you anti-all-war or only anti-war when it suits your political and self-survival convenience?

When the Vietnam War ended, I slapped out a column predicting that we had seen the end of this country's distaste for blowing up distant foreigners.

I thought I was right, but I wasn't 100 percent sure.

Now I know. Never underestimate the hypocrisy of draft-dodging moralists.

5

POLITICS AIN'T
BEANBAG

the "Fix?"

There are many things wrong with our society. But even the
harshest critics have to admit that we respect the sanctity of
the fix. When a bribe is accepted, you can usually expect to
get your money's worth, which is not something that can be
said about most goods and services. . . . Chicago is a great
city because it has been, since pioneer days, a city where a
man's fix is his bond. With rare exceptions, when you buy
somebody, they stay bought. In matters of official dishonesty,
this is an honest city.

—*Chicago Daily News,* March 6, 1974

Aldermen?

History teaches us that when any two aldermen begin whispering, a grand jury ought to immediately issue subpoenas.

—*Chicago Sun-Times,* March 24, 1982

Nixon Halfway to a Mandate

Richard M. Nixon is one of the most inspirational success stories this country has ever produced.

The traditional American success formula is that if you work hard and lose, you just work harder, improve yourself, and then you will win.

The trouble with that idea is that a lot of people who lose and work harder don't get any better.

Nixon proves that they, too, can win just by hanging around.

He is like a racing driver who chugs along in 10th place, but wins when nine other drivers lose tires or hit the wall.

Or he might be compared to the ungainly young man who finally wins the pretty girl—after all the other young men get drafted, arrested, or run over by beer trucks and she becomes desperate.

He is most like the salesman who keeps coming back, over and over again, until the weary customer signs up just to get rid of him.

This is not meant to be critical of Nixon. To the contrary: I feel it is a good thing for a loser to win once in awhile. It is the enthusiastic loser who keeps the poker game going.

Nixon's election record tells it.

He has run for major office on his own three times—twice for president and once for governor of California.

Here is how he did in total vote and percentage:

1960: 34,108,000; 49 percent.

1962 (California): 47 percent.

1968: 31,770,000; 43 percent.

The message is clear: The longer the American voter looks at Nixon, the more eager he is to vote for somebody else.

But that is why his victory this week was so inspiring. Every time he lost, he tried again. And when he tried again, he did even worse than before.

The whole thing gets even more inspiring when you consider what he was up against this time. Few candidates have faced anything like it.

Nixon was opposed by an administration that was losing an unpopular war, which is not considered a political asset. He was opposed by a party that was split more ways than a large pizza.

The country was said to be fed up with just about everything. The polls showed that nobody liked anybody or anything but color TV.

Nixon came running to the rescue and 57 percent of the troubled, tormented people told him to go away.

How often does a drowning man look at the lifeguard and say: "I'd rather drown?"

But he won. The American people have given him a mand.

A mand is about half a mandate.

The difference is that a mandate for a president sort of means:

"We have faith in you, we want you, we are behind you."

But a mand says:

"Well, I guess we've got to hire somebody for the job, so it might as well be you. But try not to mess things up, huh?"

In a way, it might be an advantage for Nixon.

Many presidents, such as LBJ, start out as very popular figures. But after a few years most people don't like them.

Nixon is coming in at what might be the peak of his unpopularity. If he does anything right, he has nowhere to go except up.

I mean, a man couldn't possibly get reelected with less than 43 percent of the vote, could he?

SEPTEMBER 17, 1971

[Editors' note: The paperback edition of *Boss*, Mike's best-selling book about Mayor Richard J. Daley, was published in early September, 1971.]

Now, About That Book

Earl Bush, Mayor Daley's press secretary and chief coat-holder, had this to say about the ban of the book *Boss* by National food stores:

"The mayor didn't know anything about it until he heard it on the radio."

Ho, ho, ho.

And a spokesman for National gave this out to the Associated Press:

"No pressure was brought—or anything like that."

Ha, ha, ha.

Come now, gentlemen, let's not kid around. If you do not want to tell the truth about who got the book banned from more than 200 National food stores, then I will.

And here it is:

On Monday, Mrs. Eleanor Daley, wife of the mayor, went shopping.

As she often does, she went to the National food store at 1920 West 35th Street. It's only a short drive from the Daley residence at 3536 South Lowe Avenue.

Mrs. Daley had not been in the store for a couple of weeks, employees say, so she saw something that brought a bit of fire to her eyes.

There, on the magazine and book rack, were the paperback copies of *Boss—Richard J. Daley of Chicago,* a book about her husband.

Mrs. Daley does not like this particular book, and she has said so in interviews. To be specific, she has described it as "trash," and the author as an "underdeveloped underachiever," whatever that may be.

(I will not debate either point. However, she also has said that the author should have gone to her husband for the true facts. The author tried to interview her husband, but her husband ignored the request.)

Anyway, there was Mrs. Daley in her neighborhood National, and there were all of those books' covers, showing her husband in the armor of a Roman centurion, striking a dashing pose.

To make matters worse, a big cardboard sign promoting the paperback version of the book stood atop the magazine rack where everyone could see it.

Mrs. Daley marched up to the book rack and turned the cardboard sign face down.

She then turned each book around so the title did not show.

That done, she sought out the manager of the store, Thomas Tamburo.

Mr. Tamburo knows Mrs. Daley on sight and he was properly respectful. He was even more respectful when he saw that she was angry.

"She was pretty mad," Mr. Tamburo says. "She said she wanted the books taken out of the store and she said she wasn't going to shop in the store anymore if they weren't removed.

"I told her that I would see what I could do to get them out of the store.

"I called downtown [to National headquarters] and told them what had happened and how Mrs. Daley felt about the books.

"In 10 minutes, I had them off the rack and put away."

That was on Monday. The paperback version had been on sale in the stores for almost two weeks without any problems.

The very next day, on Tuesday, a directive went out from National's executive office to the manager of every store, ordering the books removed and returned to the distributor.

And that is the story of how the book happened to be "banned in Bosstown," as one headline writer put it.

Frankly, I'm awed by Mrs. Daley's power. I can think of only one other person in Chicago who could get thousands of copies of a book that doesn't have even one erotic scene swept under the counters.

And I'm impressed by National's eagerness to please a customer. I remember when some of Ralph Nader's local lady raiders were trying to get National to be more specific about the age of its food products.

National gave those ordinary housewives a pretty rough time. One might even say National was arrogant.

I'm glad to see that they have mended their ways and are so quick to respond to a complaint.

But National better damn well hope that Mrs. Daley doesn't take a dislike to their milk or eggs.

A book is one thing. But have you ever tried to return an egg to a chicken?

FEBRUARY 16, 1973

What's Behind Daley's Words?

Several theories have arisen as to what Mayor Daley really meant a few days ago when he said:

"If they don't like it, they can kiss my ass."

On the surface, it appeared that the mayor was merely admonishing those who would dare question the royal favors he has bestowed upon his sons, Prince Curly, Prince Larry, and Prince Moe.

But it can be a mistake to accept the superficial meaning of anything the mayor says.

The mayor can be a subtle man. And as Earl Bush, his press secretary, once put it after the mayor was quoted correctly:

"Don't print what he said. Print what he meant."

So many observers believe the true meaning of the mayor's remarkable kissing invitation may be more than skin deep.

One theory is that he would like to become sort of the Blarney Stone of Chicago.

As the stone's legend goes, if a person kisses Ireland's famous Blarney Stone, which actually exists, he will be endowed with the gift of oratory.

And City Hall insiders have long known that the kind of kiss Daley suggested can result in the gift of wealth.

People from all over the world visit Blarney Castle so they can kiss the chunk of old limestone and thus become glib, convincing talkers.

So, too, might people flock to Chicago in hopes that kissing "The Daley" might bring them unearned wealth. Daley, or at least his bottom, might become one of the great tourist attractions of the nation.

The Blarney Stone has become part of the living language in such everyday phrases as "You're giving me a lot of blarney."

That could happen here, too. People who make easy money might someday be described as "really having the gift of the Daley bottom."

That is one theory. Another, equally interesting, goes this way:

Throughout history, the loyal subjects of kings and other monarchs have usually shown their respect with a physical gesture of some sort.

In some places, it was merely a deep bow or a curtsy when the ruler showed up or departed.

Others, who were even more demanding, required that the subjects kneel or even crawl on all fours. (A few Chicago aldermen engage in this practice.)

In some kingdoms, those who approached the big man were expected to kiss his ring or the hem of his royal clothing.

Daley has already ruled Chicago for longer than most kings reigned in their countries.

At this point, many of his loyal subjects view him as more a monarch than an elected official. It seems obvious that he intends to pass the entire city on to his sons, which is a gesture worthy of a king.

So it would be only natural that he might feel the time has come when he is entitled to a gesture of respect and reverence that befits his royal position.

And what he suggested would be simply a variation of kissing a ring or a hand. Instead of kissing the royal hem, we would kiss the royal ham.

Although I have not read of any king expecting a kiss in precisely the area the mayor described, why not? One of the hallmarks of Chicago is that we do so many things in an original manner.

What other city has made a river flow backwards? What other city makes traffic flow backwards?

And it would be quite original if we had a leader who greeted us backwards.

Where else would a leader turn his back on his people and be cheered for it?

History also tells us that in some ancient kingdoms, a person who had some terrible illness thought he would be cured if he kissed the feet of the king.

Could it be that the mayor is launching a low-cost, and low-slung, health program for us?

I am sure there will be some people who won't want to show their affection for the mayor this way. As one man put it, when he heard what the mayor had said:

"If Daley wants me to do that, then he sure has a lot of cheek."

But there also are the loyal followers, typified by radio disc jockey Howard Miller, who declared over the airwaves that the mayor has "more brains in his bottom" than his critics have in their heads.

While I might disagree with Miller on the quantity of cerebral matter, I won't quarrel with the location.

In any case, we will maintain our efforts to find out what the mayor really meant.

We hope to get to the bottom of this story. Or should I say, to the story of this bottom.

OCTOBER 19, 1973

A Law City Should Keep

The City Council intends to repeal my favorite old-time ordinance.

The aldermen say the ordinance is cruel and inhuman.

That may be so. But they are acting hastily. At least part of the ordinance should be retained because if it were enforced, it would make this a much better place to live.

This is what the ordinance says:

"No person who is diseased, maimed, mutilated, or in any way deformed so as to be an unsightly or disgusting object or an improper person [is] to be allowed in or on the public ways or other public places, [or] shall therein or thereon expose himself to public view, under a penalty of not less than one dollar nor more than fifty dollars for each offense."

Obviously, the first part of it—that which bans people who are diseased, maimed, or mutilated—should be repealed.

But the rest of it should be retained. There has been a crying need to get people off the streets who are "unsightly," "improper," or "disgusting objects."

I first came across this ordinance several years ago, and I immediately wrote a column demanding the arrest of all the politicians who march at the front of the St. Patrick's Day parade.

Anybody who has seen them come wheezing down the streets, toting their heavy wallets, would agree that many of them are unsightly, some of them are disgusting, and all of them are improper every chance they get.

Many's the time I've stood on the curb and heard citizens remark:

"Look at that improper-looking object—what is it?" They are amazed when I tell them the object is an elected official.

I doubt if any jury would look at them and not agree that they are guilty of violating the ordinance, and a lot of other things, too.

I thought it would be a fine opportunity for some young policeman to make a name for himself, herding them into a paddy wagon with an: "Up you go, you unsightly, disgusting objects." But none did. Lack of ambition, I guess.

But I still think that if this ordinance were enforced, nothing but good could come of it.

Decent people would no longer be set upon at shopping centers and commuter stations by disgusting, unsightly candidates who want to shake their hands. In any election year, they're all over the place, one more unsightly and disgusting than the last.

Enforcement of this ordinance would keep disc jockeys off the streets, and TV weathermen, former vice presidents, Chicago Bears quarterbacks, and men who wear the new F. Scott Fitzgerald-style clothes.

I know of no other law that could bring such a fast improvement in the quality of urban life.

The aldermen say they want to repeal it out of a sense of decency and compassion. I guess it is possible for aldermen to display these emotions. Wolves have been turned into house pets.

But I suspect that they are looking out for themselves. They feel threatened by the ordinance.

Anytime an alderman darts out of City Hall and scuttles down LaSalle Street, he is on a public way. And chances are he is plotting something improper. They have to make a living.

Strollers frequently say "Eek" when an alderman appears on the street, especially one of the more disgusting ones. Under this ordinance, they could be seized for displaying themselves that way.

But it won't happen, because one of the only good ordinances in the municipal code will soon be gone.

The strange part of it is that nobody knows why it was passed in the first place back in 1939.

Nothing in the council records shows why City Hall suddenly decided to make it illegal for somebody diseased, maimed, or mutilated to appear in public.

But I have a theory.

Big Ed Kelly was mayor in those days.

I think he was worried that a one-armed Republican might run against him.

JUNE 10, 1974

Mr. Ambition at Your Service

One way to measure the size of an officeholder's ambition and ego is by how his subordinates answer the phone.

A modest, humble, self-effacing politician will have his people answer the phone by identifying the office or specific department.

An example of this would be Coroner Andrew Toman, who is about as modest a politician as you'll find. Coroner Toman has under his jurisdiction the Cook County Morgue.

Thus, if Toman wished, the morgue's phone could be answered: "Coroner Andrew Toman's morgue."

By doing this, the loyal morgue attendants would be spreading Toman's name among those people who have reason to telephone a morgue, and Toman would reap whatever political benefits this might generate.

In theory, he would be building a potential following among the county's bereaved voting bloc.

But the attendants simply mumble: "Cowny Morgue." And this shows that Toman has few ambitions beyond keeping his stiffs properly toe-tagged and iced.

At the other extreme is Cook County Clerk Stanley Kusper. According to a phone survey we made by calling various offices, Kusper possesses the most hot-eyed, panting ambitions.

Kusper has many departments in his domain, doing all sorts of things. They sell wedding licenses, keep track of birth and death certificates, handle countywide elections, keep maps, register businesses, compile tax rates, and sock away records on this, that, and everything else.

Presumably, then, the citizens who call any of these many offices are interested in one of the services the county clerk provides.

Vital statistics, for instance. Most people who call want a copy of a birth certificate.

Yet, when I phoned, the person who answered said: "Stanley T. Kusper, county clerk."

So I said: "I must have the wrong number. I wanted a statistic that is vital."

"This is vital statistics," she said.

"But you said this is the cuspidor office."

"I said Stanley T. Kusper."

"What is a Kusper?"

"He is the county clerk."

"So what?"

"Excuse me?"

"Do I see him about getting a vital statistic?"

"No, you come to this office."

"Then what do I care who he is?"

She had no ready answer, because there is none.

Then I tried the county clerk's map department, and the person who answered the phone said: "County Clerk Stanley Kusper's office."

"Let me speak to Kusper," I demanded.

"He isn't here. This is his map department."

"Then why tell me his name?"

"Pardon?"

"Forget it."

The man who answers phones in the tax extension department put even greater gusto into glorifying his boss. He answered the phone with:

"County Clerk Kusper's office—may I help you?"

"This is County Kusper?" I asked.

"What?"

"You said this is County Kusper. Is that like County Cork?"

"No, no, the clerk is Kusper."

"He's the clerk of County Kusper?"

"Of Cook County."

"But I don't want anybody named Kusper. I want the tax extension department."

"That's what you have."

"But you just said it was County Clerk Kusper's office."

"This department is under the county clerk."

"Good. Let me talk to him."

"He's not in this office."

"Is he in County Cork?"

"What?"

"Forget it."

I finally called County Clerk Kusper's main office to ask him why his employees keep saying his name so much.

"County Clerk Kusper's office," his secretary said.

"Is this Mr. Kusper's office? His actual office?"

"Yes it is. Can I help you?"

"This isn't his map office, or his vital statistics office?"

"No, it isn't. Can I help you?"

"Sure. Let me talk to Mr. Kusper."

"He's not in."

"Is he in County Cork?"

"What?"

"Forget it."

Slip Off the Old Block

It appears that state Senator Richard M. Daley has a delicate nature, of all things.

A few days ago, he gasped that Mayor Jane Byrne is "ruthless," and he accused her of using "coercive powers."

Richie was upset because the mayor has made a practice of firing pay-rollers who happen to be sponsored by people she considers to be her political enemies.

And lately, while chopping several hundred city employees for budget reasons, she got rid of some who are from the Bridgeport neighborhood, the Daley family's political plantation. She also has fired quite a few who are sponsored by Cook County Assessor Tom Hynes, a chum of Richie.

Well, I share Richie's shock. A ruthless Chicago mayor. Fancy that! Whoever heard of such a thing.

Ah, for the good old days when Chicago mayors were kindly creatures who wouldn't dream of doing something ruthless or using their powers in a coercive way.

I'm thinking, naturally, of the late Mayor Richard J. Daley, who Richie used to call Dad, while the rest of us called him Boss. Now, there was a sweet-natured man.

I recall once when the mayor wanted to hold a campaign fund-raising party in the Art Institute of Chicago. The directors of the institute sent back word that a party would be impossible because it would violate their not-for-profit, tax-free charter.

A ruthless mayor would have used his coercive powers. He might have ordered the Art Institute to paint underwear on all its nude ladies. But not Daley. He simply smiled and shrugged it off.

And a few days later, the city's building inspectors swarmed all over the Art Institute. When they finished doodling on their clipboards, it cost the institute about $250,000 to comply with the city's nit-picking building code.

Then there was the man who owned a restaurant at Milwaukee and Ashland avenues. He happened to be a pal of Daley's opponent in a mayoral election. Being a good pal, he put up a huge banner urging votes for Daley's opponent.

Did Daley say even one harsh word to the restaurant owner? Did he go in and order soup and scream that there was a fly in it, as a ruthless mayor would do? Then not leave a tip?

Of course not. Daley knew that an honest difference of opinions is what makes politics such fun.

And a few days after the man put up the campaign sign, the city's building inspectors stormed in. Before they were done with him, the restaurant owner almost went out of business, his repairs were so costly.

You may also remember the late Ralph Metcalfe, the popular congressman from the South Side.

For most of his long career, Metcalfe was an obedient member of the Machine. As an alderman, he always voted the way he was told. As a ward boss, he made sure his precinct captains dragged out the vote for Daley. As a congressman, he followed Daley's suggestions.

But then a friend of Metcalfe's had a nasty experience. The friend, a doctor, was mistreated by some Chicago cops. His sole crime appeared to be that he was black.

That gave Metcalfe an interest in police brutality, and he began digging up similar cases. He went to Daley to complain about the treatment of blacks by some police, but Daley brushed him off.

So, for the first time in his long career, Metcalfe showed some independence. He went to the public with his brutality complaints.

Did Daley do anything ruthless, such as having the cops beat Metcalfe on the head? Of course not. Daley believed that a congressman has a right to point out a loathsome social condition.

All Daley did was strip Metcalfe of every patronage job he controlled as a ward committeeman. Daley also did everything he could to destroy Metcalfe's congressional career.

Some people may also remember when City Hall's insurance business was dropped into the lap of one of Daley's sons. At the time, the kid was a rookie insurance salesman. In fact, he had only recently obtained his state insurance license through fraud.

But City Hall's business gave the little Daley a windfall commission of more than $100,000.

The reporter who dug up the story went to the city official who handled the insurance and asked why Daley's son, of all the city's insurance peddlers, had been lucky enough to receive the $100,000 plum.

The city official was so surprised by the question that he told the truth.

He said Mayor Daley had ordered the insurance business transferred to the little Daley's agency.

Did Mayor Daley ruthlessly throw this city official out of his office window for opening his mouth that way?

Not at all. The mayor wouldn't punish a man for simply telling the truth.

All he did was order him to clean out his desk, get the hell out of City Hall, and find another job.

Because Richie grew up in such a loving, benign atmosphere, I'm not surprised that he is horrified by a mayor who would single out her political enemies for a knee in the groin.

Richie himself would never do anything like that. Just ask some of the people who were in the Illinois Legislature with Richie when Mayor Daley was alive.

"Richie wouldn't knee you in the groin," one of them said. "He'd just walk on your chest."

Although I don't mind seeing the payroll trimmed by 1,500 snoozers, I can sympathize with Richie. If Mayor Byrne keeps chopping Bridgeport people from the payroll, Richie's power base is going to shrink. Payrollers don't keep ringing doorbells and bringing out the vote if they aren't payrollers anymore.

And without his Bridgeport power base, Richie is less likely to run for mayor in three years, which is what he hopes to do.

Too bad. It would be nice having a sweet-tempered, forgiving mayor again. I still yearn for the days when Boss issued his famous "shoot to kill" order during riots after Martin Luther King Jr. was killed, and a reporter asked him if that included children. He sweetly said:

"You wouldn't wanna shoot children. But with Mace you could detain them."

If Richie is going to continue to remain wide-eyed about the "ruthless" way Mayor Byrne operates, then I will try to console him with the words of George Washington Plunkett, the legendary Tammany Hall politician, who once summed it all up this way:

"Politics ain't beanbag."

And Chicago ain't no playground, Richie.

MAY 7, 1984

Land of the Free, Home of the Fix

Sometimes newcomers to Chicago have a hard time grasping how government works in this city.

For example, there was a big story few days ago about Mayor Harold Washington's radical new plan for providing city services.

He said that when Chicagoans require city service, they should just phone City Hall and ask.

Aldermen and other ward politicians immediately cried that Washington was being sly, political, power-hungry, and clearly up to no good.

This led a recent arrival to Chicago to tell me: "That's very confusing."

Why?

"I've lived in other cities, and that's the normal way of doing things. If you have some problem with a city service—you have a broken curb or a dead tree or something like that—you just call the City Hall. I don't understand what the controversy is about. Why shouldn't it be done that way?"

Because it's wasteful.

"Why is it wasteful? It seems like the simplest, most direct way of doing it."

It's wasteful because it squanders opportunity. And since this is supposed to be the land of opportunity, it shouldn't be wasted.

"I don't understand. What kind of opportunity is a broken curb?"

It is a great opportunity, and I explained.

Under the system used in most cities—and the one Mayor Washington wants to use here—you dial City Hall for a broken curb or some other problem.

There you talk to an anonymous bureaucrat, a functionary, a faceless voice on the phone who takes down your name and address and tells you to "have a nice day."

You don't know this person, and that person doesn't know you or really care if you have a nice day or a disastrous day. You are just a voice on the phone, a name and address on a complaint form.

But the Chicago system always has been different.

In the traditional Chicago way, you saw that your curb was crumbling. So you walked down the street and rapped on your precinct captain's door and said: "Tony, I've got a broken curb."

He would say: "I'll see what I can do."

The precinct captain now had an opportunity to do something for you, which is what he lived for, and why he had a patronage job as a city earthquake inspector.

He would then tell the alderman that you had a broken curb, thus demonstrating to the alderman that he was keeping right on top of problems in his precinct. And the alderman would say: "I'll see what I can do."

So now the alderman also had an opportunity to do something for you.

The alderman would then call his wife's brother, an assistant supervisor in the Department of Streets and Sanitation, and tell him about your curb.

The assistant supervisor, who owed his job to the alderman, would now have an opportunity to show his gratitude. He would say: "I'll see what I can do."

He would then tell a crew foreman, who also owed his job to the alderman, about your curb and ask him to get it fixed.

The foreman, who would want to show his gratitude, would wake up a repair crew and go out and fix your curb.

Then the precinct captain would come to your house and point at the curb and say: "I took care of it."

Later he would drop by and say: "The alderman is running for re-election, you know. I'd appreciate it if you could give him your vote. And your wife's vote. And your grown kids'. And your mother who lives in the basement flat. And maybe you could put one of the alderman's campaign posters in your window?"

This would give you an opportunity to show that you were grateful for getting your curb fixed, so you would say: "I'll see what I can do."

Thus, one broken curb would open up opportunities for the precinct captain, the alderman, the assistant supervisor, and the foreman of the crew to dispense clout.

And you, your wife, your grown children, and your mother would have an opportunity to show that you had clout.

Waste not, want not.

After I explained this, the newcomer said: "That sounds like an awful lot of bother. I still think the other way is more efficient."

Ah, but what if you phone City Hall directly and the curb isn't repaired. Then what do you do?

"Then I call back and complain."

And who would you complain to? Still another disembodied voice on a phone. Somebody who just takes down your name and address and tells you to have a nice day.

But under the Chicago system, when the precinct captain came around asking for your vote for the alderman, you could say: "You didn't get my curb fixed. In my house, we're all voting for the other guy."

And on election night, when the precinct captain took in his tally sheet, the alderman would say: "Your totals are slipping." And the precinct captain would be demoted from earthquake inspection to the office of wild snake control.

The next day, the party chairman would look at the ward totals and tell the alderman: "You're slipping." And he would lose three patronage jobs, including his brother-in-law's.

"All that from a broken curb?" the newcomer said.

It's possible. From little acorns and all that.

"Well, it just sounds to me like a lot of people doing political favors and putting in the fix and showing off their clout."

We prefer to call it participatory democracy.

MAY 17, 1988

Alderman's Brain Is a Museum Piece

You may remember Alderman Ernie Jones. He's the statesman who recently said female cops take too many days off because of their "minister periods."

I'm not sure who was more confused and offended—the lady cops or their ministers.

Now Jones has turned his pea-sized intellect to other pursuits—art criticism and constitutional law.

Jones was one of the City Hall hysterics who took it upon themselves to yank a painting out of the School of the Art Institute because it offended them.

By now, most Chicagoans know the story. A student-artist thought it clever to draw the late Mayor Harold Washington in women's undergarments.

Why did he do this? Who knows? Why did Warhol love Campbell's Soup cans? Why did Van Gogh cut off his ear? History tells us that many artists are kind of weird.

This young man's painting was exhibited at a private—I repeat, private—display at the school. It was part of a showing of works by graduating seniors.

Someone called a black alderman or two, and they spread the word among their colleagues and everybody went berserk. Several rushed to the Art Institute—probably for the first time—to seize the painting.

But fearing that the students might splatter them with watercolors, they backed down and had the police confiscate the painting for them.

The police justified the seizure by saying that a painting of Washington in female undies might incite black citizens to riot.

Actually, if anyone was inclined to riot, it was this handful of alderboobs. Only the students and faculty knew about the foolish painting until the alderboobs started yelping about it.

There certainly were no reports of blacks milling about the public housing complexes at the Taylor Homes or Cabrini-Green, or on West Side streets, saying: "My man, have you heard about the offensive portrait of Harold at a private showing in the School of the Art Institute? Shall we show our displeasure by going there and trashing a Monet or two?"

As I said, one of the aldermen who took part in this art raid was Jones. I single him out because I find certain parallels between that painting and this alderman.

Jones says the painting was offensive, and I agree with him.

However, many policewomen told me they found Jones offensive for saying they stay home for their "minister periods," and I agree with them, too.

Jones clearly believes that if a painting is offensive to a segment of the population, it can and should be taken to jail.

Then why wasn't Jones taken to jail when he offended a segment of the city's population?

If anything, I find a painting far less offensive than an alderman. A painting is nothing more than an inanimate object. You just hang it on a wall and it stays there. Some aldermen are inanimate, too, but you can't hang an alderman that way, although it would be fun.

Name me one painting that has ever taken a kickback. Has a painting ever upped your taxes? Has a painting ever put its idiot cousin on the city payroll?

So here you have this alderboob Jones, sitting in the legislative branch of one of the great cities of the world, and what does he babble about? The "minister periods" of policewomen.

The least one might expect is that he go to the dictionary and find the correct word. (In fairness to Jones, some observers insist that he said the women missed work because of their "minstrel periods." I doubt that. It's been decades since minstrel shows have been seen in Chicago.)

But I digress. My point is that it is not the job of aldermen to go around snatching paintings, as offensive as they might be.

The aldermen should be content with their traditional role of snatching votes, or seizing gratuities for city contracts, zoning changes, and license fixes. If they would work at their own art more diligently, they wouldn't always be getting caught by the feds.

Some civil libertarians fear that the picture-snatching might lead to other forms of illegal censorship by the alderboobs. As a concerned liberal said: "What is to stop them from going into bookstores and libraries and seizing books they don't like?"

That's possible. But it would take more effort than seizing a painting. They'd have to find someone to read the books to them.

AUGUST 17, 1988

Bush's Selection Really Hits Home

I didn't think George Bush could do it, but he picked a running mate who will lure me into pulling the Republican lever in the voting booth.

That's because Senator J. Danforth Quayle, Bush's surprise choice, is my kind of guy. In fact, in reading his biographical material, I was amazed at how much we have in common.

To begin, J. Danforth used to be a newspaperman.

And he was quite successful at it. When he was only 27 years old, he became associate publisher of the *Huntington Herald-Press* in Indiana.

Although it isn't a major paper, few newspapermen become associate publishers of any kind of paper when they're as young as J. Danforth was.

I'm sure his father was proud when J. Danforth came home and said: "Dad, I have terrific news. I've just been named associate publisher of the *Huntington Herald-Press.*"

On the other hand, J. Danforth probably didn't say that to his dad, since his dad was the publisher of the *Huntington Herald-Press* when J. Danforth became associate publisher.

But J. Danforth didn't stay with newspapering. He decided to go into politics. And he managed to get elected to the U.S. House of Representatives before he was 30. And eight years ago, when he was only 33, he became a United States senator.

It's not easy to become a U.S. senator when you're that young. For one thing, you have to go around to newspapers and try to get their endorsements. And some publishers might not have confidence in someone so young.

But it appears that J. Danforth made a good impression on the powerful and enormously wealthy man who owned some of the biggest papers in

Indiana, including the *Indianapolis Star*. I'm not sure how the conversation went, but it might have been something like:

"Young fellow, we think you will make a fine senator, and our papers will support you."

"Thank you, Uncle."

"You're welcome, Nephew."

But to get back to things J. Danforth and I have in common.

My generation had its war. And although I wasn't eager to visit Korea and did nothing heroic when I got there, I put in my time and dutifully attended all of the chaplain's VD lectures.

And J. Danforth did his duty, too. His generation had its war in Vietnam, and he was in uniform. Between 1969 and 1975, when the fighting was fierce and heavy, he was a proud member of the Indiana National Guard.

Now, I don't want to hear any snickering from those blue-collar types who were in Vietnam. Had the Viet Cong shown up on the outskirts of Indianapolis, I'm sure J. Danforth would have been there with guns blazing. And after driving them back, he could have returned to his office and written an editorial condemning the threat of communism to all decent Hoosiers.

But let me return to the things we have in common.

As those who have seen him on TV know, J. Danforth looks remarkably like Robert Redford, except much younger.

In fact, when he first ran for the Senate, Redford sent him a telegram asking him to stop publicizing the fact that they looked alike. I guess Redford, a liberal Democrat, didn't like the idea of a conservative Republican cashing in on his good looks. And I can understand how Redford felt. Because Redford was older, Redford looked like Redford long before J. Danforth looked like Redford.

On the other hand, it wasn't J. Danforth's fault that he looked like Redford. For all we know, he might have preferred looking like Paul Newman.

J. Danforth responded by informing Redford that he wasn't bragging about their resemblance or even using it in his campaign material. He said the media kept bringing it up.

And to this day, they're still doing it. Only this week, reporters in New Orleans asked him about the resemblance.

According to one report, he sighed, his blue eyes flashed, he brushed back his blond hair, and he said: "I've had that stigma since I first ran for the Senate. It's stuck ever since."

I know how he feels because I, too, have the stigma of looking like a movie star. Not Redford, though. Jimmy Durante.

I've had that stigma since a nurse in the maternity ward pointed it out to my stunned parents, and it's stuck ever since. But I'll say one thing for Durante—he never complained or asked me to have my nose removed.

All things considered, I think Bush made a brilliant choice.

We now have a Republican presidential candidate who comes from a wealthy, prominent family—part of the Eastern elite.

And he has a vice presidential running mate who comes from a wealthy, prominent family—part of the Midwestern elite.

That's what I call a balanced ticket.

AUGUST 23, 1988

Letters, Calls, Complaints, and Great Thoughts from Readers

NAOMI FOLKERTS, Wheaton: About Dan Quayle. I would like you to recall the days of the 1960s when the media helped young men believe the Vietnam War and anyone that served in it was a bad word.

So I would think that those of you in the media would be smart enough to know that those who didn't care to go to Vietnam were simply a product of what you made them.

COMMENT: You do Quayle an injustice when you imply that he was swayed by "the media." His family owned the biggest, most influential newspapers in Indiana. These papers were super-hawkish about the Vietnam War. But it's obvious that he didn't let those papers stampede him into doing anything rash. The lad had willpower, bless him.

ELLEN KAMSTRA, Lansing: Here's a smart, good-looking young man whose family happens to have money, and the media and journalists are tearing him apart.

You get the award for being the most cruel, insensitive, sarcastic reporter in the country.

COMMENT: I accept. What time does the awards banquet begin, and is there a cocktail hour?

LOUISE HASTINGS, Downers Grove: After reading your stupid articles defaming George Bush and Dan Quayle, I'm sending my financial contributions for their campaign.

I'd like to get you by the scruff of your neck and stuff your head in a bucket of manure.

COMMENT: Thanks, but I already have dinner plans, so you and Mr. Hastings go ahead without me.

B. SWANSON, Chicago: When I saw George Bush on TV at the Illinois

State Fair, pointing that machine gun at the media creeps, I wish he hadn't been joking and had pulled the trigger and blown the whole rotten pack of you away. I can just see you jumping up and running.

COMMENT: That would have been a hair-raising experience. On the other hand, if we had had a few moments' notice, we could have asked our fathers to phone Bush to get us off the hook.

JOYCE LEWIS, Chicago: Hey, who cares? If Senator Quayle had gone to Vietnam, it would have still turned out the same way. So what's the big deal? He was smart enough to get out of it. If other guys weren't as smart, that's their problem. So let's lighten up.

COMMENT: You're right. So to lighten the mood I'm going to shift gears and we'll have a little poetry. It is from . . .

JEFFREY LAWRENCE, Schaumburg:

> *J. Danforth Quayle, the Third*
> *Thought war was brutal and absurd.*
> *So he said: Daddy,*
> *I'd rather be a Guard Major's caddy,*
> *So please have your friends put in a word.*

> *J. Danforth survived to run for Veep*
> *While others, less wise, are six feet deep.*
> *Let's praise George's choice*
> *For our nation's second voice,*
> *But of his war record don't make a peep.*

COMMENT: Maybe we ought to have a Dan Quayle poetry contest. Let's see, what rhymes with dodger?

Hail a Taxidermist for This Public Body

It was an unusual question. Is a Chicago alderman a public body?

The question came up when some do-gooders wanted Alderman Bernie Stone to disclose how he spends his city expense account. Stone refused to reveal that information, arguing that an alderman is not a public body. So the do-gooders sued him.

A Chicago judge ruled that Stone is not a public body. The case was appealed, and this week a higher court upheld the earlier ruling.

I mentioned this to Slats Grobnik, who is an ardent alderman-watcher, a hobby that is similar to bird-watching. Like bird-watchers, he often becomes excited at an unusual sighting, saying: "Look, isn't that a Pinky-Ring Two-Hand Grabber? Ooops, I was wrong. It is a Red-Nosed Wink and Nodder."

When I told him about the legal decision, he said: "Well, I'm no lawyer, but I have sighted Alderman Stone a couple of times, and I don't think the public would want his body. I sure wouldn't. What would I do with it? I suppose I could stick it out on my lawn to scare away those lousy neighbors' dogs, but it would lower my real estate values. No, I think the judges were right. The public has already got enough burdens without being stuck with any aldermen's bodies."

Sam (the Greek) Sianis, who was behind his bar in the Billy Goat Tavern, spoke up. "I dunno. I wouldn't mind have alderman's body, if I get it free. I already got stuffed billy goat on wall. Customers like goat. If I get alderman's body, I stuff it and put it next to goat. Then when tourists come in, they'd ask: 'What's that thing?' I tell them: 'Genuine Chicago alderman body.' They write home about that on postcard, I bet."

Slats nodded and said: "If you're going to make it a tourist attraction, don't put it on the wall. Stand it up in the corner, the way hunters do with their stuffed bears, then the tourists could pose for pictures with it. That would be something for conventioneers to show the folks at home."

At that moment, Patrick Whitehair, a defrocked Chicago judge, lifted his head from the bar and said: "Excuse me, I could not help overhearing your profound discussion, and I will be glad to offer you my legal expertise free, which I never did when I was wearing my robe, which is why I sit here in sodden disgrace. It is my opinion that you could not display an alderman's body in a public drinking establishment. It might be considered a violation of the municipal health codes."

Slats said: "I don't understand that. The city just said that this couple can keep a pet pig in a condo. So if you can keep a pig in a condo, why can't you keep an alderman's body in a public bar?"

"Because," the defrocked judge said, "the sight of a cute pig would not make your customers retch, but an alderman's body very well could. That is the health hazard."

Sianis said: "I don't understand dees. If two or three aldermen come in here and seet at table and whisper about deals, that's legal?"

"Perfectly legal," said the defrocked judge, "unless the FBI has bugged their beer steins."

Sianis shook his head. "But eet's not legal if I got alderman's stuffed body on my wall? I don't understand."

Slats said: "Yeah, but the question is whether an alderman's body is public or ain't it?"

The defrocked judge said: "I think not. The parks are public because when the trees and grass and flowers bloom, they are pretty and help refresh the spirits. The streets are public because they serve a necessary function. But aldermen aren't pretty, they don't refresh the spirits, and they seldom serve a necessary function."

"Sometimes they make us laugh," Slats said.

"True," said the defrocked judge. "But at those prices, you could hire Rodney Dangerfield. Besides, aldermen's bodies are of little practical or aesthetic use. I doubt if there is any great public demand for them."

"We pay for them, don't we?" said Slats. "So they ought to be the public's bodies."

"Yes," the defrocked judge said, "but you pay to have your waste products processed and removed. Would you want them in your home?"

"I guess not," said Slats.

"Now, if you wanted something worth having, it would not be an alderman's body," said the defrocked judge, "it would be an alderman's wallet. Ah, that would be a prize."

Sianis nodded. "Eef I get one of dose, I put it on wall above the goat."

"Yes," said the defrocked judge, "but be sure you have the building checked to see if it can withstand the weight."

MARCH 17, 1992

Hillary Clinton Is Fair Political Game

Until a few months ago, I didn't know Hillary Clinton from the sandwich maker at the corner convenience store.

But now I know that she grew up in the Chicago suburb of Park Ridge, was a teenager for Goldwater, excelled at Yale Law School, became a big-time attorney and an advocate of many liberal causes, has a daughter named after an English landmark, is married to the governor of Arkansas, and much more.

Unless you've been living in a cave, you've probably seen Hillary on TV, shouting an introduction of her husband into a microphone: "And I give you the next President of the United States . . ."

In other words, she's not exactly a political wallflower.

So I don't understand why Bill Clinton became so huffy when Jerry Brown tossed in a zinger about Hillary during the debate among Democratic presidential candidates. Something to do with her law firm doing business with the state her husband governs.

Clinton played the chivalrous spouse, telling Brown he wasn't fit to stand on the same stage with Hillary. This put Brown, a bachelor, at a disadvantage, since he couldn't say that Clinton wasn't fit to be on the same stage with Linda Ronstadt, whom Brown used to date. Or with Mother Teresa, with whom he nursed the needy. Then Paul Tsongas could have chimed in that neither of them was fit to be in the same swimming pool with him. If the campaign lasts long enough, who knows?

Later, while performing for the cameras at a Polish restaurant on Milwaukee Avenue (Arkansas governors just love Polish food), Clinton said he could handle political abuse but would "hit" those who maligned his wife.

I assume that he meant he would hit with words, not fists, although nothing would be a surprise in this campaign. However, if he challenges Brown to duke it out, Brown will probably say his choice of weapons are the laser swords used by Luke Skywalker.

But what is so terrible about Brown or any other candidate taking a political shot at Hillary?

She's not simply a wife tagging along on the campaign trail, gazing adoringly at her candidate/husband while being bored to death. She is one of the key players in the campaign, involved in strategy, spin, buzz, and all the other modern political voodoo.

And if he's elected president, she's going to do more than redecorate the White House living quarters and keep her eye peeled for writer Kitty Kelley's spies.

She has her own agenda of ways the federal government can be used to make our lives richer, fuller, and bureaucratized. She'll instantly become one of the most powerful figures in American government.

So if she's out there grabbing for power as eagerly as her husband, there's no reason why she should be above the political brawl.

It would be different if she were sitting home, quietly watching the soaps, collecting recipes, and pasting Bill's clippings into a scrapbook, and Brown had said: "I have it on good authority that Mrs. Clinton watches all the corniest soaps and makes a very bad meatloaf."

If that were the case, Clinton would have had good cause to pop Brown in the snoot for intruding into the privacy of an old-fashioned wife. Nobody ever sniped at Bess Truman, Mamie Eisenhower, or Pat Nixon, who were classic stay-at-home first ladies.

But Hillary is a modern woman: independent, successful, and ambitious. That's fine, because if Bill ever falls upon hard times, she can support them both.

Since she's reaching for the brass ring as avidly as her husband is, it shouldn't be necessary for him to play the protective husband.

If Brown had tossed a barb at Clinton's media huckster, his pollster, his advance man, his issues manager, his spin doctor, or any of his other professional campaign hucksters, Clinton wouldn't have talked about hitting him. Imagine Clinton saying: "You aren't fit to be on the same stage as my campaign strategists." Or, "I don't care what they say about me, but if anybody insults my pollster, I'll hit them." It would sound weird.

If he's nominated, he's going to pick someone with voter appeal as his running mate. And that person will have to expect the usual political bombardment from the Republicans. I wouldn't expect Clinton to say: "If anyone says bad things about my running mate, I will hit them." That would sound even more weird.

The fact is, Hillary will have far more power than any vice president. Based on her political activities, she'll be almost a co-president. Or, as they might say in parts of Arkansas: "There goes Ma and Pa President."

To paraphrase Harry Truman's old saying: "If you can't stand the heat, don't get out of the kitchen."

NOVEMBER 4, 1992

Bush's Wish Isn't Voters' Command

It happened almost four years ago. Or so the legend goes.

A tall, lanky man walked a lonely beach near Kennebunkport in Maine.

He was deep in thought, head down, hunched into the winter wind.

Then he stopped. Something caught his eye. He bent over and picked up an oddly shaped bottle that had washed ashore.

He looked at it, shook it, then twisted out the cork stopper.

Smoke puffed from the bottle. Startled, the man dropped it and jumped back.

The smoke poured out, became thicker, then whirled and materialized as a human form that yawned and stretched.

"Who in the dickens are you?" the lanky man said.

"I am a genie," the creature said. "I have been trapped in the bottle for ages. You have released me, so you are my master."

"Golly. Barbara will never believe this," the man said. "Wish I had my camera."

"Your wish is my command," the genie said, and a camera appeared in the man's hand."

"Jimminy cricket," the man said, "how'd you do that?"

"I am a genie," the genie said. "That is what I do. I can grant you 10 wishes for freeing me. But since you wished for that camera object, you have but nine remaining."

"Wait a minute," the man said, "are you saying you can actually grant wishes and make things come true?"

The genie shrugged and said: "Hey, it's a living."

The lanky man began talking excitedly. "Look, I just was elected to my first term as president. Do you know what that means?"

The genie pursed his lips. "I would guess that it means you are the punjab, the top maharajah, the big fez."

"Well, since Nixon's days, we usually call it the big enchilada," the lanky man said, with a piercing laugh. "But I think you have the picture."

"So what do you wish, master?"

"Well, I've been walking this lonely beach, as presidents have done since JFK made it de rigueur, trying to figure out what I'd do the next four years. You see, that's when I have to run again. And I'm already concerned. I might not get lucky and draw a prissy little Greek from Massachusetts."

"I do not understand such matters, master. I merely grant wishes."

"Anything?" the lanky man said.

"Within reason. Nothing kinky. Against genie rules. Nor can we interfere with the movement of the sun or planets. But routine miracles, you need only ask."

"OK. So tell me this: Can you make Soviet communism collapse? Greatest threat to world peace, you know. Kids'll get a good night's sleep with it gone."

"Granted. What else?"

"Golly. There's this wall in Berlin. Symbol. Ugly. Repression. Can you bring it tumbling down?"

"As good as done. Next?"

"Wowie. OK, inflation. Don't like it. Give me the lowest inflation rate in umpteen years. And low interest rates, too."

"Your wish is my command. Next?"

"Lemme think. I got it. How about a war? Not a big one, but something splashy. Bad guy starts it. Invades helpless neighbor. I move fast. Decisive. Warn 'em. Won't take it. Won't let it stand. Rally the world community. Hit 'em hard, hit 'em fast. Win it. Brilliant strategy. Great victory. Yellow ribbons. Parades. TV ratings way up. Critics way down. How about it?"

"Granted, master. You still have five wishes."

"Right. OK, let's talk polls. Yeah. After I win the war, can I have the highest approval ratings in history?"

"Easier than a wabbit out of a hat, master."

"OK, what's next? Yes, my opponents. Cuomo, makes me nervous. Liberal, but talks good. Can you make him drop out?"

"He will be out, master. What next?"

"All of 'em, the big Democrats. They thought I'd be a sitting ducky-wucky. Give 'em a scare. Make 'em go run and hide. Get rid of them. No real opposition."

"Your wish is my command. They are vanquished."

"But I must have an opponent. Wouldn't look good otherwise. OK, let's find a real patsy. How about a governor nobody heard of. From a tiny state. Arkansas. Nobody's ever been to Arkansas, even the people who live there. That's it. And give him an Elvis haircut, just for laughs. And make him a draft dodger. Can you do that?"

"You have it, master."

"And a scary liberal wife."

"You have it, master. Shall I make her a lawyer, too?"

"Good touch. Look, I hate to impose. But is there any way that almost from the day this fella runs, there's some tall blond bombshell who goes on TV and says they were, you know, significant others? In an illicit kind of way? The scandal thing. The Gary Hart thing."

"It will be done."

"Gee willikers, I love it. Then for my last wish, I want to win in a historic landslide."

"I'm sorry, master, but you have used up your 10 wishes. I cannot give you a historic landslide."

"Y'can't? Well, it won't matter. Communism, collapsed. Berlin Wall, down. War with bully, won. Inflation, scrunched. Top Democrats, hiding. Pathetic opponent, unknown governor of a teeny state. Draft dodger, sex scandal. Golly. With all that going for me, I can't possibly lose, can I, genie?"

"I am only a genie, master, not a pollster. Now I must return to my bottle. Please replace the cork after I'm in and throw me back into the sea."

As the lanky man tossed the bottle into the surf, he shouted: "Thanks to you, genie, my next election will really clinch my place in the history books."

And a faint voice came from the floating bottle: "I think you can count on it."

NOVEMBER 10, 1995

Democrats Just Got Boost from GOP Without Even Trying

It seems like only yesterday that the Democratic Party had one foot in the grave and was being given its last rites.

Those bright young Republican clones of Newt Gingrich had seized Congress and launched their yappy-yuppie revolution.

Sure, the Democrats still had the White House. But Newt's lads were almost laughing in the face of President Clinton, who couldn't seem to get anything right. And when he happened to, he'd change his mind the next day and get it all wrong.

So the question wasn't whether Clinton could be reelected. That thought was laughable.

The only question was whom the Republicans would choose to evict Clinton and finally and mercifully put an end to the suffering of the Democratic Party.

The pundits saw it that way. Newt's lads did, too. So did all of those weary Democrats in Congress who decided the end of political life was near, and they didn't want to run again.

We were about to enter the greatest era in Republican history. By the new century, liberal Democrats would be as rare as conservative war veterans.

Except that we forgot that Republicans have as great a talent for goofing up as Democrats.

And boy, oh boy, did they do it.

A few days ago, they had a potential candidate who would have peeled Clinton as easily as a tangerine.

Yes, I'm talking about Colin Powell. Distinguished military man, but not a chest-thumping bully. Mature, yet still youthful. Articulate, but not a bull-shooter. An intellectual, but not dogmatic or superior. Quiet, but not weak. Confident, but not arrogant. Of humble origins, but without sullen resentments.

Just about as perfect a candidate as either party could imagine. And to boot, he is of African-American ancestry, although he doesn't make a big deal out of it.

You would think that every sensible Republican in the country would have said: "We haven't had anyone like him since Ike. Patriot, hero, statesman, charmer. He will not only get our votes, but he will also bring us the young, since they are not saddled with our racial bigotry; he will bring us the growing middle-class black vote; he will bring us rootless liberals and independents. And he has no soiled political baggage. Poor Clinton—all he'll get is the afternoon-rate motel vote."

Yes, the Republicans could have grabbed it all. Instead, they chose to assure us the survival of the two-party system.

Just when it appeared that Powell would declare his candidacy, the right wing of the Republican Party rose up in all of its nastiness.

It appeared that Powell didn't pass all of its knee-jerk, right-wing lit-mus tests on gun control, abortion, and affirmative action. His views re-flected those of the majority of Americans.

But after more than 30 years in the Army, he was viewed by Republi-can right-wingers as some kind of dangerous liberal.

They started whispering about his military record. One wax-faced, non-elected spokesman for the rigid right went on TV to question Pow-ell's military record. He said Powell was merely a "milicrat"—a uni-formed desk-bound bureaucrat—instead of a true battlefield warrior.

That from someone who—like most of the right wing's leaders—wan-gled one campus deferment after another during the Vietnam War. They are probably the toughest-talking draft dodgers in our history.

They also managed to leak into print and broadcast the fact that Pow-ell's wife takes medication to control depression. That gives her some-thing in common with about 50 million other adult Americans.

It's assumed that her depression is caused by an imbalance in body chemistry. Or maybe it has to do with her husband becoming a Republi-can and having to associate with klutzes.

They should have been kissing his shoes. Instead, one after another, the spokesmen for the rigid right made it clear that while they wouldn't mind Powell becoming a Republican and helping them win elections, he wasn't their idea of a presidential candidate.

So he took the hint and got out and they were happy.

But they got up the next day and looked around, and those who weren't stupid or dogmatic saw what they had done.

They left themselves with as motley a collection of candidates as either party has ever had.

Senator Robert Dole is now the front-runner. I admire him, but he's over 70, comes off as a grouch, and his time has passed. Senator Phil Gramm sounds like Lyndon Johnson's dim-witted kid brother. The oth-ers? You can't name them, and this time next year you still won't.

Now they're even talking about Newt as their candidate. They appar-ently hope the average American voter is as indiscriminate in his choice of heroes as Congress babblers are.

By chasing off Powell, the Republican rigid right did something the Democrats couldn't do—they clinched a second term for Bill Clinton.

Those people are even more dangerous than they realize.

MY KIND OF TOWN

HEY, MIKE, WHADDAYA THINK ABOUT . . .

Paying Bribes?

The federal indictment of 29 city electrical inspectors has so unnerved Mayor Michael Bilandic that he says he is going to send letters to businessmen telling them that they don't have to pay bribes to city employees. This is probably one of the few cities in America in which a mayor would think people have to be officially informed that they aren't required to pay bribes. But I expect the letter to accomplish nothing more than to touch off confusion. Upon receiving the letter, many Chicagoans will probably write him back and ask: "Dear Mayor: If I don't give the bribe to the inspector, who gets it?"

—*Chicago Sun-Times,* November 17, 1978

Saloon Etiquette?

Never talk to someone who drinks with his eyes closed. Never laugh at someone who is weeping while singing a sentimental song about his mother. Don't sit next to someone who leans at more than a forty-five degree angle. Avoid making eye contact with guys who have bottle scars on their noses and tattoos on their arms. Never ask a lady in a bar to dance if she has bottle scars on her nose and tattoos on her arm. Never call a bartender who has an eighteen-inch neck "my good man" or "fellow." South of Twelfth Street, don't play the jukebox while the White Sox game is on the TV. In a strange bar, never use the phone more than twice or they will think you are planning a stickup. Never pet a tavern dog that has a purple tongue and yellow eyes. Never flirt with a barmaid who has a purple tongue and yellow eyes; her husband might be offended.

—*Chicago Sun-Times,* March 29, 1979

Slats Grobnik, Sidewalk Man

The police in suburban Arlington Heights are said to have put some kind of ban on the playing of sidewalk hopscotch.

If they are serious, which I doubt, it could not be enforced. It would be a violation of an unwritten common law that says sidewalks belong to kids.

Adults may use them for walking on, plunging to, or shoveling off, but basically sidewalks are really long, narrow playgrounds.

The best place for a child to play and learn is on a sidewalk. It is his natural environment. If you take a child into the woods, he can fall out of a tree and break a leg and ruin the weekend.

Nobody liked sidewalks more than I did, except Slats Grobnik. To this day, if he walks on grass for more than five minutes, his feet blister. His attitude toward lawns and gardens is summed up when he looks sick and says: "Worms live in that stuff."

When the rest of us would go to Humboldt Park, Slats would shake his head and stay behind, saying: "Anything that can hide behind a fireplug is small enough for me to handle, but how do I know what kind of creep is in the bushes?" He feared being kidnapped and held ransom because he knew his father didn't believe in touching the savings.

When we built a tree house, Slats wouldn't come up. He said:

"If people was meant to live in trees, the squirrels would slip some nuts to the city building inspector."

So Slats always stayed on the sidewalk and did the things all kids do. And some that nobody had heard of before.

One summer, he spent all of July pitching pennies. He got so good that one Sunday morning he made 14 straight liners. The precinct captain had that penny bronzed and it was hung up behind the bar of the corner tavern. Later, Slats' mother put it in with his bronzed baby shoes and his first tooth, a one-inch molar, incidentally.

Naturally, he sold lemonade on the sidewalk. We all did. But Slats was the only one who could sell it when the weather was cold. Even in November he'd have a dozen customers lined up.

One day a plainclothes cop happened to get in line and that's when they found out that with every glass you got to look at the dirty pictures Slats found in his father's dresser. And that was years before Hugh Hefner came along.

There were days when Slats would just draw or write on the sidewalk with chalk or stones. Mostly dirty words. Then he'd hide in a gangway and peek out to see if ladies were offended. If they were, he'd go "hee-hee." Slats would have been a natural hippie.

Sometimes he'd spend the day just lying on the sidewalk, face down, forehead pressed against the pavement, not moving a muscle. He'd be watching the ants in the crack. People from outside the neighborhood were startled, especially when he'd hiss: "Boy, they're murdering each other."

Once a drunk came out of the tavern and tripped over him. Slats pretended to have a broken rib and the drunk gave him $5 to keep quiet. Slats moaned louder and he got $5 more. For a long time after that, Slats thought about going to law school.

Even when he didn't feel like doing anything, Slats did it on the sidewalk. He liked to lean against a wall and spit. That wasn't as disgusting as it sounds, although it was pretty disgusting.

He'd just stand there, not moving or saying anything, and every two or three minutes he'd go "phtt" between his two front teeth. He'd keep it up all day, quitting only when he felt weak from dehydration.

A big event for Slats was when a new section of sidewalk was put down.

He'd sneak out at night, take off his shoe, and put his footprint in it.

His feet are hard to describe. They were very big and shaped kind of funny.

So people got nervous when they saw the print. But a man from a museum came out and said there was nothing to worry about because whatever made the print had been dead for millions of years.

What Slats was best at was walking on a sidewalk without stepping on lines. We all did that for good luck when we happened to be walking, but Slats would go walking for hours just to avoid stepping on lines.

One day he decided to try for a world's record and he left without telling anybody. He was gone for three days, walking all over the city, avoiding stepping on lines.

When he got back home, he yelled: "Don't worry, ma, I wasn't kidnapped."

His father waved the bank book and triumphantly said: "See, I was right. There was no reason to disturb the interest."

The True Story of Twinkies

Many people are suffering from a controversy hangover. They say they want to read about something that is good, popular, and harmless, and offends no one.

There aren't many things, besides our mayor, that can be described that way. But fortunately I am an expert on another one.

It is Twinkies, the world's most popular cake snack, and a delight to gourmets everywhere.

There is nothing more harmless and decent than Twinkies. Things would have been different in Chicago if the demonstrators at last month's Democratic National Convention had thrown Twinkies at the police, and the police had hit demonstrators with Twinkies.

Mayor Daley, when Senator Ribicoff offended him at the convention, might simply have opened a package of Twinkies and offered to share them with the senator. The world would have been moved by such a simple gesture of peace and good will.

There is not one recorded case of anyone committing a felony immediately after eating Twinkies, or driving recklessly while under the influence of Twinkies.

When the police stop and frisk someone, they usually let him go if all he is carrying are Twinkies.

I'm sure we'd all agree that it is hard to say something unkind about Twinkies. Many of us have been eating them in great quantity since childhood. When Slats Grobnik couldn't have Twinkies, he used to scream and roll around on the floor, which always upset the mess hall sergeant.

But how much do we know about Twinkies? Yet, any schoolboy knows about the history of the airplane, the telephone, the H-bomb, and other popular gadgets.

It is time the story of Twinkies was told, if for no other reason than to provide readers with something offbeat to drop into cocktail party conversations.

It all began back in 1930 in an office in Chicago's Continental Baking Company. An executive sat down and wrote a memorandum saying the company should produce a finger-shaped cake that would be sold in pairs.

The higher-ups accepted the idea.

The man's name? Nobody remembers, because the idea flopped. They had called the cakes Little Short Cake Fingers, and who would go into a store and ask for something called Little Short Cake Fingers?

All the bakers were depressed. They were stuck with a great stack of pans, good for nothing but making Little Short Cake Fingers.

That is when a man named James Dewar, then running an outlying Continental plant, revealed his genius.

He thought of squirting a tasty filling into the Little Short Cake Fingers.

This was done. They passed the product to all the boys at the office, who ate them up. "You've got something here, Dewar," the top brass said.

But they still had to come up with another name.

Somebody suggested Creme Filled Little Short Cake Fingers. He was demoted. Somebody else thought of New, Improved Little Short Cake Fingers. He was assigned to the day-old bread division.

Then a historic conversation took place.

Dewar was taking a ride with another Continental man. They passed a shoe factory and saw a sign that read: "Home of the Twinkletoe Shoes."

The other man said: "You might call your new baby Twinkle Fingers."

Demar said: "If we are going to be corny, let's call them plain Twinkies."

Before long, all the little Great Depression children were wolfing down Twinkies, which probably explains why they became such a law-abiding generation.

And Dewar rose to be a vice president of Continental, a little enough reward for his genius.

No one knows what happened to the man who invented the Little Short Cake Fingers, any more than we know the man who discovered the wheel but failed to come up with a good name at the time.

I can't think of any message in this story, except that success comes to someone who fills a losing product with creme to make it taste better.

That ought to make the person who wrote the mayor's official version of the convention disorders feel optimistic about his future.

JUNE 16, 1969

Change Bugs an Old Square

I walked past Bughouse Square the other night, and there wasn't a soapbox orator in sight. The little park at Clark and Walton streets was almost deserted. Only a wino asleep in the grass, and a pair of slim young men rolling eyes at each other.

It's the kind of change that takes place in a city without anyone really noticing.

Just a few years ago, original thinkers and plain loonies still went there to mount vegetable crates and loudly explain how they would reshape the world.

Since the turn of the century it had been Chicago's unofficial open-air forum for radical speakers. If your wife wouldn't listen, or if the bartender threw you out, of if you were mad at the world, you just got up on a box in Bughouse Square and yelled about it. Somebody would pay attention. Maybe they'd laugh, but they'd be there.

No subject was too touchy. On a good summer night, you'd have a choice of hearing about the comforts of socialism, the evils of communism, the cruelty of capitalism, the logic of atheism, the glory of God, the hell of war, the elusiveness of peace, the cruelty of bosses, the agony of marriage, and the certainty of the end of the world in 14 days or less.

Regardless of what a speaker said, nobody lobbed tear gas, and the FBI didn't take his picture for the files. The only punishment in Bughouse Square was being ignored.

It had all kinds of speakers over the years. Some sounded like they had staggered over from a nearby tavern. Others were as confused and vague as an alderman.

But there were real pros, often self-educated workingmen who lived alone and liked to research an offbeat subject at the library, talk about it in the park, and pass the hat for the price of a meal or a binge. In a way, they were the professional ancestors of today's TV commentators.

Serious radicals from across the country made Bughouse Square a regular stop. Before both world wars, the park echoed with antiwar sentiments. Advocates of the labor movement were safe from billy clubs in the square.

Long before today's generation was born, soapboxers talked about hunger, slums, inequality, the draft, and giving poor people a voice in governing themselves. Audiences heckled and laughed when they listened to pipe dreams about the 30-hour week, social security, and free medical care for the aged.

The audiences were seldom as intense as the speakers. Most people drifted over because it was a good place to get an evening of free entertainment. Tourists liked it. They could go home and say they heard a dirty man talk about free love right there in a public place.

If the speakers were dull, which was unusual, somebody might be playing a washboard. And prizefights were held on the grass a few times.

Local Bohemians and intellectuals hung around the park, and they were fun to gawk at. It was something like an early-day Old Town, but without the gloom of today's youths.

By losing its voice, Bughouse Square has completed a cycle.

Originally a cowpath, it was given to the city by its original owner in 1842 to be used as a park. And for many years it was just a quiet little city park—formally known as Washington Square.

When it became an orators' haven it was dubbed Bughouse Square. Now it is just a quiet little city park again.

There is no mystery to why it has stopped being Bughouse Square.
Who needs it today? The whole country has become Bughouse Square.

So, It's Over and Out, Roger!

There were 30 minutes to go before the private screening of his first movie, so screenwriter Roger Ebert nervously asked the bartender for a shot and beer chaser.

That was bold drinking for so young a man. Sure enough, he coughed on the shot.

Then he stuck me with the bar bill.

"Remember," he said, "I'm saving you $3 by inviting you to my free screening."

"I have heard about your movie, and you aren't saving me a nickel."

He lapsed into a glum silence. Ebert, the popular, talented movie critic of the *Chicago Sun-Times,* had done something few critics would dare. He had written a screenplay—for the film *Beyond the Valley of the Dolls.* Even before it opened here, critics in other cities put aside any fraternal affection they may have felt for him.

"It is sure to disgust you!" raved a West Coast critic.

"Don't miss missing it," said another in New York.

Using Ebert's own movie rating system—four stars for great and one star for terrible—he was averaging about one handful of crater dust per review.

The critics had generally agreed that it was dirty, violent, and not much fun.

I seldom see these kinds of movies, since a normal day in Chicago can be dirty, violent, and not much fun, but Ebert had arranged for this screening. He wanted his friends to see it.

We got there a few minutes late. A breast was already bounding across the screen.

"Did we miss the first act?" I asked.

"Yes," answered a voice from the darkness, "an abnormal one."

It's not easy to read notes that were scribbled in darkness, but I can transcribe these from my note pad:

"Bare breasts . . . bottoms . . . naked couples . . . in bed . . . grief . . . haystack . . . toe fetish . . . old man, young girl . . . young man, old girl . . . young man and old m . . . only half over . . ."

I can't report on my notes for the second half, which is when the violence came in, because it is difficult to write when you have both hands clapped over your eyes. It was something like the final cattle chute in the Stock Yards, except the movie used people.

When the lights went on, I was glad for Ebert that the room was filled with his friends. Strangers might have beaten him with the chairs.

My reaction, once I got outside and breathed the fresh polluted air, was one of puzzlement. I had always assumed, since I didn't know any better, that creeps wrote all the dirty, violent movies. In fact, I had hoped they were written by creeps, because this would keep them busy and they wouldn't be climbing up my rose trellis and peeking in my bathroom window.

But Ebert is not a creep. Just the opposite. He is a peaceful, pleasant, thoughtful young man, only 26 or 27, with a cherubic face and a great writing talent. While still a student, he wrote a history of a university, and it was a clean book, which used to be possible when writing about universities.

Later, as we all leaned on a bar, Ebert asked his friends what they thought. We told him. This time, he ordered a double shot and a beer.

"Why did you write a dirty, violent movie?" I finally asked him.

"It was written as a parody of dirty, violent movies," he said.

"Did the producer and director know that?"

Although I am not a movie critic, I think I have figured out what went wrong, how so talented a writer and so decent a young man could be involved in that dog.

Ebert's problem is that he is not a dirty old man. If a dirty movie is going to be any good, it has to be written by a dirty old man. You wouldn't let an ROTC student write a war movie, or a Republican write a book about Chicago politics.

I believe that every young man is entitled to one big mistake, despite what the alimony court judges may say. And this movie is Ebert's, and I urge you to avoid it.

Someday he will write another movie, and I'm confident that it will be excellent. Even if it is dirty, it will be better. I'll be his technical adviser.

APRIL 12, 1973

A Requiem for a Tavern

It was 5 o'clock and dusk. In the cocktail lounges along Michigan Avenue, the martinis were starting to flow. The eager young glands were beginning to congregate in the singles bars on the Near North Side.

But in Swastek's Tavern on the Near West Side, there were only Stanley the owner, a friend, and the sleeping watchdog.

Stanley was explaining why, after almost 70 years in his family, the corner tavern was being shut down at the end of the month. A glance down the empty bar would have been enough.

"Just look around the neighborhood. So many of the people are old, living on their pensions. The young people move away as fast as they can afford to. The Puerto Ricans go in their own place. By the time I pay for my license and dram-shop insurance, it costs me almost $2,000. So I think it's time to lock it up."

He took out a copy of an antique-dealers' magazine. "Look. I put an ad in for all my fixtures."

The ad described the bar: 26 feet long, solid mahogany, built by Brunswick in 1886.

Stanley slapped the reddish wood. "When my father opened this place, the bar cost $3,700. That was 70 years ago, and you could buy a good brick two-flat for that money in those days."

The back bar was in the ad, too. Also mahogany, with ornate carving, pullout wine racks, and one of those huge mirrors that movie cowboys are always throwing things at.

"Some dealer called me from Kentucky. He said he saw the ad and he was willing to take it off my hands for $1,200.

"I laughed at him. Look at it, the cigar counter, the package cabinet, they're mahogany, too. Look at this ancient cash register. It rings up quart, pint, half-pint. You know it wasn't designed for any grocery store. I told him to start talking at $8,000. I don't think he understood what he was getting."

It's too bad history can't be put in an ad because Stanley's fine mahogany has had a lot of it spilled across the top.

When John Swastek, his immigrant father, opened the place, three-cents-a-ride streetcars clanged past. Men with lunch pails and accents came in after work and ordered their nickel shots and nickel beers. They sat at the tables and played pinochle, banging down the cards until their knuckles were swollen.

"Some people say TV killed the tavern business," Stanley said. "You know what did it? When the police knocked out the sociable card games. People want to do more than just drink in a tavern. Look at the English pubs with their darts."

Or the singles bars, for that matter, with their strenuous games.

In those days, a good tavern was a political center. A candidate could get more votes by buying a round than making a speech. And if he bought enough rounds, he could make a speech and the customers wouldn't even laugh.

Some famous political bellies bellied up to Swastek's mahogany. Mayor William (Big Bill) Thompson came in with the local cigar-puffers.

So did Mayor Anton Cermak, an anti-Prohibition hero. Martin Kennelly came around before he was mayor. And one of the regular customers was Steve Kolinowski, the chief deputy coroner. He would thrill customers with accounts of the latest body found in a trunk.

The social evil of Prohibition closed a lot of bars, but not Swastek's.

"My father made the proper arrangements with the politicians, and we kept operating. We got our beer from the Touhy gang. His driver always wore two pearl-handled pistols strapped to his hips.

"Our biggest problem during Prohibition was Tubbo the cop, remember him?"

Captain Daniel (Tubbo) Gilbert, a political badge who became known as the world's richest cop. For years he ran the Cook County state's attorney's police. And he ran the state's attorney, too.

Tubbo liked to lean on the mahogany bar. But there wasn't a glass in his hand.

"In those days, he was in charge of the district station. He'd come in here, and if we took in $10, he figured his share was $20. No wonder he was the world's richest cop. He could have retired on what he took from us."

Federal Prohibition agents closed the place once. But that turned out for the best.

"The agent got talking to my father, and when my father told him about putting his kids through school, and some sickness in the family, the agent said he didn't believe in closing up family joints. He was a family man himself.

"So he not only let us reopen, but he sold my father a load of bonded whisky. Good stuff, too."

Stanley took over the place in 1937, when his father died. He died right behind the mahogany bar.

It happened the night a young man named Jesse James Jackson came in. He worked in a grocery store, but he pulled one robbery a week. Talk about the work ethic.

"He ordered a bag of peanuts, and when my father turned, he said it was a holdup. My father grabbed for a gun in the drawer, and Jackson shot him four times.

"Then he headed for the door, and my father shot him four times. They both fell over dead."

Stanley has run it since, and until a few years ago, it did its share of business.

But now it is dark outside, and the first good cash customer hasn't come in the door.

Stanley looked out the window at the store on the other corner. It sells junk. "That used to be a drugstore, and it had a running fountain and goldfish swam in it." Next to the junk shop was still another junk shop. "That used to be a real estate agency." So on down the street.

He talked about the softball teams his tavern sponsored, the great feasts in the back room when the neighborhood men came back from hunting ducks and deer and picking mushrooms, the kids coming in for a pail of beer for their fathers, the many breweries that used to make beer in Chicago, the three-piece bands—accordion, piano, and drums—that played on Saturday nights.

But he has no complaints, now that it's all over.

"Why should I? Listen, this place was good to us. My father managed to put us all in college. Two of my brothers are doctors, and another one is a lawyer. I went, too, but I liked this business. Now my son is a teacher, and my daughter is a nurse.

"So I can't complain. This old bar has been good to us."

Solid mahogany, and they don't make them like they used to.

JANUARY 21, 1976

Ladies Miss Goat's Flavor

A lady from the leafy Chicago suburb of Barrington recently made her annual trip downtown, as she put it, "to sample the sights and sounds of the big city."

Part of the trip was a disappointment, she complained, and I am responsible.

"After lunch," she said, "I prevailed upon my companions to visit the Billy Goat Tavern, hoping to glimpse some of the colorful people about whom you write."

It is true, as she noted, that I have written a few things about this scruffy joint, which is located in the dark hollow beneath Michigan Avenue. I once wrote about how the owner, a stubby Greek, threw out the same belligerent drunk six times in one night, and about a man who drank for 12 hours without once visiting the men's room, both athletic achievements worthy of mention in the *Guinness Book of World Records*.

But the Barrington lady and her companions did not find it interesting.

"The Billy Goat was a disappointment," she complained. "There were no colorful savants offering their views. And the appointments were lackluster."

I suppose I owe her and her companions an apology for the inconvenience and disappointment of their trip to this dive, and for the absence of "colorful savants" and other amusing characters.

But it was never my intention to encourage Barrington ladies to pop in for some tea and gawking at the amusing characters. Basically, this is just a simple saloon that happens to be in the downtown area, frequented by people who go in taverns to drink, not to philosophize. It doesn't even have peanut shells fashionably scattered on the floors, as many suburban pubs do. You are far more likely to see some of the regular customers fashionably scattered on the floor.

There are several reasons why they were disappointed in their search for colorful characters.

For one thing, colorful bar characters are not like paintings hanging in a museum, available for scrutiny any time you come in, or musicians at Orchestra Hall, who perform on a given schedule.

A colorful character might sit there for hour after hour, quietly, even morosely, knocking them back, before he finally does something colorful. And even then, it might be only to topple off his chair.

The Barrington ladies might have been there at the wrong time of day. Even colorful characters have to earn a living, or rest so they can deliver fresh wit and bon mots. If you try to be witty and colorful day and night, the cirrhosis is sure to chew up your liver.

Had they come by when Walter the horseradish maker was there—and he drops in only on certain days and early hours—he would surely have shoved spoons of fresh horseradish into the ladies' mouths and said: "Bet you never tasted nothing this good, huh?" What a droll story that would have been for the next bridge party.

And it would have been a memorable visit if Romantic John had been there. He is a migrant loafer by trade, and every time some strange ladies walk in, he gives them the eye. Disgusting, really. It's made of glass, and he takes it out and slides it down the bar at them. But he means well.

If they had been lucky, "the sea captain" would have been having a drink, and telling tales of his adventures as commander of his own ship. It is one of the fleet that takes tourists on two-hour cruises on the river and along the lakefront. He might have told of his greatest adventure, which is when he spotted a body floating in the river. Without hesitation, he blew his whistle, snatched up the microphone and yelled:

"Ladies and gentlemen, if any of you brought your cameras, just ahead of us is a genuine Chicago dead body. Get a shot before it sinks."

Had it been summer, they might have seen a gathering of the softball players, the most dedicated of all athletes. One day I saw a sweaty player down six straight boilermakers and collapse into a distraught crying jag because he felt he had let his team down in the clutch. And that was before the game began.

It's quite possible that some of the colorful players and "savants" were present during the visit of the Barrington ladies. But they might have been subdued because they feared the ladies might whip out cameras and take their picture to show as a slide presentation at a Travel Club meeting. Some of the natives are superstitious about having their pictures taken by tourists. They fear somebody with an old warrant might recognize them.

Warren the bartender, usually friendly, probably clammed up because they could have been wives who had come downtown looking for their husbands. The presence of such people always casts a depressing mood of doom over the place.

While apologizing for the disappointment, I must defend the "appointments" in Billy Goat's, which the lady described as "lackluster."

It has two cigaret machines, two pay phones, a TV that sometimes works, a juke box that has both rock and Greek music, and a men's urinal that has never once backed up.

What more do you want?

AUGUST 28, 1990

If Only the Acorn Could Play It Again

There are bars and there are bars. Some are just fast-drink emporiums where you grab one before hopping a commuter train. Some are places where you can sit, sip a beer, and actually talk to other bipeds. There are mean joints where one cross word gets you a facial scar, and friendly joints where you might meet the girl/boy/mutant of your dreams.

I know a lot about bars. More, I'm sure, than is good for my health. It was my family's business in the long-gone days when the neighborhood tavern was the working class equivalent of the country club. The corner tavern was—as the theme song of the TV series *Cheers* puts it—"where everybody knows your name."

So I must take a moment to mourn the closing of one of the best gin mills in Chicago. (Which is saying something. I doubt that any other city has a bar called "Stop and Drink." There, a shot is a shot, a beer is a beer, and a corporate lawyer and a tuckpointer can belly up as equals.)

The "Acorn." Or more formally, "The Acorn on Oak." Or, as some of us called it: "Buddy's."

It's closed down. Damn progress. Damn real estate prices and rentals. Damn the changing drinking habits of the American public. We have lost one fine bar.

A minute or two after 11 o'clock. Not a.m. If you're a morning person, the Acorn wasn't for you.

Buddy Charles would shake a few hands along the front-door bar, let go with his boisterous laugh, and slide onto the bench in front of his upright piano.

A bar wrapped around Buddy's piano, and it seated maybe 15 or 20. I never counted. All that mattered was *the rule*. When Buddy played, you shut up.

The first time I went in there, many years ago, I was skeptical. I'd heard a lot of piano-bar players banging out junk, second-rate Liberaces grabbing for the conventioneer's tip.

Then Buddy smiled across the piano. Only one smile like it. With his lean face and sharp-pointed beard, he was the Devil incarnate. Except he wasn't. The man actually teaches Sunday school.

"Anything special you'd like to hear?" he said.

I threw him the curve. I've whipped it by piano-bar players from one coast to the next. They always expect that you'll ask for "Send in the Clowns" or some toned-down Beatles banality.

"Yeah, play 'Black and Blue.'"

He grinned. "Don't get many requests for that."

Then wham, his fingers raced in a flourish from low E to high E, he leaned back, his eyes half-closed, with a devilish grin, and his piercing tenor froze the place:

"Cold empty bed/springs hard as lead/pains in my head/feel like Ol' Ned/hey, what did I do/to feel so black and blue."

And that was the beginning of a very fine friendship. During my bleakest years, before I met and married the blond, I spent many a night listening to Buddy. He made them less bleak.

Name the song and he played it. And it wasn't just the playing. He gave it style. When he played Cole Porter or Irving Berlin, I could imagine them sitting there saying: "Exactly as I intended."

Some of you reading this have been there. Midnight, 1 o'clock, 3 o'clock. You know what it's like when you're feeling low, lonely, miserable, and you want to go somewhere where the dark hours start throwing sparks.

That's what the Acorn on Oak was.

I did a TV show some years ago. Interviewed celebrities and all that nonsense. I twisted the arm of the TV producer—a classic nonentity of his craft—to end the show with a performance and chat with Buddy.

Buddy talked about the kind of people who come into late-night bars to have one or two pops and listen to a piano player. He talked about widows and widowers and the kind of music they liked. Good music. And when the show ended, he slid into "One for My Baby, and One More for the Road."

We didn't do another show. The producer said the first one was too depressing. Being a TV creature, he paid no heed to our rating—highest in our time slot—or more importantly, Buddy's unique style. He suggested that I replace Buddy with a one-man band—thumping a drum, banging a multipurpose keyboard. I suggested things that are unprintable.

So the Acorn is closed. The post-midnight gang feels homeless.

What to do? I don't know. I've been writing for a living a long time. Maybe I'll open a joint. Let me know. Is there anybody out there who appreciates the world's best rendition of "Black and Blue"?

NOVEMBER 21, 1995

Even a U.S. Senator Can Botch a Recipe for Success

This simple little quiz is directed at those who love hot dogs. Not any hot dog, but the true, classic Chicago hot dog. The finest hot dog known to man.

Look at the following recipe and see if something is wrong. If so, what?

Chicago hot dog: Vienna beef hot dog, poppy seed bun, dill pickle, jalapeños, relish, mustard, ketchup. Place dog in bun. Cover with jalapeños, relish, mustard, and ketchup. Serve with dill pickle.

The flaws are so obvious that by now those with civilized, discriminating Chicago taste buds are snorting and sneering and flinging this shameful recipe to the floor and spitting on it.

It deserves nothing less.

But not merely because it includes ketchup and omits sliced tomatoes, chopped onions, and that miraculous dash of celery salt.

No, I won't condemn anyone for putting ketchup on a hot dog. This is the land of the free. And if someone wants to put ketchup on a hot dog and actually eat the awful thing, that is their right.

It is also their right to put mayo or chocolate syrup or toenail clippings or cat hair on a hot dog.

Sure, it would be disgusting and perverted, and they would be shaming themselves and their loved ones. But under our system of government, it is their right to be barbarians.

The crime is in referring to the above abomination as a "Chicago hot dog." And who did it?

Brace yourselves for a real shocker.

Some time ago, a hot dog recipe book was put together by the American Meat Institute, the National Hot Dog and Sausage Council, and other groups that promote the eating of dead animal flesh.

They got their recipes by calling the offices of United States senators. Being publicity freaks, most of the senators responded.

Most of the recipes are ridiculous, since most senators are ridiculous.

And this shameful recipe was contributed by Senator Carol Moseley-Braun.

Yes, Senator Moseley-Braun, who claims to be a Chicagoan, actually told them that a Chicago hot dog includes ketchup. And that it doesn't require chopped onion or sliced tomatoes or celery salt.

I don't know what could have possessed her to do such a thing. She is a liberal Democrat, so I can understand her deep yearning to seize our money and throw it hither and yon like so much political confetti. That's part of the natural order of Washington creatures.

But to publicly state that you put ketchup on a Chicago hot dog? And overlook celery salt? It is said that power corrupts. I didn't know that it brings on utter madness.

Apparently Senator Moseley-Braun pays little or no attention to my efforts to maintain standards in those things that are unique to Chicago.

If she did, she would have noted a column that appeared here in July of 1993. In it, various hot dog experts commented on ketchup.

Maurie Berman, who owns Superdawg on the Northwest Side, where I've been eating classic hot dogs for about 40 years: "I see more and more desecrations of the Chicago hot dog. Yes, we provide ketchup, but we have the customer defile it himself.

"We say, 'Sir, the ketchup bottle is on the side. We'll ask you to squirt that yourself.'"

John Miyares, who serves hot dogs at Irving's near the Loyola University campus, says: "No ketchup, no kraut. That's the law. But when you're younger and your mom lets you put ketchup on the hot dog, you get used to it, I guess. The people about 35 and over, they get upset if you mention ketchup, especially if they're born and raised here. And even more if they're South Siders.

"But we get a lot of students from out of town, and they all want ketchup. Except if they're from New York. They want steamed sauerkraut."

Pat Carso, manager of Demon Dogs on the Mid-North Side, said: "You have to ask for it. And more people are asking. I don't know why. Maybe parents think it is better for their kids. But we choose not to put it on. Even if they say 'everything.' In here, that does not include ketchup. We don't even keep ketchup up front. We have a little bottle in the back if people ask for it."

These men are keepers of the flame. They are cultural and culinary descendants of the short Greeks who used to take their pushcarts into every

Chicago neighborhood and would have thumbed the eyeballs of anyone who dared ask for ketchup.

But here we have a United States senator, allegedly representing Chicago and the rest of Illinois—even the Downstate yokels—and she shames herself and the rest of us by displaying her ignorance of what makes a hot dog a true Chicago hot dog.

I'm sure Senator Moseley-Braun has the usual excuse: Someone on her staff did it.

Well, forget it. That only proves that senators hire boobs.

No, the buck and the hot dog stop here.

There is time for Senator Moseley-Braun to mend her ways. But if the election were held today, I'd have to vote for just about anyone running against Senator Moseley-Braun.

Letters, Calls, Complaints, and Great Thoughts from Readers

MIKE VOLGESBURG, Chicago: Why is it wrong to put ketchup on a hot dog? Until you can give a logical explanation, how can you state something is wrong when in fact you can't give a reason as to why it's wrong?

COMMENT: It is wrong because it is not right. Would you put whipped cream on a pizza? Would you put mayo on pancakes or salt on ice cream or pour milk on French fries? Remember, the Romans started putting ketchup on their hot dogs and look what happened to their empire. Within two or three generations, it was overrun by guys with names like Volgesburg wearing fur underwear.

CATHY ARNOLD, Memphis: I grew up in Chicago's western suburbs. But for the past 14 years, I have been living in Memphis, where I discovered the most heinous hot dog crime of all.

My children's Southern friends not only request ketchup for their dogs, but—are you ready for this?—they slather large amounts of mayonnaise on them too. It's enough to make your hair curl.

COMMENT: If it's enough to make my hair curl, I'm going to try it.

RAGING AGAINST THE NIGHT

How History Is Taught?

If American history had been taught in the schools—really taught, not used as a dull, memory-testing exercise—the country wouldn't have gone into open-jawed shock when the civil rights movement began and the black man finally walked out of his shack and said enough is enough. If people weren't disgorged by the public schools with their ignorance of government intact, they wouldn't scream "traitor" every time the Supreme Court affirms a constitutional safeguard. They wouldn't be so muddled about what a free society is that they want to preserve it by tossing all dissenters into a dungeon. For a country to be as steeped in racism, prejudice, internal hatred and distrust, and as fond of TV situation comedy as we are, the educational system has got to be about as vigorous and effective as a 90-year-old gigolo.

—*Chicago Daily News,* January 13, 1970

Lakefront Isn't a Wasteland Yet—But It Will Be

When I was a kid, the best days of the summer were spent at the beach.

The cinder-covered school yard was too hot and dusty for softball. The alleys were so choked with flies and garbage smells that hunting bottles for their two-cent deposits was no fun.

So we grabbed our itchy wool trunks and a fried-egg sandwich, rode a North Avenue streetcar to the end of the line, and there it was—the big, blue, cool, clean lake.

You could smell it and taste it long before you saw it.

We threw our bony bodies at the waves, sprawled on the sand, stared in boyish awe at the older girls, and went home exhausted and ready for 10 hours of deep sleep.

Sometimes we went to fish. I was lucky because the local tavern gentlemen didn't mind taking a kid along. Tiny the fat man, Chizel, and Clem were good conversationalists as well as fine fishermen.

They sat for hours on the rocks, guzzling bottles of cold beer, talking about the Cubs' pennant chances (this was a long time ago), and pulling fat, needle-boned perch from the lake with their bamboo poles.

So I like the lake. I like knowing that Indians used it, city kids used it, and hundreds of thousands of people still use it.

And I get sick and angry when I hear someone like Thomas H. Coulter, chief executive officer of the Chicago Association of Commerce and Industry, say:

"Our lakefront is not much more than a wasteland. Oh, it has some trees, but the only time I've been on the lakefront in the last 30 years has been to McCormick Place.

"I'm sure that is true of the 20 million other persons who have gone to McCormick Place, not so much for commercial or business meetings of various kinds, but for cultural programs, art, theater, ballet. . . ."

As a newspaperman, I've had to listen to some odd ideas—from Skid

Row winos, aldermen, singing mice, and editors—but I've heard nothing to compare with Mr. Coulter's blather.

He was making a pitch for a lakeside expansion of the McCormick Place convention center, the grotesque Temple of $$$ built on lakefront park land after the *Chicago Tribune* bludgeoned politicians into putting it there.

Mr. Coulter is paid to say things like that. He works for and with the city's commercial and business interests.

But even from a paid mouthpiece, it was in bad taste. His rich crowd has misused the beautiful lake. And a gentleman doesn't speak badly of a lady he has misused.

The lakefront is not yet a wasteland, despite what Mr. Coulter says. But it is on its way. And who has caused it?

When I went swimming, I took a shower in the bathhouse and left the lake as clean as I found it. When we caught fish, we took what we wanted to eat.

Ah, but what of Mr. Coulter's employers—the rich, smoke-belching industrial fat-cats? They've poured enough slop into the lake to make a million pigs sick.

They've stunted and killed the fish and are rapidly making most of the shoreline unfit for humans. Beaches on the Far South Side and in Indiana have become sewers. Thank you, commerce and industry.

And the view from the shoreline? The swimmers, cyclists, fishermen, picnickers, and golfers didn't blot it out. But the real estate interests are crawling to the water's edge for their rich, high-rise profits.

A wasteland? Not yet, but some day it will be. And it won't matter a bit to the commerce and industry crowd. They have their spacious suburban surroundings, their backyard and country club pools, and their summer homes.

They don't use the lakefront except for yachting. So they dispatch a handsome, manicured, Canadian-born, Pennsylvania-educated suburbanite to inform us that it is a wasteland.

He probably thinks it is, because he doesn't go there to see the hundreds of thousands of ordinary yahoos using the beaches, parks, and paths.

From a suburban patio, one can't see that Chicago's lakefront is draped with humanity on warm weekends, from the Far North Side to the Far South Side.

Oh, it is true that many of the users—especially south of McCormick Place—are Negroes. But even the most ignorant or the richest bigot shouldn't kill a lake because Negroes are dipping their toes in it. Yet a red-nosed politician once told me: "I don't care what happens to Jackson Park. Niggers have took it over."

The "lake-is-a-wasteland" people have wonderful arguments. Remember, they are doing something noble while pouring industrial wastes into the water and gobbling up the shoreline. They EMPLOY people. They put food in our mouths, clothes on our backs, roofs over our heads. So when you are eatin' regular, what is a Great Lake or two?

Spare me that soul-talk. They employ people so their companies profit and they can make $70,000 a year plus stock options and early retirement plans.

And living the good life is worth the price of creating a concrete-walled septic tank bordered by four states.

Putting McCormick Place on the lake was a mistake. Expanding it on the lake is a mistake.

It should have been built in Cicero or near the Rush Street night life district. That's where the action is. Conventioneers aren't looking for sunshine or moonlight glittering on the water. Ask the vice cops.

But it is there and the people who put it there are committed to it. And if they say the lakefront is a wasteland, they must be right. And they will do everything they can to prove they are right—including making it a wasteland.

[Editors' note: This column was instrumental in fueling a civic movement that blocked lakefront expansion of McCormick Place—it went inland instead—and secured new pollution controls.]

APRIL 8, 1968
[Editors' note: Martin Luther King Jr. was murdered on Thursday, April 4, 1968.]

Trace of Hope Was Lacking

It was almost 10 o'clock Saturday night. That's when the casual crowd, the slacks-and-sweater crowd, stops in the place for a bite.

They come from the movies for a pizza. Or they step out for some martinis and a butt steak. It's a comfortable place people like when they don't want to dress up but want good food and drinks.

And it's the kind of neighborhood, Far Northwest, where people don't worry about the food budget if they drop an extra $10 or $15. Not rich, but comfortable. The kids have cars.

A color TV flickered at the end of the padded bar and somebody on the screen was screaming and running from door to door on an empty street. A killer was after him and the tough TV detective Mannix wasn't there to help.

The chatter faded for a moment. Nobody knew the plot or why he might get killed, but it was good terror in itself. He screamed and ran, Mannix didn't show, the killer squeezed the trigger, and the man twitched, spun, and died.

"Waitress, another martin with a twist, please. Make it two."

A man in a turtleneck came in and took a stool at the bar. The stools have padded backs on them and they swivel.

"What do you hear?" he asked, thumbing at the TV.

"Nothing yet," the bartender said, "but I hear it's bad. Daley called in the Army."

It was bad, 10 or 12 miles away. That's where the flames were eating a hole in the ghetto, where people were shooting at each other, where the hospital emergency rooms were overflowing. It was so bad that there were more troops in Chicago than at Khe Sanh during the Tet offensive.

But that restaurant-bar with its regular Saturday night crowd was a more important place than Chicago's raging ghettos.

What was said and felt and thought in that bar was more important than what was said and felt and thought on the fifth floor of City Hall, where the mayor was losing weight fast.

What the people in the bar said was more significant than what the ministers in the churches would say the next morning.

If there was a glimmer of hope, it would have to show here. These were the people who would determine which way society would go.

They had already made that decision, probably, when they talked about open housing, busing, and all the other things that were entwined in the distant fury. They had said that you can't legislate what's in a man's heart, right? Right, they answered themselves.

There would have to be some understanding here, a new outlook, if America was to change direction. That's what everybody in high position was saying, anyway.

And they are right. This was a neighborhood where two congressional candidates fought it out on a single issue: which one was more opposed to Negroes coming in. This is where only two members of a PTA talked up for busing.

The people here hadn't liked Martin Luther King Jr. when he marched and sang. And now he was dead. But they HAD cared about Mannix's friend.

Mannix avenged his friend, and the TV slid into the news. There was only one story.

Looting was shown. A couple of black kids walked out of a store carrying things.

A young man at a table loudly said: "They ought to kill 'em. Right there, kill 'em." The young man's lady, a pretty, soft-eyed blond, nodded. Had their sense of justice been stirred that violently by slum rats, lynchings, or Mrs. Viola Liuzzo, the civil rights activist from Detroit who was murdered in Alabama?

A tall man stared at the screen while slowly chewing his sandwich. The waitress watched his table closely because the man's name is Harry and he is one of the city's best-known Democratic politicians. He used to run the Chicago branch of a huge federal agency and now he holds an elective office.

The screen showed some black people who had lost their homes in the flames. One of the people at Harry's table, a woman, said: "That's a shame. They lose a down payment when that happens."

Harry's face twisted. "Down payment!" he scoffed. "They haven't reached that level yet."

He never talked that way when he was rooting around for the black vote. But this was his neighborhood, and you can relax in your own neighborhood.

The TV brought King into the room. Old film clips. He was preaching against violence. Somebody called out: "Waitress, another martin, huh? With a twist, no olive."

A couple got up to leave. The man stretched and patted his tummy. As he walked to the door with a roll, he glanced back at the TV. King was exhorting his audience to be peaceful. "They should've killed him then," the stomach-patter said. His quip drew chuckles from several tables, and he giggled at his own words.

Somebody at the bar said: "Hey, for chrissakes, enough is enough, huh?" The bartender turned the TV knob. King left. A comedian appeared. There were grunts of appreciation, and the conversation lifted. Laughter returned.

Whatever they disliked about him alive, they disliked about him dead. And all that happened this weekend was that there was another riot. Bigger, maybe, but just another riot. Another martin, please, with a twist, no olive.

JUNE 7, 1968

Laugh It Up, It's Violence

Somewhere in the sky, at that moment, a jet plane was crossing this country with Senator Robert Kennedy's body as its cargo.

Down below, a thin young man in a T-shirt hurried through the afternoon crowd on Randolph Street. He took out his wallet as he walked.

He pushed three $1 bills at the cashier at the United Artists theater. As she gave him his ticket and 80 cents change, he glanced at the ad posters.

"Strung up. Whipped. Tortured. McCord gave them 'A minute to play and a second to die.'"

He went in the middle aisle but it was crowded, so he went to the next aisle and slid into a seat. He sat low and put his legs up. The movie began, and he got what he went there for. Blood, guns, death. Kicks.

There hadn't been enough death, apparently, on his TV screen during the past 36 hours. And the terrible black headlines in the papers hadn't satisfied him.

None of it had been enough for the biggest crowd at any Loop movie house Thursday—the same day Senator Kennedy died, the day after he was shot in the head.

In the United Artists, shortly after noon on a work day, there were . . . take a guess: 50? 100? 200?

There were at least 250 people there. Probably 300.

The manager said: "Something like this outdraws anything else downtown."

Why?

"People like the violence. That's the big thing today."

Like most of today's movies, the color is great, the camera work is imaginative. Technically, today's B movies make yesterday's Academy Award winners look like home-made jobs.

But the technical excellence isn't what draws those crowds.

A few minutes after it began, the hero—a thief and a killer—shot his first man. In the head.

Then he made another man kneel, and he put the gun to his head. He smiled and slowly squeezed the trigger. It took a long time, and the victim registered terror. The audience laughed.

Get that: The audience laughed. You would have thought it was Abbott and Costello.

The gun clicked. The man gasped with relief that he was not going to have a bullet in his brain. The audience howled.

There was a bigger laugh a few minutes later when two bad guys beat a priest's face bloody with their fists. Then one showed him the contents of a bag—a human head. The priest screamed and ran hysterically to the altar. Laughter. They shot him.

One killer said: "It is bad luck to shoot a priest." Belly laughs.

During the final mass blood-bath scene, the laughs ran together from one death to another.

A wounded man fell into a fire. Funny. Another lost his gun, and the hero kept shooting his feet until he fell backwards off a cliff and screamed all the way to the bottom. The laughter drowned out his scream.

After almost two hours, it ended. They came out, swaggering a bit, smiling, gorged with vicarious kicks.

They are easy to describe. They look like the next 300 men you'll see on the city's streets. Black and white, most in casual clothing, some in summer suits. They looked like ordinary American men.

And as they left, others like them were coming in, filling the seats.

It began again. The man knelt and trembled at the thought of a bullet crashing into his brain. And the audience laughed. The priest screamed. The audience laughed.

Outside, people were asking what was wrong with this country, why it kills the way it does. The world was asking if the United States is that sick and corrupt.

Inside the United Artists, and in theaters across the country, guns were barking, blood was flowing—and people were laughing.

They laughed and laughed. And by then the plane had landed. Now, his family would bury him.

APRIL 14, 1971

Fred Hampton at the Ballot Box

It was a night more than 16 months ago. The people in the 2300 block of Monroe Street on Chicago's West Side were snapped awake by the sound of gunfire.

There could be no mistaking it for a car's backfire. Shot after shot, dozens of shots, were booming through the neighborhood.

Many people, fearing that a riot had broken out, dived for their floors. Others called the police.

When the firing stopped, people peered from their windows and saw squad cars filling the streets and policemen going up the stairs into one of the old buildings.

Then they saw black people being brought out on stretchers. Some were still alive, some were dead. They were loaded into the paddy wagons and driven away.

After the police left, lights began going on along Monroe Street, and on nearby Adams, Jackson, Western, and Oakley. People came out, asking each other what had happened.

That was when they learned that right there in their neighborhood, Fred Hampton and Mark Clark, two leaders of the Black Panther Party, had been killed and four others had been wounded during a raid ordered by Cook County State's Attorney Edward Hanrahan.

When the Panthers opened the apartment to the public that morning, the people from there in the neighborhood were the first to go through and see bullet holes and blood-stained beds.

Then they watched as for days thousands of people from all over the West Side and the rest of the city came to the apartment. Day after day, from dawn until late at night, the line of people waiting to enter the apartment was there. The cars kept coming into their neighborhood.

The state's attorney's men went on TV for that famous reenactment, telling in great detail of Panther bullets tearing through doors as police officers knocked, of shotgun blasts answering pleas to the Panthers to surrender. But the reenactment meant nothing to the people from the neighborhood, because they had gone through the flat and seen the evidence with their own eyes, and they knew. They knew it was mattresses and bedroom walls—not doors or doorjambs—that were ripped by bullets.

Famous people came to the flat. The people from the neighborhood heard men like the Reverend Ralph Abernathy—president of the Southern Christian Leadership Conference—say: "We are going to fight. Even though my fight will be nonviolent, it will be a militant fight."

The shock waves spread from the neighborhood to other parts of the city. More than 100 black organizations banded together to issue a statement that said, in part:

"The responsibility for these acts and the behavior patterns which strangle this city and country as a consequence rests with every level of political . . . leadership in this nation."

Students walked out of their classrooms to protest the deaths of Hampton and Clark. Pickets marched around the Civic Center Plaza. Black congressmen came to Chicago, and they went to the house on Monroe Street and looked for themselves.

Black leaders railed against the raid, most of them saying it was an attempt to squash political minorities.

Much later, a federal grand jury investigated, and it found that one shot, at most, had been fired by the Panthers, but that almost 100 bullets had been poured into the apartment by the raiders.

These findings didn't surprise the people in the 2300 block of Monroe Street, or on nearby Jackson, Western, Adams, and Oakley, because they had been the first to go into the flat to look, and they had known.

Last week the people in that neighborhood went to the polls.

One of the candidates was Mayor Daley, who heads the political machine that put Edward Hanrahan into office.

It was Daley's police department that provided Hanrahan with the 14 predawn raiders and his police department that was accused of trying to whitewash the case.

And this week the official vote canvass was announced in City Hall.

It showed that the people in that precinct, the people who heard the gunfire, saw the bodies, and were the first to walk through the flat and see for themselves, had cast five votes for Richard Friedman, the Republican nominee for mayor.

They cast 219 votes for Daley, who remains Hanrahan's political leader and booster.

For years, blacks have been castigating whites for our indifference. Maybe it is time they started talking to themselves.

JANUARY 24, 1973

Hollow Ring of Peace

Mike, the newsstand man, was alone at the corner of State and Madison streets, shivering in the cold night.

"Nah, nobody's been around celebrating," he said. "What's to celebrate?"

The end of the war. Mr. Nixon said it on TV, half an hour ago.

He shrugged. "That so? Now maybe we can take care of things in this country, huh?"

A young couple came around the corner, heads down in the wind. They disappeared down the subway ramp and the corner was again empty.

It wasn't like 1945, when the end of a war brought a million people downtown to cheer.

Now the president comes on TV, reads his speech, and without a sound the country sets the clock and goes back to bed.

And that's as it should be. There is nothing to cheer about this time, except that it is over. Even the announcement could have been put more simply. Mr. Nixon's efforts to inject glory into our involvement were hollow. All he had to say was that it is finally over.

"Peace with honor." He had to use the wilted phrase that has been with us most of the war. He said we obtained it.

It is hard to see the honor.

We have just finished 10 years of pounding a little country that most of us hadn't heard of until we went there.

We threw everything, short of The Bomb, at them. At one point, we put more than half a million troops into it. We killed them up close on the ground and from on high in the air. We used old-fashioned infantry tactics and modern electronic warfare. We scorched their forests and bombed their cities. Nobody will ever know how many of them were killed.

With all that, we got a draw.

Before it ended, the word "frag" was introduced into our vocabulary. That's when enlisted men murder their officers. Drug addiction replaced VD as the GI's ailment. Before it ended, we had put our own men on trial for murdering civilians; pilots were refusing to drop any more bombs.

After all that, why even talk about honor?

"Let us be proud," he said, "of those who sacrificed, who gave their lives that the people of Vietnam might live in freedom."

More hollow words. Almost 20 years ago another war ended in a draw, and we were told that our boys had died for somebody's freedom. Now the South Koreans live under a dictatorship.

And so will the South Vietnamese. If it isn't communism, it will be some other form of iron rule. They will be told what they can say, write, read, or think. They are almost there already. When they step out of line, they will be tossed into jail.

Why kid ourselves? Our men didn't die for anyone's freedom. They died because we made a mistake. And we can't justify it with slogans and phrases from other times.

It was a war that made the '60s the most terrible decade in our history. It tore us internally. It left many with a lust for revolution, and others with a lust for repression. It saw young people crossing borders or going to prison rather than fighting.

If we insist on looking for something of value in this war, then maybe it is this:

Maybe we finally have the painful knowledge that we can never again believe everything our leaders tell us. For years they told us one thing while they did another. They said we were winning while we were losing. They said we were getting out while we were getting in. They said the end was near when it was far.

Maybe the next time somebody says that our young men must fight and die somewhere, we will not take their word that it is for a worthy cause. Maybe we will ask them to spell it out for us, nice and slow, and nice and clear.

And maybe the people in power will have learned that the people of this country are no longer willing to go marching off without having their questions answered first.

I hope we have learned these things, because there is nothing else to show for our longest war. If we haven't, then we are as empty and cold as the intersection of Madison and State.

SEPTEMBER 16, 1975
Nero Would Love Chicago

On a side street near Division and Damen is a house my grandmother used to own. I drove past it the other day. It had burned and was boarded up.

An old man who lives a few doors away was walking by. I asked him if he knew anything about the fire.

He shook his head. "Somebody burned it," he said. Who? He shrugged. "Somebody. Nobody knows." He waved his hand, as if taking in the whole neighborhood. "Somebody burns, but nobody knows who."

That's the way things are in the neighborhood known as Humboldt Park. And it is amazing, if you really think about it. A sizable slice of the city slowly burning away. Drive through and you'll see street after street pocked with gutted hulks of recently burned buildings. People are living in terror because arsonists are on the prowl.

Nobody knows who and nobody knows why. And that includes the police. Except for a couple of kids who set themselves on fire while burning a building, the police haven't been able to catch anyone.

But it's not that amazing if you think about it a little more.

For instance, think about the fact that there are only eight cops assigned to the police department's arson squad. Eight, to investigate arson throughout the entire city of Chicago.

To bring that figure into a sort of nutty perspective, consider that about 25 cops are assigned to the unit that chases hookers and raids massage parlors.

That's right. Three times as many cops are concerned with what is occurring on a waterbed in the Velvet Touch Bath House than with who tossed the Molotov cocktail through the living room window and burned down Stanley and Mary's three-flat.

They work harder at catching some grown woman rubbing oil into the pores of adult males in the Harem Leisure Spa than they do at catching somebody pouring gasoline on the back porch of Walter's bungalow.

If you wonder why they have such peculiar priorities, the answer is that the mayor doesn't like thinking about the things that occur in massage parlors. It makes his face red. So the police please him with their frenzied pursuit of public bores like porn impresario Weird Harold.

That's why Weird Harold has been arrested more often than all of Humboldt Park's arsonists combined.

And while the cops enforce the mayor's blushing Bridgeport morality, terrified old women sit all night by their windows and watch the street for someone carrying a can of gasoline.

For further perspective, consider that at least 20 cops, and as many as 50, are assigned to every game played by the Cubs, Sox, Bears, Bulls, and Blackhawks.

If that much manpower were assigned to investigate the Humboldt Park inferno, you couldn't light a cigaret on Augusta Boulevard without being questioned.

Or consider the number of policemen who are assigned to guard the mottled hides of Chicago politicians and union bosses.

I can't give an exact figure because that's a big secret, says the police department. But at least twice as many cops act as drivers and body-guards for politicians as investigate the fires that destroy the life's work of ordinary people.

Even former Cook County Assessor Parky Cullerton, who no longer holds any public office, still rates a cop as a full-time companion. They sit in Parky's home and play gin rummy.

Then there is the political snoop unit. There were something like 25 undercover men assigned to spy on people like Alderman Bill Singer, author Studs Terkel, TV commentator Len O'Connor, and other critics of the mayor. If Smokey the Bear came to Chicago, they'd put together a dossier on him.

More people work in various police public relations functions than in the arson detail. Their job is to spread the word about what a great job the mayor's police department does.

That's nice. When Chester's three-flat is burned down, he can go to police headquarters and they will give him a tour of the crime lab and a brochure with the mayor's picture on the cover.

More police man-hours are expended on the yearly St. Patrick's Day parade than in investigating the mystery of who is burning up an entire neighborhood.

That is some way to run a city.

On the other hand, who am I to criticize the way Mayor Daley wants to run things? As everybody knows, he is the greatest leader a city has ever had.

At least since Nero.

MARCH 4, 1976

Busing a Whip to Flog Liberals

Busing is the most wonderful thing that could have happened for racists like George Wallace and all the righteous conservatives. It has permitted him to take one issue, which almost everybody concedes was a mistake, and use it to flail away with the phony idea that everything else that has come out of liberal efforts during the last 25 years was also a disaster.

Regardless of where a conversation with a Wallaceite or a Reaganite may begin, they eventually steer it around to "What about busing?"—as if this were the end-all of human relations.

They clutch at busing as the ultimate proof that they were right all along about everything that, to them, busing represents.

The fact is, while busing is a failure, they themselves were wrong all along about almost everything else.

Wallace likes to point at busing as evidence that he was a prophet years ago when he warned about the evils of the federal government coming into the South and stomping all over the rights of the decent folk down there to live their lives free and unfettered.

Free and unfettered to do what? To put on the white robes and hang somebody from a tree?

Who is Wallace kidding? He's not kidding anybody who spent time in the South when it was the South that Wallace wanted left free and unfet- tered. I lived for a year in the Jim Crow South and saw people free to treat blacks—or niggers, as they were called even in polite society, and to their faces—as little more than cattle. Actually, the cattle were treated better.

Twenty-five years ago, black citizens of this country could be, and were, killed for looking the wrong way at their betters, for walking into the wrong bar or restaurant, or because some white clod drank too much and was feeling sadistic.

So busing is a mistake. Big deal. Was it a lesser mistake when some of Wallace's fans got a slap on the wrist for killing civil rights workers and hiding their bodies in a pigpen? Was it just a minor mistake when a man was lynched while his children looked on? Nobody asks Wallace about these kinds of grass-roots efforts at "social engineering."

And I'll be damned if I can remember any of the conservative pundits who now crab about busing speaking up in the '50s and '60s about rigged laws that prevented masses of black people from voting or using public facilities, about tar-paper shacks and rat-filled slums, and about malnu- trition in cotton-field babies.

It didn't bother them that American citizens could be barred, because of their skin, from state universities, hospitals, public recreational facili- ties, voting booths, jobs, buying homes, traveling, or simple justice. That poverty and ignorance were not only tolerated but imposed on masses of citizens didn't get them noticeably upset.

What did anger them was when somebody ELSE spoke out about these conditions. They didn't give a hoot if people were pushed around. But let Paul Robeson complain about it, and they would scream for Paul Robeson's scalp.

Since the 1950s, the efforts of black activists and white liberals have been responsible for the biggest gains by blacks and other minorities since this country's founding.

In every area—education, jobs, housing, justice, politics, government, and business—there has been enormous progress. Yes, I know how bad things still are in many ways. But I'm also old enough to remember how bad things were. And there is no comparison.

These changes occurred without the help of the people who today scream about busing, and despite their hindrance.

And just as it was a waste of time to pay any attention to them when they stood in the schoolhouse door, or blocked the bridge at Selma, or yelled that Chief Justice Earl Warren should be impeached, it's a waste of time—and a bore—to pay attention to the overworked issue of busing.

If busing is the biggest mistake the liberals ever made, then they have nothing to be ashamed of. It beats hell out of burying a body in a pigpen.

FEBRUARY 5, 1981

Talk Won't Save Life

I would appreciate it if the handgun lovers would once again share their wisdom with me.

As we all know, one of the most cherished arguments of the handgun lover is that almost anything can be used as a weapon, so why pick on guns?

I have been lectured by them on the potential dangers of the kitchen knife, the table fork, hat pins, baseball bats, tire irons, clothing irons, beer bottles, automobiles, coffeepots, shoes, toilet seats, house bricks, piano wire, leather belts, ashtrays, rolled-up newspapers, plastic toothpicks, and pantyhose.

As the handgun lovers point out, these and almost any other object can be used to take a life. Therefore, they smugly ask, why don't I urge that these objects be banned?

Their logic is so devastating that I'm always left with the lame response that these objects weren't designed for killing, but handguns are. My feeble rejoinder never satisfies them.

So that's why I'm asking them to enlighten me on something.

On Tuesday, there was a tragic incident on the South Side of Chicago.

Two men standing across from an elementary school were quarreling about an $8 gambling debt. Apparently they had been feuding for a long time.

Several children, just out of school, gathered to listen and watch.

Then, with the kind of madness that erupts every day somewhere in this country, one of the men drew a pistol and fired it six times.

Four of the bullets hit the other man, killing him. And one bullet ripped into a 12-year-old boy, killing him, too. Still another struck a second boy, wounding him.

Now I know that the handgun lovers, in their wisdom, are already chanting another of their favorite slogans: "Guns don't kill, people kill." That's true, of course, just as nuclear weapons don't kill, people kill; poison gas doesn't kill, people kill; and biological warfare weapons don't kill, people kill. Which is why I've never understood why we don't legalize the sale of nuclear weapons and poison gas.

But that's not the point here. What I'm interested in finding out is how that boy could have been killed by some of the objects I mentioned in the third paragraph.

Let's say that the man had been armed with a kitchen knife instead of a handgun.

There's no question that he could have whipped the knife out, plunged it into the chest of the other fellow, and killed him just as thoroughly as he did with the handgun. Of course, the other man might have grabbed his wrist and fought him off. But for the sake of argument, let's say that he killed him.

How, then, would the 12-year-old boy, an innocent bystander, have been killed? That's what I'm asking the handgun lovers to explain.

I guess there are ways, as the handgun lovers will point out. If the man had been stabbed, I suppose he could have *fallen* on the boy, becoming a blunt object himself, and breaking the child's neck.

And if the knife were long enough, and the man skinny enough, it could have gone all the way through him and also pierced the child.

Or, let's say that the killer used a baseball bat or a tire iron instead of a handgun. Handgun lovers delight in pointing out that these objects can and have been used to commit murder.

When the argument reached its peak, the killer could have whipped out a bat or tire iron. Actually, I don't know how he could whip these things out, since they are hard to conceal unless you have huge pockets in an extremely baggy suit. And chances are that if he had approached his victim carrying a bat or tire iron in plain view, the victim might have been smart enough to run.

But let's say he somehow produced a bat or tire iron and used it to beat the other man to death. How would he have managed to also kill the boy?

On his backswing? Yes, I guess that's possible. I've seen softball players conked with bats when they've stood behind a teammate who was taking practice swings, although none died of it.

Or on the ricochet? I guess that's possible, too. The killer could have hit his victim a glancing blow with the bat or tire iron, and the bat or tire iron could have bounced off the man's head and continued on several feet to hit the boy. But I would think one glancing blow wouldn't be enough. So then the killer would have had to hit his victim several glancing blows, and each time the bat or tire iron would have had to bounce off and continue on, hitting the boy. I really can't remember anyone ever having been killed this way—by repeated, accidental, secondary blows—but maybe some handgun lover has a better memory.

And we have the piano wire. Or any other wire or cord. The handgun lovers like to point out that these can be deadly strangling weapons, as anybody who saw *The Godfather* movies would agree.

During the quarrel, the man could have produced a piano wire or a length of cord, looped it around the other man's neck, and done him in. But once again I ask if he could have killed an innocent bystander.

The answer from the gun lovers will probably be yes. There's the victim-as-blunt-instrument principle, which I mentioned earlier.

And in theory, I suppose if he began with a wide enough loop, he could have swept the boy up and strangled him with the other man. For that matter, he might have accidentally swept up the entire group of children and strangled all of them, although I've never heard of innocent bystanders being strangled the way they are often shot.

But the handgun lovers will explain all this, I'm sure. Just as they will say that if the killer had been trained to respect guns, as they are, this wouldn't have happened.

He was trained. He had been a security guard, went through handgun training, and was licensed to carry the gun, even though he had long been unemployed.

And they will also snarl that the answer is not to ban handguns, but to really be rough on those who commit crimes with them.

Well, I'm sure this killer will be severely punished. He'll probably spend the rest of his life in one of our hellhole penitentiaries.

Which brings me to my final question for the handgun lovers:

How will severe punishment for the killer bring back the life of that 12-year-old boy?

APRIL 8, 1981

Feel Guilty? Me?

They tell this story about a guy who once fought Archie Moore, the former light-heavyweight boxing champion.

In the first round, Moore really slammed the guy. He was hit so hard and solidly that he was unconscious when he was carried from the ring. He was still out when they got him to his dressing room. And it took about 15 minutes on the training table before he finally came to.

Then he staggered to his feet, and on rubbery legs and with crossed eyes he lurched to Moore's dressing room and said:

"Mr. Moore, can I have your autograph?"

I thought of that story when I read in *Time* magazine that President Reagan has told visitors to his hospital room that he is still against stricter gun-control laws.

You might think that somebody who just had a bullet taken out of his lung might not feel kindly about a system of inadequate laws that permit a loonybird to easily buy a cheap handgun for the purpose of shooting a president.

You might think that a bullet passing through the brain of his press aide might cause Reagan to reconsider his *Death Valley Days* views on handguns.

But not Reagan. His views on guns might be foolish, but, hole in the chest and all, he is faithful to these foolish views.

And that's why I was not overwhelmed by the sense of horror that some people say swept the nation when TV brought the assassination attempt into our living rooms.

I never feel overwhelmed when someone who opposes strict handgun laws is shot. In fact, if the only people who were ever shot were those who believe in the easy ownership of handguns, I wouldn't favor handgun controls at all. My attitude would be that if they want to shoot each other to pieces and leave the rest of us alone, let them. I'd sell them guns at cigar stands.

Then there are those alleged feelings of collective shame and guilt. You've read about them. "It is another blot on the national conscience" ... blah, blah, blah ... "there is some deep sickness in this country" ... blah, blah, blah ... "we are all demeaned by an act of violence of this kind" ... blah, blah, blah ... "all of us had our hand on that trigger" ... blah, blah, blah. And more blah.

Well, I don't feel guilty about the shooting. My conscience is fine. And the majority of Americans have no reason to feel any guilt.

What happened was that a crazy man was able to buy a handgun and ammunition, then go shoot at a president. It's as simple as that.

It's as simple as that almost every time some prominent person is gunned down. Or when some obscure person is gunned down, for that matter.

There is not much that can be done to prevent crazy people from moving about in our society. We can't lock them up. And we shouldn't. Most of them aren't dangerous.

And we probably don't have a greater percentage of crazy people than any other modern industrialized nation.

But the difference is that no other supposedly civilized country arms its crazy people. If, for example, France's laws made it possible for every nut in Paris to buy a gun, Charles de Gaulle would have spent most of his public career trying to duck bullets.

Since every poll shows that the majority of Americans favor strict, effective handgun laws, these Americans have nothing to feel guilty about. If Congress listened to these sensible people, Reagan wouldn't have caught a slug in his chest, Jim Brady's brain wouldn't have been pierced, and tens of thousands of other lives wouldn't be lost.

Instead, Congress listens to a minority that should feel guilt and shame and has blood on its hands.

The National Rifle Association, for example. Its political blackjack tactics have blocked effective handgun laws for years. Nobody wants to take away the hunter's rifle, and nobody wants to take away the target shooter's rifle. Nobody even wants to prevent the honest, clear-headed citizen from keeping a rifle or shotgun in his home for his own protection.

Yet the NRA and its members have done more than any other group to make it possible for somebody like John Warnock Hinckley Jr. to buy a cheap pistol and shoot a president.

And guilt should be felt by those individual handgun lovers who bombard politicians and newspapers with their inane slogans about people, not guns, killing, and about how knives and forks and baseball bats can be used to kill, too, so why not outlaw them?

I invite any such moron to explain how John Warnock Hinckley Jr., armed with a knife, a fork, or a baseball bat, could have gotten close enough to Reagan to stab or club him and to also damage the brain of Brady and seriously wound two lawmen.

I would invite any such moron to also reveal when the last time was that a president was assassinated with a knife, fork, or baseball bat.

While the handgun lovers cling to their feeble defenses of loose handgun laws, thousands die.

Even John Warnock Hinckley Jr. has no reason to feel guilt, since he's obviously insane. If an insane person is able to get a gun and uses it, who's guilty—him or those who armed him?

So with all the talk about guilt and shame, let's put it where it belongs—on those who do the arming.

Looking at it that way, Reagan helped point the gun at himself.

APRIL 14, 1981
Letters, Calls, Complaints, and Great Thoughts from Readers

GLADYS SMITH, Chicago: At a time when I and other good Americans were praying for their president, you had the low taste to write a column that lacked any sympathy and compassion and was nothing but a piece of propaganda against guns.

I don't believe guns are the real problem. But that aside, how can you be so heartless? How can you be so cold and unfeeling? Do you dislike Reagan that much? You are a nasty man.

COMMENT: Well, at the time that you were praying for the president, other good Americans were being shot dead because of the lack of effective handgun laws, and the victims included children. I happen to believe guns are the real problem. So how can you be so cold and unfeeling? Do you dislike children that much, you nasty lady?

MRS. REVA HORWITZ, Chicago: When Nancy Reagan visited her husband in the hospital, the first thing he said to her was: "Honey, I forgot to duck."

I would like to suggest a new slogan to replace the National Rifle Association's stupid and tiresome cliché:

"Guns don't kill; people don't duck."

COMMENT: Yes, but although the Reagans still don't believe in strict gun controls, Nancy offered an insight: She said violent movies might be the real problem. So next time the president sees someone brandishing a box of hot, buttered popcorn, he should duck.

PHIL COOPER, Chicago: I wish you would stop trying to make people think that those of us who favor the ownership of handguns are some kind of nuts. You are the one who is crazy, and we are the normal, straight-thinking people.

COMMENT: Sure, I'm always hearing from normal, straight-thinking people, such as the man who wrote the following letter:

S. R., Chicago: I hope someone shoves a gun up your [bleep] and blows your brains out. You can go [bleep] yourself and your anti-gun paper. You need hanging. I'd like to run into you in a public place sometime.

COMMENT: Fine. The next time the attendants aren't watching you, just climb over the fence and come around.

W. C. CHAPMAN, Chicago: Come on, get off this dumb handgun kick. You're not going to accomplish anything, so why bother trying?

I'm sick and tired of reading all that drivel. It is boring, boring, boring.

COMMENT: During the years of the Vietnam War, more Americans were killed by handguns in this country than died in that war. If you find that boring, what does it take to spark your jaded interest—the Black Plague?

MARCH 26, 1991

After All, This Is What We Fought For

Despite its having been ravaged by war, there is encouraging news coming out of Kuwait.

Shortly after Kuwait City was freed, some residents began publishing a newspaper. It began very small as a mimeographed tip sheet on where people might find medical care or something to eat. But it soon became a more professional journal, and its popularity increased.

But about a week ago, a government official went to the newspaper's office and told the editor that he would have to cease publication immediately.

The official was upset because the newspaper had criticized the government for its bumbling efforts to provide food, water, electricity, medicine, and other services to Kuwait City's miserable inhabitants.

The editor asked the government official what he had to do to keep publishing. The official said he needed a government license. The editor asked how he could get a license. The official said he could apply for one, but he didn't know if or when it would be issued.

So that was the end of Kuwait's first postwar independent newspaper.

Now various international press organizations are criticizing Kuwait's rulers for shutting down the newspaper. They are making the predictable statements about press freedoms. But their criticism is misguided. In this case, the government did the right thing.

It must be remembered that we fought the Gulf War to restore the "legitimate government" of Kuwait. And at considerable expense in human lives and money, this "legitimate government" was restored.

So how does it look, after we have gone to all that expense and effort, to have the legitimate government we restored accused of being a bunch of bumblers? Is that the impression a newspaper should be giving—that to restore a bunch of bumblers to positions of power, we killed more than 100,000 Iraqis and devastated their country?

Besides, it's quite possible that the newspaper was mistaken in its criticism. True, there wasn't much being done in the way of making life tolerable for the people of Kuwait City. But the paper may have overlooked the fact that in such difficult times, the government has to establish priorities.

That paper should have been aware that while it was carping about food, water, medicine, and other matters, the government was faced with the urgent tasks of preparing a palace for Kuwait's ruler, Emir Jabir al-Ahmad al-Jabir al-Sabah.

It was essential that the palace be made livable so that the emir could return in triumph from the hardships of his temporary quarters at a luxury resort in Saudi Arabia.

So Kuwaiti engineers and other craftsmen joined with the U.S. Army Corps of Engineers to do an almost miraculous job of fixing up one of the emir's several palaces. The one they chose was built several years ago at a cost of a few hundred millions of dollars.

The job wasn't easy. They had to order and install dozens of gold-plated toilet paper rollers, gold-plated shower heads, new marble toilets and sinks, crystal chandeliers, cut-glass ashtrays, and the finest fabrics and wall coverings. And the most sumptuous furniture for the dozens and dozens of rooms. To get that kind of stuff, you don't just pop into a Home Depot or a Wal-Mart. It took a gigantic logistical effort to bring it in from Saudi Arabia.

But that was the easy part. Naturally, the emir and his clan would need water. And not just to brush their teeth. The palace has a huge fountain inside, so the palace has its own reservoir that holds two million gallons. It was filled from the city's water supply, and the fountain gushed in all of its prewar glory.

Then there was the problem of electricity. It takes a lot of juice to light up the bulbs and get the air conditioners working in a joint about the size of the Pentagon. So three monster generators were put back in order and everything worked: the stereos, the TV, the electric tooth flossers.

This had to be done because the emir is the ruler of the nation. And until he was back in Kuwait, the "legitimate government" wouldn't really be restored. But without a palace to come home to, how could the emir return? And without the emir safely in his palace (the bulletproof glass was also installed), how could we claim victory?

So that nagging newspaper was clearly out of line. Yes, the citizens of Kuwait City could use water. But can their needs be compared to the needs of the emir's great fountain? Electricity? Would they have their emir walk into a room that wasn't properly cooled? They want food and medicine at a time when trucks are urgently needed to haul the emir's new furniture?

You have to wonder what kind of whining ingrates we fought this war for.

SEPTEMBER 25, 1992

War's Toll Doesn't End with Last Bomb

There was this squib of a news story the other day. It wasn't much longer than a baseball box score.

"Boston (AP)—The death rate among Iraqi children rose dramatically in the months after the Gulf War, largely because of an outbreak of diarrhea caused by disabled water and sewage systems, researchers reported today.

"In the first seven months of 1991, about 46,900 more children died than would have been expected, according to a study in the *New England Journal of Medicine*.

"It said the death rate for children under five was triple that before the war.

"The study was conducted by Dr. Alberto Ascherio of the Harvard School of Public Health and other researchers from the United States, England, New Guinea, and Jordan. It was paid for by the United Nations Children's Fund.

"The researchers said they worked independently of the Iraqi government."

That's it. About 15 lines of newspaper type.

But then, it's old news. The war has been over for a year and a half. The parades have ended, the yellow ribbons have been taken down, and the last proud, chest-thumping speech has been made.

Still, if you like numbers, 46,900 is an interesting figure. And you can play with it in different ways.

For example, there are baseball and football stadiums that have a seating capacity of about 46,900.

So we might try picturing one of these stadiums with every seat occupied by a child.

Try it. Close your eyes and imagine Comiskey Park in Chicago or Shea Stadium in New York with a little kid in every seat.

That's a lot of noisy kids.

Now, imagine that somebody pulls a switch and sends a jolt of electricity into the seats, and every one of those 46,900 kids dies.

That would be a lot of dead kids. So you'd better open your eyes, since it isn't a pleasant thing to imagine.

Or we can look at it another way. The biggest hotel in the world is in Las Vegas. It has 4,000 rooms.

So if you put 11 kids in each room, you'd have stuffed the place with 44,000 kids. Put the extra 2,900 in the grand ballroom.

Let's imagine that someone pushes down a plunger, setting off a huge explosion that blows the hotel away, really flattens it.

Now that would rate more than a squib of a story. It would be front-page headlines all over the world: "Hotel explodes killing 46,900 children."

Which just shows that bad water leading to diarrhea and other intestinal disorders doesn't have the same dramatic impact of an explosion, although the results are the same.

Or we can play with the number another way.

The average daily attendance at Disney World is 72,233.

Of course, all 72,233 people aren't there at the same time. Some come in the morning and are gone by mid-afternoon. Some come in the afternoon and leave when the big parade is over.

So let's take a guess and say that at about 2 p.m. on an average day, there are about 46,900 people there, many of them children.

And a terrible thing happens. A giant meteor comes roaring out of space and lands smack dab on Disney World, leaving nothing but a giant crater. (Scientists say something like that could happen, but it's a zillion-to-one shot, so don't change your vacation plans.)

Now that would be a super-big story. It would stun the world and would go down in history as one of the greatest disasters.

Which shows that if you want to make history, get hit by a meteor instead of stomach cramps.

Which also shows that there is more to modern wars than that which the Pentagon allows us to see on CNN.

What we see on TV is kind of fun, all those videos from high above of targets far below suddenly blossoming like tiny flowers when a bomb lands. The graphics are not yet as good as Super Mario 4, but maybe by the next war, they'll catch up.

And we see the parades, the strutting politicians, and the cheering sports bars that have become cheering war bars.

But what we don't see is described in the full report by the doctors who made this study:

"The destruction of the supply of electric power at the beginning of the war, with the subsequent disruption of the electricity-dependent water and sewage systems, was probably responsible for the reported epidemics of gastrointestinal and other infections.

"These epidemics were worsened by the reduced accessibility of health services and decreased ability to treat severely ill children."

In other words, we don't see those invisible but deadly killers in the water or the children screaming because their stomachs hurt and their fevers are raging. And we don't see them weaken, fade, then die.

But who would want to see a downer like that, anyway?

In a classic understatement, the doctors concluded: "War is never good for health. But the full effect of war and economic sanctions on morbidity and mortality is difficult to assess, and the number of civilian casualties caused indirectly is likely to be underestimated.

"During the Gulf War, it was suggested that by using high-precision weapons with strategic targets, the Allied forces were producing only limited damage to the civilian population.

"The results of our study contradict this claim and confirm that the casualties of war extend far beyond those caused directly by warfare."

Forty-six thousand nine hundred kids. Give or take a few tots.

So what color ribbon do we wear for that triumph?

THE TROUBLE WITH
EVERYWHERE ELSE

HEY, MIKE, WHADDAYA THINK ABOUT . . .

the Moon?

We stopped going to the moon and haven't gone to Mars
and other places for one very simple reason. There's nothing
much to do there. . . . When we got to the moon—at enormous expense—it turned out to be exactly as expected. It
was barren and bleak and dusty and had an awful climate.
Well, how many people want to visit a place like that? When I
get the urge to go somewhere that is barren and bleak and
has an awful climate, I hop in my car and drive to Indiana.

—*Chicago Tribune,* July 21, 1994

Wisconsinites?

Those of us in Chicago sometimes poke affectionate fun at
our rustic neighbors to the north. We tease them for wearing
red long underwear to weddings and other formal events—as
an outer garment. We call them cheeseheads and chuckle at
the way they chomp their bratwurst, drink their brandy-beer
boilermakers, and happily thump their distended tummies.
The men too.

—*Chicago Tribune,* November 8, 1995

Hicks Get Their Licks

I hadn't realized that people in Indiana are so excitable. Every time I've been there, they've seemed tranquil. So tranquil that many appeared to be asleep on their feet.

So you can imagine my surprise at the wild-eyed way they reacted to a bit of mild criticism I directed at their state in a recent column.

All I said was that I thought the Indianapolis 500 race was America's most stupid major sporting event, that Indiana is probably the most miserable state in the nation, and that Indianapolis was the dullest of big cities.

I quite accurately said: "For most males in Indiana, a real good time consists of putting on bib overalls and a cap bearing the name of a farm equipment company and sauntering to a gas station to sit around and gossip about how Elmer couldn't get his pickup truck started that morning. . . ."

And I noted: "Its only large cities are Indianapolis and Gary, which give you the choice of dying of boredom or of multiple gunshot wounds."

Now most mature people can accept constructive criticism, which is exactly what those comments were. What could be more constructive than telling the residents of Indiana how unfortunate they are to live in such an awful place?

But did they take it that way? Just the opposite. They got mad and started shrieking and hopping up and down.

After that column appeared in an Indianapolis paper, Mayor William H. Hudnut III called a press conference to denounce me.

Mayor Hudnut said, "It's easy to write out of ignorance, but not very responsible." And he added that my mind was like concrete: "All mixed up but too set to change."

The state's lieutenant governor, John M. Mutz, fired off a statement saying: "You know those nasty things you said weren't true." And he challenged me to come to Indianapolis so he could show me the city's exciting sights.

Even worse, my phone has been clanging with calls from those people who are the worst threat to clear, logical thinking—hosts of radio call-in shows.

"Why did you say all those things?" demanded one talk show babbler.

"Because they were what I had in my heart," I honestly told him. "And somebody had to say them."

He became angrier. "You talked about Indiana men wearing bib overalls and talking about whose pickup truck wouldn't start?"

"That's right, I did."

"But I've seen men do that in Ohio and Arkansas and even in Downstate Illinois."

"That doesn't make it right," I said. "Just because they do it in other places is no excuse."

Another airwave defender of the faith snarled:

"You said Indianapolis is a big hick town. Are you aware that we have a new convention center? And that we are building a domed stadium—the Hoosier Dome?"

I showed admirable restraint by not laughing aloud. Can you imagine—the Hoosier Dome?

If there is anything that marks a town as being a genuine hicksville, it is the innocent belief that a new domed stadium is the height of progress.

The greatest cities in America do *not* put protective plastic bubbles over the heads of their dumb athletes. Yankee Stadium has none. There's none in San Francisco. And, of course, none in Chicago.

And they're going to call it the Hoosier Dome. The Hoosier Dome?

Of course they are, since they call themselves Hoosiers.

Do you know why they are called Hoosiers?

There are two explanations. One is the one they prefer, and it's not accurate. The other is accurate, but they don't like it.

The Hoosiers will tell you that the word "hoosier" came from the tendency of early Indiana settlers to say "Who's here?" when somebody rapped upon their cabin door.

Over the years, their habit of saying "Who's here?" evolved into something that sounded like "Hooshere?" And finally "Hoosier."

(That could explain why so many settlers kept going west when they got to Indiana. Who'd want to stay in a place where everybody was yowling: "Hooshere? Hooshere? Hooshere?")

But most reputable scholars, which are the only kind I deal with, say that the word "hoosier" came about this way:

The early settlers of southern Indiana were mainly unwashed, uncouth mountain folk from Kentucky.

They were usually referred to as "a hoojee" or a "hoojin." As in:

"Quick, lock up the girls and the livestock—there's some of them hoojees and hoojins comin'."

And as years passed, the words "hoojee" and "hoojin," meaning "a dirty person," according to one reference book, evolved into "hoosier."

So maybe they should call their new stadium the "hoojee-dome" or the "hoojin-dome."

A lady who phoned one of the call-in shows said: "But what about all of the famous people who came from Indiana?"

I had to tell her that I wasn't aware of any famous people coming from Indiana, but later I realized I was wrong.

Indiana should receive credit: John Dillinger, America's most famous bank robber, was a Hoosier. But Chicago's Biograph Theater must be credited with being the place where he was finally shot down.

And further research has shown that George Ade, a wonderful writer at the turn of the century, came from Indiana. It was Ade who once said:

"Many smart young men have come out of Indiana. And the smarter they were, the faster they came out."

But I have an open mind. So I'll probably accept the invitation of the lieutenant governor to take a tour of Indianapolis and see all the great sights. It shouldn't take me more than an hour.

And when I get there, I'll take the advice of an airline stewardess who was on a plane that recently landed in Indianapolis. She cheerfully announced to the passengers:

"We have just arrived in Indianapolis. If you wish, you can turn your watches back 25 years."

JUNE 17, 1982

Letters, Calls, Complaints, and Great Thoughts from Readers

MARY GIBBINS, Indianapolis: You, sir, deserve to be horsewhipped for the disgusting things you have said about the great state of Indiana.

And if you ever come to Indianapolis, I'm sure some of our decent, God-fearing men will give you the thrashing you deserve.

Fortunately, your opinion of Indiana is of little importance. I'm sure most Chicagoans appreciate what a fine state this is, especially considering the kind of sewer your city is.

COMMENT: I'm sorry to have to tell you this, but most Chicagoans share my opinion of Indiana. I recently conducted a poll of 1,000 typical

Chicagoans and asked them this question: "Would you be willing to go to war if Argentina seized Indiana?" Exactly 999 of them said no. Among their comments were: "Are you crazy? It's not worth shedding American blood over. . . ." "Absolutely not. There's nothing there that we need. . . ." "Go to war over a few sheep and rustic bumpkins? Never. . . ." "I think we should negotiate rather than fight. Maybe we could sell it to them." The only person who didn't say no was undecided. He said: "I don't have any opinion because I don't know what an Indiana is. Is it vegetable or mineral?

CLEM C. SKELTON SR., Huntingburg, Ind.: How could you, living in a cesspool of rotten politics and gangsterism, be so unfair to the great state of Indiana?

Have you forgotten that Abraham Lincoln was a Hoosier?

COMMENT: It's true that Lincoln lived in Indiana for a while, but he moved out. However, his memories of Indiana never left him, which is why he always looked so depressed.

K. D. BARTEY, Indianapolis: Indiana, which is my home and the state where my children have been raised for 18 years, is a little conservative and morals-oriented compared to liberal areas like Chicago and New York.

We do not aspire to your crime rate, congestion, traffic problems, pornographic opportunities, or egotism as espoused in your column.

COMMENT: See? No ambition.

JUNE 27, 1982

Iowa's the Real Pits

All those unflattering comments I've made about Indiana in recent weeks—I take them all back.

It appears that I've made a terrible mistake, and I owe the people of Indiana an apology.

I discovered my error this way:

A friend of mine, who is a Hoosier, had suggested that he take me on a tour of Indiana.

"Believe me," he said, "when I show you what a wonderful place it really is, you'll change your mind."

"Never," I said. "I've been to Indiana and nothing you can show me can convince me that it is not the dullest, most miserable state in the union."

"That's what has me confused," he said. "I don't understand how you could say that about such a lovely state."

"Because it's true," I said.

"Why don't you take one more look," he said. "I appeal to your sense of fairness."

"All right," I said. "But I warn you that nothing you can show me will change my mind because I've already seen it."

So we set out for Indiana.

Within an hour, I knew something was wrong.

"Isn't that a pretty sight?" he said, pointing out a part of the countryside.

"You're right," I conceded. "I don't understand how I could have overlooked it."

A little later, he showed me something else.

"Isn't that beautiful?" he said.

Once again I had to agree.

Finally I blurted out, "Something's wrong. I'm thoroughly confused. I've never seen any of these things before."

He said: "I can't understand that. If you've been to Indiana, then you couldn't have overlooked these pleasant sights."

"Are you sure this is Indiana?" I said.

"Of course," he said. "I lived here most of my life."

"Then there's something I have to confess," I told him. "I don't think I've ever been in Indiana before. This is all new to me."

He said, "But you said you had been in Indiana. You wrote that in your column."

"I meant it. I thought I had been in Indiana. But none of this is familiar."

It was a baffling mystery. But we finally got to the bottom of it and discovered how I had made the mistake.

First, I have to explain that I'm not very good at reading road maps. They all look the same to me, and I'm always turning onto the wrong highway.

Also, I have a poor sense of direction—especially when I go beyond the city limits, which is why I seldom travel outside the city. I was once lost in suburban Schaumburg for two days. It was such a frightening experience that my hair turned white almost overnight.

So what apparently happened was this: When I went to Indiana, I must have turned onto the wrong road. And I ended up somewhere else.

But the question was, where?

My friend provided the solution. He got out a book that has pictures of towns, cities, and the countryside in every state. And we went through the book, page by page, hoping that I would see something that looked familiar.

"How about this?" he asked.

"No. There were no mountains where I was at."

"All right. What about this?"

"No. There was no seashore with a rolling surf. I'd remember something like that."

"And this?"

"No. Those are skyscrapers. I didn't see anything taller than a silo. Lots of silos."

We were about to give up when he turned a page and I said, "That's it! I've seen that town before—that's Indianapolis."

My friend shook his head. "No, that's not Indianapolis."

"Then what is it?"

"That's Des Moines, Iowa."

"Iowa?"

"That's right. When you thought you were in Indiana, you were actually in Iowa. And when you were in Des Moines, you thought you were in Indianapolis."

"So all those things I said about Indiana . . ."

"You were really talking about Iowa."

"Amazing."

"Well, mistakes will happen. But you really should apologize to the people of Indiana.

He was right.

So, in the immortal words of Emily Latella, the lady on the original *Saturday Night Live* shows:

Never mind.

APRIL 9, 1984

Just Take Your Oranges and . . .

When he phones, he usually begins the conversation by asking: "How's the weather out there?"

He lives in southern California, and they always ask that question, especially if it is winter in Chicago. And he ends the question with a small laugh. No, it's not even a laugh. More of a self-satisfied snicker. A "hnk-hnk-hnk."

Then he always says something like: "Well, it's terrific here. Beautiful day. I was just out in my backyard picking some oranges."

I've never understood why being able to pick an orange in their backyards is significant to so many people in California or Florida. I mean, if

I want an orange, I can go to my refrigerator and get one. I told him that once, and he said:

"Oh, but that's not the same. This is right off the *tree*. And I've got dozens. Hundreds. I can't count them."

That also puzzles me. How many oranges can a person eat? Besides, monkeys pick food off trees, but that doesn't mean I envy their lifestyle.

When he finishes talking about his orange tree, he usually gets into golf. "I played 18 this morning," he'll say.

"So did I."

"But it's snowing there, isn't it?" (They always know our weather. Watching our weather on TV is one of the highlights of their day. Besides picking an orange.)

"Golf is better when it's snowing," I tell him. "The course isn't crowded."

He usually ends the conversation by saying: "Just took a dip in the pool. I told you we put in a pool, didn't I?"

"About a hundred times. By the way, I just read an article in a science magazine. They found that too much exposure to chlorine makes men impotent."

"Well, you have to come out here for a visit. Get away from it all."

"Thanks. But I like it here. Bye."

He called a few days ago, but this time he began by saying:

"I suppose you heard the news."

I knew what he was talking about, but I pretended not to. "No, what news? Your oranges have blight?"

"C'mon. You know. You heard about the census figures."

"Oh, that. Yeah, think I heard somebody mention it."

"Well, how does it feel to be," he said, pausing for dramatic effect, "*number three*"?

He was referring to some figures that have come out of the federal government that allege that Los Angeles has now passed Chicago in population. Which, if true, means that L.A. is now the second largest city and we are third.

"Well? How does it feel?" he said.

I've tried to avoid getting involved in something as silly as this. But I suppose it is a subject that has to be faced.

So I said: "It feels fine. Great."

"Oh, c'mon. You're probably all eating your hearts out. No more Second City."

"We don't care. Really. Besides, I'm told that the new figures include everybody in Los Angeles asylums."

"So what?"

"Well, if you subtract the asylum inmates and count only normal people, if you have any, then you probably wouldn't be any bigger than Peoria."

"Is that so? Well, the Chicago figures probably include everybody in your jails, and without them you wouldn't be as big as Rockford."

"You don't have to be rude."

"I'm sorry."

"The fact is, we're pleased for a number of reasons."

"I'll bet. Hnk-hnk-hnk."

"But we are."

"Why?"

"Because everybody knows that southern California attracts those who are strange. This can only mean that if our population went down, and yours went up, people have moved from here to there. And chances are, they are the kind of people who believe men in outer space are sending them messages through their dental fillings or bed springs."

"No matter what you say, we are now the second-biggest city in the United States."

"City? You aren't a city. I've been there, and I looked around and I couldn't find any city. You have no downtown. You don't even have a subway. Every real city has a subway. London. Paris. New York. Chicago. You are a giant suburb."

"Say what you will, but you are now looking up at us."

"It means nothing. Remember, Indianapolis is bigger than San Francisco and New Orleans. Do you hear anyone singing, 'I Left My Heart in Indianapolis?' Did Louie Armstrong ever sing about the Hoosier Dome? Numbers are meaningless."

"You are eaten up with bitterness."

"Nonsense. All this means is that with more people in your city, there is more weight. And it is just a matter of time until the San Andreas fault cracks—the way Lex Luthor, bless him, intended—and you will slide into the ocean."

"I hope you get mugged on a subway."

"Have a nice mud slide."

"I hope a blizzard engulfs you."

"Have a pleasant forest fire."

"Remember, we are number two."

"Depending on the meaning of that phrase, I think I agree."

AUGUST 20, 1984

Regional Tastes Hard to Swallow

It's often said that because of mass communications, Americans have lost their cultural differences. We watch the same TV shows and movies, read the same magazines and books, drive the same cars on the same interstates, wear the same clothes, eat the same food, live in the same houses, listen to the same music, drink the same liquor, and play the same games.

But while driving to Texas for the Republican convention recently, I discovered that this isn't entirely true.

I stopped in Texarkana, a blotch of motels and fast-food joints on the Texas-Arkansas border, and asked a gas station attendant if he knew of a good place to eat.

"Ya want somethin' hah claise?" he asked.

Of course. I always prefer a hah-claise joint.

So I wound up dining in the Cattleman's Steak House, which had red flocked walls, dim lights, and no cattlemen visible.

Something on the menu puzzled me, so I asked the waitress, a pretty young woman, if she could tell me what Turkey fries were.

"Uh, you mean the Turkey fries?"

Yes. Right here, listed under appetizers. Turkey fries. What are they?

"Uh, well, they're, uh, they're kind of, uh, they, uh . . ."

Yes, yes, what are they?

"Well, uh, sir, they're kind of hard to explain. You get a whole bowl of them, and you dip them in a sauce."

I see. But what are they? Could you be more specific?

She stammered, flushed, then said: "Sir, it's really hard to explain."

Well, are they part of a turkey?

"Yes, sir, they are part of a turkey."

So, what part?

She stammered and flushed some more. Then a man at the next table who was wearing a string tie leaned over and drawled: "I'll tell 'im, honey. The *cojónes*. They're the turkey's *cojónes*."

You mean they are the testicles of a turkey?

"That's right," the man said, returning to his food.

The waitress nodded somberly. "That's what they are. We sell a lot of them. You want to order some?"

I think I'll have the shrimp cocktail.

The man in the string tie leaned over again and said: "Ya ought to try 'em. They're purty good."

I'm sure. But I have to avoid fried foods.

"Uh-huh."

Very unusual dish, though. Tell me, how do they go about obtaining them?

"Well, I guess ya just catch yourself a turkey and, snip, snip. Ya know what I mean?"

I couldn't help but think about that for a while. Actually, to serve them by the bowl, a person would have to chase down a whole herd of turkeys and, as he put it, snip, snip. Poor birds.

I had to wonder: Do turkeys have thoughts? If so, what do they think when somebody is abusing them that way?

And what about the people who do that to turkeys for a living? How does a person get into that line of work in the first place? Does it require special training, lengthy experience, certain physical skills such as keen hand-eye coordination? Do you put it on your resume before you go into the personnel office? If so, how do you describe this particular job skill?

It also seems to me that in social situations, it might be a line of work that would be difficult to explain.

For example, a young man who does that to turkeys might find himself in, say, a singles bar. I'm sure they have such places in turkey-tormenting country. And he might find himself responding when a young lady asks what he does for a living. Which could lead her to say:

"You do WHAT to turkeys? My goodness, why would you want to do something like that?"

As I was paying the restaurant check the man in the string tie asked where I was from and I told him. He said:

"Don't serve Turkey fries up there, huh?"

Just French fries. But fortunately for Frenchmen, it's not quite the same thing.

"Well, you folks don't know what you're missing."

We do now. So if anybody interested in new dining experiences happens to be down around Texarkana, you might give them a try.

If you can handle fried foods, that is.

OCTOBER 5, 1990

Thank You, Cubs: The Pressure's Off

One year ago, my nerves were frazzled. I was manic-depressive and was swinging between bouts of incoherent babbling and crouching in a dark closet to hide from the world.

It was the result of being afflicted with pennant fever. The Cubs had won 25 percent of a world championship and were in the playoffs, and I foolishly believed they would go on to win the other 75 percent.

The tension was such that in less than a week, I lost 75 pounds, all of my hair turned white (even under my arms), my face looked like a melting candle, and I kept swallowing my tongue, as well as my thumb. By the final and fatal out, I was in a hospital bed, curled in a fetal position and wearing a diaper, tubes dripping nourishment into my gaunt body, while a team of psychiatrists tried to bring me back from the dark depths of melancholia.

When my eyes finally opened, and I saw the relief on the faces of my loved ones and my bookie, to whom I owed a tidy sum, a nurse cheerfully said, "Wait'll next year," and I went into shock and was out for another week.

But now it is next year. And thanks to the Cubs' aggressive charge back to mediocrity, my health has returned. Now I can sit back and watch the autumn baseball ritual as a cool, detached, casual observer.

Of course, it would be un-American of me not to temporarily attach my loyalties to one of the four competing teams. In this country, we don't mealy-mouth or stand timidly on the sideline unless we're elected to leadership positions. Besides, baseball can be such a slow, dull game, that if you aren't pulling for one of the teams, you might fall asleep before the first player spits.

So some people form a temporary attachment by betting. Others cheer blindly for the American League or the National League. Some make a regional choice. Those who lack character always cheer for the favorite. Those who lack brains always pull for the underdog.

I have my own approach, as some readers might recall. It has nothing to do with the league, teams, individual players, or part of the country.

My choice is based on need and compassion—which city's population has the deepest craving for the joys of victory and is most deserving of it.

For example, San Diego should never be in a World Series because they have sunshine and beaches and serve sushi in their ballpark. But Detroit should, because the people of Detroit have to live there. The federal government refuses to evacuate them to safety.

It is also based on cruelty and vindictiveness. Which city do I dislike the most? Was I ever served a lousy meal there? Mugged? Does an old girlfriend whom I hate live there? And will her fat husband choke on a potato chip if his team flops?

As I said, I try to be objective.

The choices this year are difficult because there is no city that is easy to hate. No blabber-mouth New York, no smug San Francisco, no goofy

Los Angeles. Nor is there a case of abject hardship, such as Dallas, where the people don't even realize that they should be evacuated.

So let us look at the choices.

Oakland. Normally, Oakland would be deserving, because it has to live with the indignity of being next to San Francisco. But it won last year, so two in a row would be gluttony.

Boston. Absolutely not. I don't care about all the hard-luck stories about the bad-bounce Red Sox. The city is crawling with Harvard types. The very worst villains of Wall Street are Harvard MBAs. Actually, I'm not sure if that's true, but it probably is. And even if it isn't, I don't trust Harvard people because I suspect that most are still loyal to the throne of England.

Cincinnati. Now here's a nice city, with good, simple folk. It's kind of like Milwaukee, except in Milwaukee they eat bratwurst and burp, but in Cincinnati they cover noodles with chili and burp. But I read that a poll showed that most people in Cincinnati didn't think that Pete Rose should have gone to prison. How can I cheer for a town that admires a tax cheat but wants to put an art museum director in jail because he displayed some controversial photos?

Pittsburgh? A fine choice. The people of this city used to work in mills. They all had tattoos on their arms. All the men, I mean. Only half the women. Now the city is more refined. And they deserve a championship because of their superior intelligence. You see, as bad as the Cubs were, they still outdrew the Pirates. That tells you something about our brains and theirs.

Take Off Mittens, Count Your Blessings

"Why are we here?" Slats Grobnik suddenly asked.

Are you talking about the meaning of life? If so, I'll move down the bar.

"Nah, I mean right now: What are we doing here?"

We're here to sip a tad of 86-proof antifreeze to help ward off the unfriendly elements that we will face when we go outdoors.

"But why are we here?"

I just told you.

"Nah, I mean why are we in Chicago?"

What a silly question. We are in Chicago because this is where we live and work. It is our hometown. We were born here. We have always lived here. We are Chicagoans.

"But the weather is so stinkin' miserable. You go outside for a few minutes, and your nose might fall off. Not that your nose would be much of a loss."

Yes, but that is part of the mystique of being a Chicagoan. Every winter we contend with such adversity: snow, cold, or both. We are viewed as hardy, sturdy, tough Midwesterners, admired, even envied. Unlike many soft Americans, we don't become immobilized by a few snowflakes or panic when the temperature drops below zero. We put on our long underwear, thump our chests, laugh at nature, and we persevere.

"I hate it."

You what?

"I said I hate it."

I am shocked. I can't believe you said that. You hate Chicago?

"This week I hate it. Come to think of it, I hate it every January. And I hate it every February and March. And I don't think much of it in November or December. And October ain't much to brag about, either."

How long have you felt this way?

"All my life. That's why I still hate my grandfodder."

What does your grandfather have to do with it?

"Everything. He's the answer to my question of why we're here."

Your grandfather? I remember him well. He barely spoke English, except for the words "Jim Beam" and "beer chaser," and "sharrup, woman." How can you blame him for your treasonous hatred of Chicago?

"Because he got off the train too soon."

What train?

"The train from New York to Chicago. He comes here as an immigrant, OK? He gets off the boat and he gets on a train. But then what does he do? He gets off here. If he stayed on the train, it would have gone all the way to San Francisco, or Portland, or Seattle, or someplace where you don't freeze your butt. And you know why he got off in Chicago?"

To seek work in a boomtown, as so many immigrants did?

"Nah. He didn't know they had a toilet on the train. So he got off to look for an outhouse, like in the Old Country. By the time he found a john, the train was gone. So he was stuck here. And my old man was born here, and me and my brother, Fats, was born here. My dumb luck because my grandpa had to go but didn't know where to go. If it wasn't for him, I could have been born in California and be a cool California kind of guy."

You wouldn't want such a fate.

"Why not? Gold chain, suntan, an earring, maybe a facelift and a hairpiece. Dump the wife, find some California girl with a real little brain. Hey, it beats the tip of my nose turning blue when I go home tonight."

But you don't want to live in California. It is no longer utopia. They have earthquakes, terrible fires, mud slides, and Michael Jackson. People have been fleeing the state.

"Awright. Then I could go someplace else."

Such as?

"One of those states down South. They don't get this kind of miserable weather. I mean, what about Florida?"

Florida? Do you really want to look like George Burns, wearing plaid pants, a long billed cap, and Wal-Mart sneakers, bent in half while taking your morning walk like a hyperactive little bird, with a portable EKG machine attached to your chest?

"Florida don't have no earthquakes."

No, they have hurricanes. Some day the entire state will be washed away. Why, recent statistics show that more than 100,000 people your age were swept out to sea last year and eaten by sharks and crabs.

"Is that true?"

No, but one never knows. Stuff happens.

"Well, what about Alabama or Mississippi or Georgia or those other states down South? I could move there and I wouldn't freeze no more."

They are not your kind of people.

"Hey, people is people."

Is anyone in your family named Bubba? Or Billy Bob or Bobby WaWa? Do you eat grits, a pallid version of Cream of Wheat? Don't you realize that anyone who lives south of 111th Street in Chicago is—and let them deny it—a beady-eyed hillbilly? You cannot become a Southerner. For someone from Chicago, it is an unnatural act. Your eyes do not meet at your nose. You would be an object of distrust.

"What about New Mexico and warm places like that?"

You go there and you will spend the rest of your days getting up in the morning and shaking your shoes for lizards and snakes. Plus, there are still a lot of Apaches there. You never know when they might start plucking hair again.

"Then I'm stuck. But I feel better because so are you. I bet you freeze before I do."

I'll take that bet.

"Bartender, more antifreeze."

NOW, WAIT A MINUTE

HEY, MIKE, WHADDAYA THINK ABOUT . . .

Rock Lyrics?

. . .brings me back to a discussion I had with several young adults at the time Tipper Gore was on her labeling kick. . . . They asked me to join them in opposing Tipper's efforts. I asked them if it was true that rock was a powerful social force, and they said it was indeed. And could any powerful art form—the music of Beethoven, the Michelangelo paintings on the Sistine Chapel ceiling, the writings of Shakespeare—elevate and enrich the human spirit? You betcha, they said. But then I suggested that if great art elevates and enriches, it stands to reason that really grubby, raunchy stuff might have just the opposite effect. Such as songs that seem to condone or encourage sadistic sexual behavior, violence, and acting like slobs. Couldn't they devalue the human spirit, warp attitudes? Maybe, they said . . . but the listeners should have the right to decide if they wanted to be degraded or warped.

—*Chicago Tribune,* July 24, 1992

the New Hampshire Primary?

There are well over 200 million of us. So why must we listen to the TV babblers, the Washington pundits, and every other self-important yapper tell us that it is of monumental importance how the vote turns out in a state that represents less than one-half of 1 percent of the American population. You could drop all of the registered voters in the entire state of New Hampshire into New York City and lose them. Oh, I wish we could.

—*Chicago Tribune,* February 2, 1996

Ringing Dissent to Criticism of Justice Douglas

When Associate Justice William O. Douglas returns from his honeymoon, it would be perfectly proper for him to do the following:

- Walk with great dignity to his seat on the U.S. Supreme Court bench.
- Sit down.
- Draw his black robes about him.
- Slowly raise his right hand.
- Touch the tip of his thumb to the tip of his nose.
- Wiggle his fingers.

This would provide a fitting message, answer, and explanation for the busybodies of America who currently are wallowing in indignation, their favorite puddle.

The busybodies are upset because Douglas, 67, married Cathleen Heffernan, 23. It was his fourth marriage, and she is his youngest bride.

The marriage occurred just when the busybodies were recovering from an earlier attack of disapproval.

Last month, many of them registered protests against the marriage of a rich young baseball player and actress Mamie Van Doren.

They haven't been this angry since the girl down the block had the baby after they used up the fingers and thumbs of both hands counting months.

It has been almost as infuriating for them as seeing all the shades in the neighborhood pulled down at once. Or discovering that the hotel room walls are thick and soundproof. Or slipping on the ladder and skinning their noses on the transom.

The fact that a man they don't know married a girl they don't know for reasons that are none of anyone else's business has a terrible effect on the tempers of many people.

Why this is, I don't know. Their psychiatrists, mothers, or closest friends might be able to explain. But it probably would be too terrible to report here.

A typical reaction to the marriage was heard yesterday on a radio talk show that seems to air the comments of listeners every time a famous person gets married, which is an unusual format.

At an hour when most people are concerned with washing their faces, downing coffee, or getting to work on time, a young man found himself deeply concerned with Douglas' marriage.

In a high-pitched adenoid-filtered voice, he cried out over the airwaves, so the listeners in four or five states would know exactly where he stood on the matter:

"I object to that marriage."

Fortunately, Douglas and his bride are honeymooning in the Far West, out of the station's range, so they survived this crisis.

The radio caller went on to say that he and his wife fight a lot, but that fighting is much better than marrying and divorcing young girls all the time. His wife, disabled or uninterested, did not volunteer an opinion.

Even in Congress, where marriage is not often discussed on the floor, there is indignation.

A Mississippi Democratic congressman, Representative Thomas G. Abernethy, raised his eyebrows and said:

"In recent years the court has given us enough trouble . . . but I doubt if any decision has lifted more eyebrows than a justice's fourth journey on the highway of matrimony with one only a third his age."

Since the highway of matrimony being traveled by Douglas does not go through Mississippi, it was not clear why Representative Abernethy was upset.

Equally indignant was Representative George W. Andrews (D-Ala.), who called for a congressional investigation of Douglas' character.

Andrews said that he has heard that Douglas had been cruel to his other wives.

He did not reveal how he happened to know details of the earlier marriages. Nor did he say whether he knew things about the marriages of congressmen, lobbyists, relatives, and the folks next door.

Representative Paul Findley (R-Ill.) said Douglas' personal life indicates a weakness in the judicial system.

"There should be a way to remove a justice from the bench without a trial for crimes and misdemeanors," Findley said.

Findley and the others left several questions unanswered:

- How many marriages will a justice be allowed before he gets kicked off the bench?
- Will he get favorable consideration for such positive things as being on time with his alimony?
- What will be an acceptable age difference in the marriage of a justice to a younger woman?
- Will a justice be permitted to marry an older woman?
- Will a justice be permitted to marry Mamie Van Doren?
- Will the marriage limits be extended to congressmen?
- What does the Alabama congressman consider cruelty to a wife? Are tear gas, billy clubs, police dogs, and shotguns acceptable on the highway of matrimony or only on the highway back home?
- And, finally, what do Findley, Abernethy, and Andrews think about when they are not thinking about someone else's marriage?

Anything?

FEBRUARY 21, 1968

[Editors' note: The film *Bonnie and Clyde,* starring Warren Beatty and Faye Dunaway, was greeted enthusiastically by many critics—and movie audiences—as the first of a new genre, successfully combining graphic violence with comedy, sex, and social commentary.]

Bonnie 'n' Clyde—the Sad Side

Jim Campbell, a pipe fitter, isn't going to see that movie about Bonnie and Clyde. He knows enough about them already.

He was 20 when the infamous couple came to his part of Oklahoma. The date was April 6, 1934, and Campbell has never forgotten it.

"My father was the constable in Commerce, a small town. The only reason he had the job was because the people liked him. He sure wasn't a professional lawman. He had been a contractor until the Depression, then he lost everything. He was nearly 60 then.

"I was very close to my father. My mother died when I was only three, so my father leaned toward me after that.

"After my mother was gone, he devoted his life to his family, keeping the four kids together.

"That's why he took that police job. It only paid about $15 a week, but it kept us eating.

"When it happened, I was 20. I was going to a junior college in the next town. Most of the time I hitchhiked. It was my ambition to be a journalist. You know, you're the first one I ever talked to.

"A farmer came to town one day and told my father some people he passed were in trouble. Their car had gone off the road. My father and another policeman—they were the whole force—drove out there.

"When they stepped from the car, my father was killed instantly. The other man was wounded. I'm sure my father didn't know who killed him. He was just going out to help someone.

"It's ironic. I don't think my father could have shot anyone if he had to. As I said, he got the job because he was well liked and needed it. He really wasn't a policeman.

"I never went back to my classes. I guess I became . . . oh . . . bitter, you might say. I didn't see much point in anything. I just brooded. He had given so much of his life to us, to keeping us a family after my mother was gone.

"I worked in a gas station and did other things like that. Now I'm a pipe fitter [at an atomic energy plant near Kennewick, Washington], a job I enjoy. I probably wouldn't have made a journalist anyway.

"As far as that movie goes, I guess Bonnie and Clyde seem glamorous. The kids are fascinated by them. You can't blame the kids for that, but they shouldn't think they were glamorous.

"They may have reasons for doing what they did. But they weren't glamorous. Certainly not glamorous."

Russell Moore, a Korean War vet and now a lawyer in Albuquerque, New Mexico, isn't going to the movie. He was less than a year old on August 5, 1932, but he knows about Bonnie and Clyde.

"You're the first person to ever ask me about this. I've wondered if somebody wouldn't think to write about this side of it.

"We lived in Atoka, Oklahoma. My father was only 31. My sisters were seven and three.

"My father's family had been wealthy. My grandmother had ranches, farms. But he was a speculator, and the Depression wiped them all out.

"My father had us to feed, so he became a deputy sheriff and was glad to get the job.

"It happened this way: My father and the sheriff, Charlie Maxwell, drove up to a dance in Stringtown to look in on things. Their car got stuck in a rut, and they walked over to a parked car to ask for a push. The Barrow gang was in the car.

"They gunned my father down with shotguns. They thought he was after them. They wounded the sheriff. He was crippled for life.

"My mother was left with three children to support. "We moved in with her parents and she got a job. There was no insurance, but fortunately my father had a burial policy. We couldn't have paid for that.

"My mother was still young and pretty when it happened, but she never married again. She hasn't had a date. Oh, we used to tell her that maybe she . . . well, let's not talk about that now.

"The roughest thing for me was growing up without a father. My grandfather was helpful and understanding. But it isn't the same."

Claude Harryman farms near Saginaw, Missouri (pop. 189). His father used to farm there until April 13, 1933.

"You know how it was. You couldn't live off the land. My father was a county constable. No regular salary, just fees for what he did. I was 20, the oldest of five children. I worked construction and helped on the farm.

"The police from Joplin came into our county. They thought they knew where the gang was. To make it legal, they got a search warrant. But they needed someone from our county to serve it. My father.

"He was on the porch with the paper in his hand when they shot him to pieces. They also killed a Joplin policeman.

"We sold the farm. I worked where I could to support the family. For a while I worked in a packing house, butchering animals for $1.50 a day. My mother sewed for the WPA.

"It was a long haul. It wasn't until my brothers and sisters grew up that I could make plans, get married, settle down on my own place.

"See the movie? No. There's nothing in it I'd care to see. I've heard about it."

Many critics say the movie is "realistic." Clyde is handsome, Bonnie is a beauty. They are fun-loving, even cute, dashing and very human. You can sympathize with them. The movie is touching, heartbreaking, brilliant. That's what the critics say. And realistic.

Of course, there's not much in it about the nameless, faceless dead men. Or the orphans and widows and the never-healing scar of a man who never knew his father.

If you put that in, how could you make a movie "realistic"?

JANUARY 27, 1978

Short-Legged Dog Has Snow-Fooling Problem

During these raging snowstorms, most public attention is given to stranded motorists, pedestrians staggering through snowdrifts, and travelers stuck at airports.

But nothing is ever said about a creature who goes through far more agony during a blizzard than any of the above.

I'm talking about dogs that have short legs.

I had not given this problem any thought until Thursday morning. That was when a neighbor of mine came huffing down the street, a look of panic on her face.

"My dog got out. Have you seen him?" she said.

"Don't worry, he won't go far in this storm," I said. "He'll probably come home when he's hungry."

"Yes, but if he's out too long, he might become frozen."

"Oh, he'll be OK," I said. "He has a thick coat."

She looked at me with disgust. "Not *there* he hasn't."

Then I remembered. Her dog was a basset. It has legs about the size of a thread spool. Just like a dachshund and a few other stumpy breeds.

And I understood her concern. The snowdrifts were already a foot or two deep. The dog's belly, and everything else in that vicinity, is only about six or eight inches above ground level.

That meant that certain parts of the creature were being constantly immersed in snow.

I couldn't imagine anything more uncomfortable, especially first thing in the morning, although it was probably a quicker waker-upper than a cup of strong coffee.

Later, while driving downtown, I heard a radio call-in show during which a worried lady called and reminded people to put bread crumbs out for the birds, or the tiny things would lose body heat and freeze.

That's fine. But what about the excruciating problems of dogs with short legs? In weather such as this, they too could freeze. Maybe not all over but, boy, even a dog shouldn't have to suffer from frostbite of . . .

So I phoned the radio station and said that something should be said on the air in their behalf.

"What do you want said?" the radio person asked.

That something should be done immediately for short-legged dogs. Who knows how many might already be going into shock.

"Yes, but what can be done?"

"Well, maybe you can suggest that people put out a shallow pan of warm water so the afflicted dog could defrost himself.

"I don't think we can say that," he said.

Then maybe you could say people should be sure to shovel their walks so that short-legged dogs don't freeze their . . .

"Uh, we can't say that either," he said, and hung up.

So I called a few veterinarians to ask how severe this problem is.

One vet was surprisingly casual. "Oh, I wouldn't worry about it," he said. "During my entire career, I've seen only two or three cases of that type of frostbite."

He probably wouldn't be that casual if he had seen only two or three veterinarians with that type of frostbite—and he was one of them.

But another, Dr. W. T. Boozer of Palos Heights, said: "Yes, it can happen to all breeds. But the closer the dog is to the ground, the more susceptible he is."

This is now a frank society, so I posed the question of how this could affect the dog's future love life and his masculine capabilities.

"If it were extreme, it might affect his potency to some extent," he said.

Dr. Algis Rimas of Park West Hospital on Lincoln Avenue agreed: "If he were out there long enough in extreme conditions, it could cause impotency or permanent damage."

That, I imagine, could lead to self-doubts, anxiety, and depression. So the danger is more than physical. It includes the possibility that a severe, snowy winter, such as this, could create a vast number of short-legged dogs that have deep psychological troubles. And whom can they tell about it?

And I had always assumed that the worst thing that could happen to a dog was fleas.

I have sometimes wondered why basset hounds have that constant look of overwhelming sadness on their faces. They always look so tragic that everybody laughs at them.

Now I understand why they look that way, and I'll never laugh at them again.

You'd look that sad, too, pal, if your men's room was filled with four feet of snow.

NOVEMBER 20, 1979

Fun with Khomeini

I can't remember when this country has had such a good time. There's nothing as invigorating as a good collective hate. And for that we can thank Iran's Ayatollah Ruhollah Khomeini.

Our students have taken up demonstrating on campus again. But this time they are rallying 'round the flag.

The federal gumshoes are out rounding up Iranian illegals like old-time dogcatchers, and only a few civil libertarians are protesting.

Iranians in this country have been warned not to travel alone so they won't be set upon and thumped by angry Americans.

Flag merchants say they can't keep up with the demand for Iranian flags that Americans want to burn.

I read an article by a sportswriter, about 30, talking about how his "lost" generation—soured by the Vietnam War—is finally having its patriotic juices stirred and would be ready to march off to Iran for love of country. (I'll believe *that* when they all rush down to enlist.)

The country has even been cheering President Carter for one-upping the Iranians by snubbing their oil before they could cut it off, and for freezing their money before they could take it out of our banks.

Because I don't like to feel left out of things, I've been looking for a way to show my displeasure with the ayatollah.

I almost attacked a swarthy man I saw holding up a placard on the street. But in the nick of time, I saw he wasn't an Iranian but was just putting up an "open for lunch" sign on the window of a Greek restaurant.

Then I considered getting into the great Iranian student hunt by setting up my own hot line—something like Chicago's "Pothole Patrol"— and offering a bounty to readers who would turn in their Iranian friends or neighbors. Someone suggested calling it "Persian Patrol," but this newspaper's accounting department turned down the idea. They were afraid people would also fink on Armenians, Albanians, Turks, Greeks, and dark-haired Americans with winter-vacation suntans, and we'd be cheated out of bounty money.

So I'll just have to sit back like everyone else and merely seethe about the mad ayatollah and hope that a pollster or TV man-on-the-street interviewer will ask me how I feel, so I can shout that we should send in the Marines or deport all the camel jockeys or nuke the greaseballs!

The only problem I have in maintaining my anti-Iran fervor is that I keep thinking how I might feel if I were an Iranian.

There is the whole business of the deposed shah being our guest in a New York hospital because Henry (Dr. Strangelove) Kissinger and David (Bottom Line) Rockefeller pressured the White House into letting him into this country.

It's said that when the shah was running Iran, his secret police force, the SAVAK, killed thousands of people whose views bothered him. They used to hold daily executions and bring in the victims' relatives to watch.

Or maybe it was tens or hundreds of thousands of people killed. No-body is ever sure of exact numbers when talking about the secret police force of a despot.

But whatever the exact death toll was, it's generally accepted that a horri-fying number of Iranians went to their graves because of their political views.

And it is also true that the shah was our boy. We put him in charge and kept him propped up. And when he used torture and murder to stay in power, we looked the other way.

We justify this, of course, by saying that it was all in our national interest. And it may have been. The shah sold us oil and was the best customer our weapons industry had, spending billions of dollars a year for the latest in boom-booms. If he had remained in power long enough, Iran might have had more American-built fighter planes than camels.

From our point of view—if we all think like Kissinger—there's noth-ing wrong with a greedy, murderous skunk being in charge of Iran, so long as he is *our* greedy, murderous skunk.

But if you look at it from an Iranian point of view, it's understandable that some Iranians might still hold a grudge against the shah.

After all, millions of Americans almost froth at the lips because they don't like the way Howard Cosell talks on TV. During the World Series, a mob of fans smashed his car and tried to maul him because his com-ments didn't satisfy them.

So if we can go berserk over a sportscaster's evil ways, it's understand-able that some Iranians might feel resentful about someone who tortured or murdered their friends and relatives, then fled their country with bil-lions of dollars of their wealth.

And I can understand Iranians being confused, if nothing else, when this country, which likes to think of itself as the symbol of freedom and justice, welcomes a greedy, murderous skunk as its guest. (Does anyone really believe the shah couldn't find skilled medical treatment in Mexico City? Where do sick Mexican millionaires go?)

Of course, I'm not trying to excuse the Iranians for seizing our em-bassy and holding our people hostage. That is a bad breach of interna-tional law and the ayatollah is a nasty guy for doing it.

But I wish I knew more about international law, because I sometimes wonder if using our Central Intelligence Agency to put deadly dictators in charge of other countries is even a misdemeanor.

Letters, Calls, Complaints, and Great Thoughts from Readers

M. J. DAVIS, Cleveland: What is wrong with the news media? Aren't you happy unless you are trying to drive a president from office?

What is it that President Reagan has done wrong? He has tried to make friends with Iran. Is there something wrong with that?

Just because he didn't blab his plan to the press, everybody is jumping on him. Why should he tell the press anything? You'll just lie and distort it anyway.

If I had my way, everybody in the media would be locked up in jail or put against the wall and shot. We'd be better off without the whole bunch of you. You just destroy our freedoms.

COMMENT: Look, Ron and Nancy, if you're going to write to me, don't use phony names.

Fulfilling Advice for Wellesley Grads

"Students, faculty, and guests of Wellesley College, welcome. As you know, Barbara Bush was supposed to be our commencement speaker. But at the last minute, she was asked to baby-sit for some of her grandchildren. Because she considers that to be a more fulfilling task, she has asked to be excused.

"In her absence, we have invited Chicago columnist Mike Royko to address you. Unlike Mrs. Bush, Mr. Royko has never been a housewife or mother. And he has a working career. So except for not being a female person, he fulfills the requirements of the 150 student feminists who signed petitions objecting to Mrs. Bush's presence. So I introduce Mr. Royko."

"Thank you, Chancellor Whatsis, Dean Whoozits, and all the rest of you rich, Eastern elitists who have gathered at this citadel of snobbery.

"First, I would ask that nobody boo, jeer, or otherwise protest my presence, as I have a nervous stomach and that will make me throw up, which, in turn, will make you nauseous, causing some of you to retch, faint, or stampede toward the exits, thereby detracting from the solemnity of this occasion.

"Now for my commencement address. I will begin by saying that I know what you think I'm going to say. You think I'm going to give you the old 'get out there and help make this a better world' routine, which is standard for commencement speeches.

"You expect me to tell you to think not only of yourself, but to do something with your lives that will help mankind—excuse me, I meant personkind. And that you should think of the downtrodden of society, the have-nots, and of all the social ills that afflict our nation and the world.

"OK, if you want to be do-gooders, that's fine, as long as you don't get obnoxious about it. But chances are you won't, because you are more concerned with your own happiness than some stranger's, so we'll leave it at that.

"Instead, I would like to talk about the crummy way some of you treated Mrs. Bush, crabbing that she wasn't a worthy choice to speak here because she dropped out of college, got married, and was never anything but a wife, mother, grandmother, and homemaker.

"Actually, I'm glad you did that, because it touched off a national debate and gave a lot of pundits a chance to get their minds off of Lithuania and ponder your silliness.

"So I'd like to ask you a question. Those of you who have ever gone through nine months of pregnancy and 12 hours of labor, raise your hands.

"That's what I thought.

"Now, those of you who have ever hauled yourself out of bed at midnight to change the diaper—non-disposable and with pins—and handle the late feeding of a baby, raise your hands.

"That's what I thought. Probably never made formula either, right? Or boiled any nipples? Or had a boy baby wee in your eyes?

"OK, now I want to see a show of hands from any of you who have been up at 5 a.m., when the baby starts crying for a bottle, and stayed up all day taking care of the kid while getting the older kids off to school, then making dinner for the whole family, and finally collapsing into bed at 11 p.m.

"Uh-huh, as I suspected.

"Young female creatures, I don't think any of you know what work really is. You think a working career is tough? Let me tell you about working careers. In most of them, when 5 or 5:30 p.m. rolls around, you lock your desk, turn off the office light, and go over to Harry's Place for a drink.

"But at 5 or 5:30 p.m. a young Barbara Bush, or a young Wanda Kowalski, isn't turning off the office light and ordering a white wine.

"She's probably sitting there with a kid going through the terrible twos, and the kid is saying: 'Why sun go down, mamma?' So she explains. And the kid says, 'Why?' And she explains some more. And the kid says, 'Why?' Ten more times the kid says, 'Why?' Before she's done, she's into the meaning of the universe, and the kid is still asking 'why?'

"Meanwhile, a pot is boiling over, two of the older kids are fighting over which channel to watch, and the dog is barking to go out before he ruins the rug.

"Or it's noon. You, in your real-world career, are going out for a power lunch. What's young Barbara, or Wanda, doing? She's just grabbed a load out of the washer, dumped it into the dryer, and is making a mad dash for the nursery school. Or maybe the pediatrician, because one of the kids has red spots all over the face and a 103 temperature.

"By the way, how many of you are adroit in the use of a rectal thermometer at 3 a.m.? Please hold up your hands. Uh-huh.

"This is an unfair question, I know, because of your ages. But have any of you taken a totally helpless infant and guided it through those important early developmental years, reading to it, playing educational games with it, then getting it through one grade after another of school, making sure it does homework, trying to teach right from wrong, providing decent, humane values, until finally one day you have before you a fully grown, mentally developed, useful, intelligent, and likable human being—your very own creation?

"Do you realize how much mind-boggling, back-breaking, nerve-frazzling, self-depriving, 16-hour days of work this takes, if you are going to do it right? And you don't consider that a career?

"A final question: How many of you consider yourselves able to hit a good tennis backhand?

"Fine. I knew you had accomplished something.

"Well, in conclusion I can only say: the back of my hand to you, too."

MAY 28, 1990

Letters, Calls, Complaints, and Great Thoughts from Readers

JANE BAPTIST, Burlington, Conn.: I am a feminist who objects to your column about Barbara Bush speaking at Wellesley.

If the "career" of wife, mother, and grandmother is so fulfilling, why are you a columnist?

COMMENT: I will have to send you a personal note explaining why I am not a wife, mother, or grandmother. If you wish, I can send photos that will help you understand. But don't show them around.

JAMES Z. HOTCHKISS, North Miami: I have just endured the nauseous experience of reading your heart-rending, tear-jerking, slobbering piece on the maternal sacrifices of Barbara Bush and have come to the dire conclusion that a lobotomy is urgently indicated for you.

Your imaginary speech would have made me nauseated, caused me to retch, faint, and stampede toward the exits had I heard it. Reading it was punishment enough.

COMMENT: Based on your symptoms, I'm wondering if you ate the column instead of reading it.

[Editors' note: Barbara Bush did speak at Wellesley on June 1, despite the protests, and invited Raisa Gorbachev to join her there while their husbands met in Washington. Both women were big hits with the students and both championed the right of women to have careers or be full-time mothers.]

SEPTEMBER 28, 1990

So Much to Hate, and So Little Time

Although the shooting hasn't begun yet, I've been trying to work up a healthy hatred for Iraq. It seems like the patriotic thing to do. And I've always believed that if people go through the bother of killing each other, they shouldn't be impersonal about it. After all, it is a very intimate act.

Although I haven't reached the point of gnashing my teeth at the thought of an Iraqi, I'm sure it will come, because I've had so much experience at this sort of thing.

The first time I developed a patriotic hatred was in 1939, when newsboys came through the neighborhood at night, waving special editions and shouting: "Extra, extra, Germany invades Poland!"

Although I was just a kid, within a couple of years I dutifully hated Germans, Japanese, and Italians. (I didn't hate Italians very long, though, because they surrendered as soon as it was convenient.)

At the same time, I loved and admired the brave Russians and Chinese because they had joined us in hating the evil Germans, Japanese, and Italians.

But as soon as World War II ended, and I could stop hating the evil Germans and Japanese because they weren't evil anymore, I had to start hating the brave Russians and Chinese, because they weren't brave anymore, but had become evil.

While I was adjusting to that, along came the North Koreans. Even though I didn't know a North Korean from a South Korean, or any Korean from a chipmunk, I went along and hated them. The North Koreans.

Not long after that, I discovered that I could still hate some Germans. Not West Germans, because they had become good and even gave us some of their ex-Nazi scientists to help us build rockets. But East Germans had become evil commies and were to be hated.

However, this created some confusion, since Poland, Czechoslovakia, Yugoslavia, and other countries had become commie, too, so I felt a responsibility to hate them. But I was told that they didn't really want to be commies: The Russians made them do it. So I didn't have to hate them as much as I hated the Russians and Chinese.

Then came Cuba. I had never paid much attention to Cuba because I didn't smoke cigars. But when a heroic Fidel Castro overthrew an evil, corrupt regime, I was urged to admire the heroic Castro, which I did, although he looked like he needed a bath. Then, almost overnight, Castro became an evil commie and I had to start hating Cuba. My hatred reached the boiling point when we had the Cuban Missile Crisis. But in recent years, it's been reduced to a simmer.

Naturally, I joined in really hating North Vietnam. And some Cambodians, although I'm still not certain which Cambodians I was supposed to hate. It's possible that in the confusion I was hating Cambodians that I should have been liking, in which case I apologize.

The 1960s may have been one of my hate-peaks, second only to the 1940s. I found myself hating the Russians, Chinese, North Vietnam, and Cuba, while still nursing an intense dislike for North Korea and not thinking highly of Albania. There were a few other countries that I occasionally cursed, but their names slip my mind.

Shortly thereafter, though, President Nixon said I didn't have to hate the Chinese anymore, although I wasn't expected to hug them. And I haven't hated them since, except for that recent month or two when I could again hate them because of the way they kicked around their students. But that seems to have calmed down and President Bush says it's OK not to hate them, so I don't.

In fact, I don't have to hate the Russians, or hardly anyone in Europe, because we've become pals and they're all eager to eat Quarter Pounders with Cheese like decent folk do.

And it couldn't have happened at a better time, because of the need to hate Iraq. I can be vicious, but I have only so much hatred to spread around.

Actually, it isn't that hard to hate Iraq. It's simply a matter of shifting my hatred a few miles. Until recently, I hated Iran and kind of liked Iraq because it was fighting with Iran. But now that it's time to hate Iraq, it's not necessary to hate Iran. Unless Iran cuts a friendly deal with Iraq, in which case I'll have to hate it again. Iran, I mean.

Fortunately, there is less pressure to hate some of the other Arab nations, which I formerly hated because they went in for terrorism. But now they say they hate Iraq, too, which means that I can like them. At least for the time being. Things can change quickly, and I might have to start hating them once more, so I'm not going to like them a lot just in case.

I wonder if there will come a time when there isn't anyone I have to hate. Nah. Not as long as there are New York Mets.

MAY 6, 1992

Bush Needs Liberal Doses of History

Looking back at Selma, Alabama, in 1965, I'm trying to remember how many liberals I saw smashing the heads of peaceful civil rights marchers. I can't remember a single one. The only liberals I saw were attached to the cracked heads.

That was the case at most of the confrontations I saw. Those swinging the clubs or shooting from ambush could probably be described as social conservatives. Those on the receiving end tended to be of the liberal persuasion.

This applied to the politics of that era. Any legislation thought to be beneficial to blacks—voting rights, access to public places, job opportunities—was opposed by most Republicans, especially the far right.

Laws that finally did pass were pushed by gutsy politicians like Senator Paul Douglas, a Democrat from Illinois and an unabashed liberal.

It isn't hard to make the argument that if it had been up to the Republican Party of the 1960s, there would be far fewer black officeholders, school teachers, police officers, firefighters, lawyers, doctors, bank tellers, reporters, business executives, and other members of the black middle-class.

And it isn't hard to make the argument that if it hadn't been for Democrats, especially those who were liberal and progressive, we would have an even worse racial mess in this country than we have today.

So I'm not sure what President Bush is talking about when he blames Democratic policies that began in the 1960s for the riots that erupted in

Los Angeles last month after a jury acquitted four white cops for the beating of black motorist Rodney King.

Is he talking about Operation Head Start? Yes, Democrats pushed that through. The idea was to start educating disadvantaged kids as early as possible.

Pre-school education isn't a radical concept in the suburbs where most of Mr. Bush's friends, relatives, and political associates raised their children. But it wasn't widely available in the slums of Chicago, Detroit, or New York.

The only thing wrong with that program is that it wasn't big enough. But even with limited funding, it was one of the most successful educational programs ever launched in this country. And it would have had even greater impact if it hadn't been opposed by so many of Mr. Bush's political allies.

Is he talking about laws that were intended to prevent discrimination in hiring and promoting? Sure, in some cases the laws were abused. And we've all heard the complaints about reverse discrimination—some valid, some sour grapes.

But I didn't notice Mr. Bush's party putting forth any bright ideas about job opportunity, other than to whine what a hardship it is for businesses if they can't be selective, another way of saying that they want their rights as bigots preserved.

Just who does President Preppie think he is kidding? Since 1968, when Richard Nixon was elected president, the White House has been controlled by the Republicans for all but four years. We've had Nixon, Gerald Ford, Ronald Reagan, and George Bush, with only one term for Jimmy Carter.

If there is anything that the 20 years of Republican presidents shared, it was an indifference, almost a disdain, for big cities—especially those big cities that have large black populations.

High-tech weapons for foreign dictators? There were always a few billion dollars to spare. Subsidies for tobacco farmers? Just ask. Huge contracts for military industries? Stop by anytime, the check is ready. Billions for savings and loan crooks? Just print some more money.

But at the bottom of the list were Chicago's West Side, New York's Bronx, L.A.'s Watts, and the other big, multiracial cities. If all these Republican presidents had an urban policy, it was this: to hell with them; they're Democratic voters anyway.

Now, after decades of indifference and neglect, a Republican president says it's all the fault of Democrats. However, he hides behind a press secretary and doesn't say just what it was that the Democrats did to cause the riots.

If I had to guess, I'd say he is falling back on that old favorite of Republicans such as Vice President Spiro Agnew and President Reagan.

Agnew and Reagan helped create that legendary urban folk-figure, the welfare mother who travels in a Cadillac, wears mink, and fills her shopping cart with lobster, filet mignon, and fine burgundy.

That was the contribution to racial harmony of Agnew, a convicted crook, now sunning his corrupt hide in Palm Springs, and Reagan, the upholder of family values, whose own kids now bum-rap him as an indifferent father. Agnew had the gall to sneer at some woman raising three kids on $300 a month, while he was stuffing his pockets with graft. Reagan did the same while on the mooch from big corporations.

Now President Preppie says it's all the fault of Democratic policies. Tune in tomorrow. He'll probably say he saw Willie Horton looting a shoe store.

SEPTEMBER 1, 1993

'68 Convention-al Wisdom All Wrong

The radio talk-show host said he wanted to do a show about the 25th anniversary of the legendary 1968 Democratic convention.

"The way I see it," he said, "we could talk about the true long-range significance of that convention."

Uh-huh. And that significance—what was it?

"How it led to a new era in American politics—the coming of age politically of the Baby Boomers, the rock generation. People such as myself.

"And it brought together young blacks and whites in the cause of reforming American politics. In that case, it was their united opposition to the Vietnam War.

"We could talk about that. And how it led to the collapse of the Daley Machine and brought on a reform movement."

Because we were talking by phone, he couldn't see the expression on my face, as if I had taken a big bite of lemon.

So I thanked him for his invitation, but I had a commitment that evening and had to decline.

Had I been truthful, I would have said he was a self-important jackass who didn't have a clue about the significance of the 1968 convention.

But he isn't alone. In recent days, there's been much strange babbling about that wild week in Chicago. So let's get a few things straight.

First, what that Democratic convention did was bring about the election of Republican Richard Nixon. And with his election came the Watergate scandal, his resignation, and the interim presidency of the unknown Gerald Ford, which led to the opportunity of the equally unknown Jimmy Carter. And that, in turn, opened the White House door for Ronald Reagan, George Bush, and now Bill Clinton.

So, yes, it was a heck of a significant convention. It altered the course of presidential history for the next 25 years.

If the convention had been orderly and boring, as modern conventions had already become, it's likely that Hubert Humphrey, not Nixon, would have been president.

Nixon won because millions of voters saw cops bashing heads, protesters gagging on tear gas, hippies chanting obscenities, and Democratic delegates shrieking about being prisoners in Richard J. Daley's police state.

And these voters asked themselves: Do I want to trust the White House to people who let a convention become a week-long riot? That's leadership? The answer of many was, hell no.

What makes the whole thing so nutty is how easily it could have been avoided.

People forget that the entire city was not under siege from hundreds of thousands of dangerous hippies, yippies, and dippies.

When the convention was gathering, only a few thousand war protesters were in town. They really weren't sure what they were going to do except make ridiculous threats.

They gathered in Lincoln Park, about eight miles from the convention site—the International Amphitheatre—and three miles from the headquarters hotel.

East of the protesters was Lake Shore Drive and Lake Michigan. If they went that way, they'd be run over by cars or drowned.

Just west waited an army of cops in riot gear. If they got past the cops, which was unlikely, they'd be in the Old Town entertainment area. Fine place for a drink, but not much to demonstrate against.

If they broke through, they'd still be many dangerous miles from the Amphitheatre. Depending on the route they took, many might have been mugging victims.

So they sat in the park, wondering what to do. I later asked one of the leaders what would have happened if the police had just let them sit all night. Maybe bellowing threats into their bullhorns every hour to keep them awake and afraid.

He told me: "We would have sat there waiting for the cops to move in. Then in the morning . . ." He shrugged. "I guess we would have been exhausted and would have gone home to get some sleep. That might have been the end of it."

Instead, police moved in after the park curfew. And the brawl was on. Network TV broadcast that first violence, and it served as a recruiting call. Other angry young war protesters came pouring into Chicago and the game was on.

By week's end, the story of the Democratic convention was not the nomination of Hubert Humphrey, a decent man and well-qualified candidate.

The story was cops battling longhairs on Michigan Avenue. Protesters in trees screaming obscenities. Cops cracking the heads of reporters.

And, of course, Richard J. Daley saying he had defended his city against the invasion of revolutionaries, anarchists, terrorists, maybe assassins. It wasn't true, but what can you say when your police force runs amok?

Now we have the myths:

Myth: The protests led to the end of the Vietnam War. Baloney. The war went on for Americans for five more years until 1973. It might have ended sooner with Humphrey's election.

Myth: It wrecked Daley's reputation and his Machine. Nonsense. Daley was even more popular after the convention because the majority of Chicagoans thought that bashing hippie heads was great sport. The Machine came apart years later, and for other reasons.

Myth: The protest heightened the political conscience of the Baby Boomers. Oh, yeah? Then why were they such strong supporters of Ronald Reagan?

Myth: It brought together young blacks and whites in a common cause. Nope. Few blacks took part in the protests. They figured that if young white suburbanites wanted their heads bashed, that was their choice. The blacks had enough troubles of their own.

But if the now-aging protesters want to boast about something, they can. They helped elect Nixon and shaped the next 25 years of American government.

You want to brag? Be my guest.

FEBRUARY 9, 1994

Time to Be Color-Blind to All Words of Hatred

When he sat down to draw his editorial cartoon, Dennis Renault wanted to make a point. But he didn't know how remarkably successful he would be.

What Renault wanted to say through his drawing was that Nation of Islam Minister Louis Farrakhan was wrong when he said: "You can't be a racist by talking—only by acting."

That's what Farrakhan said in defending the most recent verbal attack on Jews by Khalid Abdul Muhammad, a senior aide.

Renault, who draws for California's *Sacramento Bee*, disagreed with Farrakhan. Most rational people do.

So he wanted to do a cartoon that would make the point that words can be enough to earn you the label of "racist."

And he came up with this idea for his drawing: It showed two loutish members of the Ku Klux Klan looking at a copy of Farrakhan's statement. And one of them says: "That nigger makes a lot of sense."

Had I been his editor, I would have said: "Fine cartoon. It makes the point."

Of course it did. If I pointed at a black person and said, "Look at that nigger," I would expect an angry reaction. Maybe a well-deserved punch in the mouth.

On the other hand, if I was talking to a black person about race relations and I said, "I consider the racist and hostile use of the word 'nigger' offensive and un-American," I wouldn't expect a negative reaction.

Intent. Context. That's how the use of words should be judged. The word "bitch" is appropriate when kennel people are describing a female dog. It's probably borderline acceptable when describing a chronic complainer as someone who does nothing but "bitch, bitch, bitch."

But you don't use that word to describe a female person, to her face or behind her back, although many black rap groups and white heavy-metal bands would disagree. But, then, we can't expect less from slobs.

Or take the word "bastard." I can use that word to describe my boss. And he can toss it back at me. No harm done, really. In fact, I have often used that word to express my sentiments about governors, senators, and—more frequently—tax-erotic presidents. I'm sure they feel the same way about me. And we're probably all reasonably accurate.

But you would not use the word in its original meaning: a child born of parents who are not married. That would be low and cruel.

So let us return to Renault and his cartoon.

It drove people wacky.

His paper was bombarded by protests, outrage, and threats from politicians, clergy, and leaders of civil rights organizations, and even some co-workers.

They demanded that the paper apologize and show remorse. (Some even asked that the paper make a larger financial contribution to black causes, which is a bit tacky.)

What were they angry about?

The word "nigger."

As I said earlier, it was used in a totally satiric, ironic sense. Intent. Context. It isn't the word, it is how the word is used.

The cartoon used it to show that Farrakhan is wrong—the use of words can be racist. Which is why Jews, Catholics, and others who were flailed by Farrakhan's aide were offended by the vile remarks.

But that seemed to go right over the heads of those who were irate about the cartoon. It didn't matter that the cartoonist was sympathetic to black sensitivities and was on their side.

He had used the terrible word. Why he used it and how he used it didn't matter. So they screamed.

And in doing so, they made his point. If he offended them with a cartoon sympathetic to their cause—the fight against bigotry—then what does that say about Farrakhan's chronic Jew-baiting and white-baiting? If one word—used in sympathy to their social causes—could enrage them, then how do they think Catholics or Poles felt about the first Polish pope being described by Farrakhan's chum as "the old, no-good pope, you know, that cracker"?

All Renault did was use a word. Well, what does Farrakhan use? It's possible that Farrakhan is the most adroit, quick-witted speaker in America.

The difference is that Farrakhan uses words in a vicious, belligerent, bigoted way. He baits Jews, he baits Catholics, he baits whites in general. While I admire him for his style, oratorical talents, good looks, and ability to tie a neat bow tie, he is a racist, bigoted, opportunistic louse.

In contrast, Renault used the word "nigger" as part of an attack on bigotry—white and black.

You might expect that he would be applauded by Sacramento's leading blacks.

Instead, they pounced on that one word and used it to justify a lot of silly indignation.

It reminded me of when blacks demanded the banning of Mark Twain, America's greatest writer, because he had a character named Nigger Jim in *Huckleberry Finn*. It didn't matter that Jim was essential to Twain's powerful statement against racism. It was the use of the word "nigger." Poor Twain. He should have had the foresight to describe him as "African-American James."

Confronted by all these threats and demands from Sacramento's black leadership, the *Bee* responded as one would expect of a corporate entity. It folded like a pricked balloon.

Its top exec wrote a profuse page 1 apology.

Its editorial page editor wrote a piece that, while taking Farrakhan to task, wound up on a hand-wringing note about the need for understanding in our society.

Yes, there is the need for understanding.

There also is a need for people to look in their dictionaries for an understanding of the meaning of "satire."

MARCH 25, 1994

Using Short Form? Try Briefs Deduction

With the income-tax deadline only a few weeks off, it's time for you to start thinking about ways to itemize deductions and save a few dollars. And I might be able to help.

First, I must admit that I'm not a tax expert or even a novice. A friend who is an accountant comes over, scoops up the paperwork, feeds the numbers into his computer, and I write a check.

For people smart enough to do it themselves, there are books, computer programs, and columns in financial newspapers and magazines that offer advice.

But I doubt if any of these products will provide the tip I'm going to give you.

Think underwear.

Yes, that simple, humble piece of clothing most of us wear beneath our outer garments could represent a tidy savings on your tax bill.

I first discovered this about eight months ago, when it was disclosed that while governor of Arkansas, Bill Clinton would donate his used shorts to Salvation Army or Goodwill resale shops and take a $4 deduction for each pair.

And it has since been revealed that he gave away long underwear and valued them for tax purposes as $12 per long john. (I don't know if they were with or without back flaps or whether it matters.)

This filled me with admiration for Clinton's financial acumen and regret that my father didn't have the means to send me to Yale Law School so I could become that smart.

Not that I think a Yale education would have led me to the White House, but it would have given me an appreciation for the underlying value of my underwear.

Because I am older than Clinton, I've been paying income taxes a lot longer: since I was 16.

All those years, I bought underwear, wore it, threw it away, bought new underwear, wore it, threw it away.

I can't even guess how many hundreds or thousands of pairs of underwear I have discarded over the decades.

And it pains me to think of all the tax dollars I could have retained. Why, by now I could be retired and taking brisk daily health walks in Florida or Arkansas.

Stupid. You can't see me, but take my word, I am slapping my forehead and saying: "Stupid, stupid, stupid."

But it isn't too late. Not for me or you.

There are 250 million people in this country. Many are infants in diapers, which might not have any tax value, but the majority are adults who own underwear. Most of us live within driving distance of some sort of charitable resale outlet.

So I would guess that at least 150 million Americans have used underwear that they could give away.

How many pairs per person? I don't know. It would depend, I suppose, on how often you change them.

But a conservative guess would be that each person replaces at least five or six pairs a year.

That would be about 900 million pairs of underwear. Almost a billion.

If we use the $4 value that Clinton placed on his underwear, we are now talking about $3.6 billion.

Then there are all those hearty souls in the wintry states of Minnesota, Wisconsin, Michigan, the Dakotas, upstate New York, Illinois, Iowa, Ohio, Pennsylvania, and all through New England.

Think of the millions of pairs of long underwear that are worn in these states. At $12 a long john, we're talking big-time money.

So the potential write-offs for the nation's used underwear would easily exceed $4 billion.

Assuming, of course, that we all place the same value on our used underwear that Clinton placed on his. And why shouldn't we? When he was governor of Arkansas, he put his underwear on the same way the rest of us do—one leg at a time. (Unless he had the state troopers or his friends put them on for him. But I'll leave that to the tabloids to ponder.)

How much money would American taxpayers save with the underwear write-off?

Once again, I can only guess. There are several tax brackets. And rich people probably buy more and fancier underwear, which would give them an even higher estimate of the value.

But we can make a conservative guess and say the average bracket would be about 25 percent.

That means Americans could save $1 billion in taxes from used underwear alone. That's $1 billion in our pockets, instead of in the squandering mitts of Congress and the bureaucrats; $1 billion we could put back into the economy by buying things. Maybe even new underwear, which would eventually become used underwear that we could write off. And think of the jobs that $1 billion would create—especially in the underwear industry.

So look in those dresser drawers at all those used drawers. Think of them as a personal and national asset. Why, that pair of shorts is almost a symbol of patriotism.

However, there could be a slight problem. Most tax experts say that $4 for briefs and $12 for long johns are outrageously inflated deductions.

And a survey I did of Arkansas thrift stores established that used underwear sells for about two-bits or maybe 50 cents.

But who do you want to believe? Some accountant or thrift-store manager? Are they Rhodes scholars and Yale lawyers? Did any of them become president of the United States and vow to revolutionize our economic structure?

Any man brilliant enough to achieve such heights and have such goals sure as heck knew the value of underwear.

So give those skivvies away and write them off.

And if you get audited, it should be no problem. Just tell the tax guy: "Hey, Bill sent me."

MEDIA MUSINGS

HEY, MIKE, WHADDAYA THINK ABOUT . . .

Today's Newspapers?

[T]here's no doubt that today's reporters and young editors are better educated and far more professional than the hell-raisers and brawlers who were around when I accidentally stumbled into this trade. Newsrooms are serious and businesslike. You can't even smoke in most of them. And despite what media-bashers say, today's newspapers are far better than they were 30 or 40 or 50 years ago. They deal with more significant subjects, and they do it more thoroughly and carefully. They are less politically partisan and less likely to slant news one way or another. So if the newspapers are better, the standards higher, and the reporters and editors better educated and more professional, why in the hell are they going around asking public figures if they have ever bopped someone besides their wives?

—*Chicago Tribune,* August 14, 1992

Journalists?

It has been said that journalists have a special public trust. I don't know about that. If we have a public trust, how come the public doesn't trust us?

—*Chicago Tribune,* July 21, 1995

An Exclusive—in Club News

A few weeks ago, reporters were invited to the exclusive Chicago Club to cover a speech by a member of President Nixon's Cabinet.

When they arrived, all but one of the reporters were admitted.

Carol Oppenheim of the *Chicago Tribune* couldn't get past the doorman because she is a woman, and such creatures are not allowed to enter the club.

In its 103-year history, women have entered the club only once. And that was when the members celebrated the 100th anniversary and wives were invited.

The situation embarrassed the speaker, Caspar Weinberger, who is secretary of health, education, and welfare, because his outfit is supposed to be working against sexual discrimination. But even his displeasure wasn't enough to make the club bend its rules.

So he made his speech to the male reporters, while Ms. Oppenheim was left out in the rainy weather on Van Buren Street near Michigan Avenue.

The incident struck me as being silly at the time. I can't think of any reason why women shouldn't be allowed in a place like the Chicago Club. Possibly the members fear that females might fill their heads with erotic thoughts, when they should be discussing high finance.

But I doubt it. I've been in the Chicago Club and most of the members pant only when they have to walk up a flight of stairs.

After Ms. Oppenheim was rebuffed, I waited to read the indignant editorial that I was sure would appear in the *Tribune*.

Newspapers always get angry and bluster editorially when they are denied access to a legitimate story. And they get even angrier when their reporters can't get in while others do.

And there is the matter of sexual discrimination. Even if an editor is a male chauvinist deep in his heart, he can't let these feelings show in his editorials. There are women out there buying the newspaper.

Boy, I thought, wait until the *Trib* gives it to those stuffed shirts at the Chicago Club.

But it didn't happen. The incident passed without even one peep of protest on the editorial page.

That was a surprise. I'm sure that if a politician pulled a stunt like the club did, he would have been peeled like a grape.

And there were so many things that could have been said. If it is wrong to keep people out of clubs because of their religion or race, isn't it also wrong to discriminate for reasons of sex?

Since such clubs are important to a person's business or professional career, is it not wrong to reject people for such arbitrary reasons as religion, race, or sex?

There is also the question of giving a state liquor license to a club that so blatantly discriminates.

And what kind of example are the Chicago Club members—some of the most famous and influential men in Chicago—setting for the rest of us? They are our civic leaders. Are they in favor of discrimination?

I would think an editorial page would enjoy sinking its chops into so juicy a subject.

But not a word appeared.

So I thought I might look into the matter and say a few things myself.

Among the things I came across is the fact that the vice president of the Chicago Club is Frederick A. Nichols.

Mr. Nichols is also the president of Tribune Company.

Hmmmm.

And one of the members of the Chicago Club is Harold F. Grumhaus.

Mr. Grumhaus is publisher of the *Chicago Tribune*.

Hmmmm.

Another member of the Chicago Club is Clayton Kirkpatrick.

He is editor of the *Chicago Tribune*.

Hmmmm. And a tsk, tsk, too.

I'm shocked, shocked, shocked to find that some of our leading journalistic figures are members of such a male chauvinist pig club.

How can they expect other people to talk to their reporters when they won't even let one of their own reporters into their own club?

Fortunately, there is a paper that spoke out on the barring of Ms. Oppenheim.

In strong terms, the *Chicago Sun-Times* told its readers that it didn't approve of such discrimination.

That was very nice. And now I hope that the editorial director of the

Sun-Times, Emmett Dedmon, and the publisher of the *Sun-Times,* Marshall Field, also tell that to the members of the Chicago Club.

They both belong to it, too.

Tsk, tsk.

DECEMBER 28, 1973

Letters, Calls, Complaints, and Great Thoughts from Readers

JAMES NELSON, Chicago: I disagree with your column about private clubs that don't admit women.

Clubs have a perfect right to discriminate. They are social organizations and a person has the right to choose his social acquaintances. You must belong to some kind of club, don't you?

COMMENT: No, I don't. And I have no intention of ever joining a club composed of men who don't want to associate with women. As Willie Hyena, the city's poet laureate, put it:

There once snoozed a club on Boul Mich
That accepted a curvaceous dish.
They gave her a squeeze,
And one of them wheezed:
"Ain't been turned on since Lillian Gish."

APRIL 26, 1981

Come Clean, Post

I'm sure that by now most normal people are bored by the story of the *Washington Post* reporter who faked a story that won a Pulitzer Prize.

By normal people, I mean the 200 million who don't live in Washington, D.C., or work on magazines in New York City.

They're far more concerned with such issues as earning a living, paying the bills, falling in or out of love, keeping their kids off dope, trying to avoid being cheated, robbed, or murdered, planting their crops, hating their boss, and getting through a day without going nuts.

So they have only a limited amount of time to spend pondering the grave, grave questions that the fake Pulitzer story has raised.

You probably know what all these grave, grave questions are because every columnist in Washington has been gravely wringing his hands about them.

Some of them have written that every journalist in America is somehow tainted by this shabby affair.

Nuts. Only the *Washington Post* is tainted by this shabby affair. After all, when Bradlee, Woodward, Bernstein, and the *Post* became national idols because of Watergate, no one said that the rest of us were also national idols. Now that they're bums, they can keep that distinction for themselves, too.

And there's been much written about the credibility of the press being endangered because of the faked story, and how the press must be even more alert to this danger.

More nonsense. The credibility of the press is most often questioned by people who find that their particular prejudice is being punctured. When the press was covering the civil rights movement in the 1960s, it was accurate and responsible. But its "credibility" dropped because many whites just didn't want to read about civil rights, so they said it was a pack of lies.

When the *Post* dug up Watergate, millions of Republicans said press "credibility" was no good because they just didn't want the truth coming out.

People have written to me and said things like: "I've been reading you for years, and I always thought you were a fair, responsible reporter. But ever since you began writing about guns, I realize I am wrong. You are a liar, irresponsible," etc., etc.

In other words, because my views conflict with theirs on one issue, I suddenly have no credibility in anything.

So credibility isn't the issue.

And there is no way the press can say this must not be permitted to happen again. Somewhere there might be a reporter crazy enough to try to fake an entire story. And he or she will be found out and fired. Lawyers are disbarred, doctors lose their licenses, a president is kicked out of office. So who can guarantee that out of thousands of reporters in this country, another one won't get carried away by blind ambition?

But there is one aspect of this fiasco that bothers me. And when a reporter from *Newsweek* magazine called for a comment on the story, it led me to say that any editor involved in approving that faked story should be fired. And not because it turned out to be faked, either. Here's why:

The story was about an eight-year-old boy who was being turned into a heroin addict by the mother's boyfriend.

The reporter told her editor that she actually saw the needle shoved into the boy's arm. But, she said, she couldn't use names because she had promised the mother that everyone would be kept anonymous. Also, the boyfriend had threatened her life if she revealed who he and the others were.

The reporter said she didn't even want to tell any of the editors who the people were.

Her editor and others went along with it. The sensational story was written, approved, went on page 1, and eventually was submitted for, and won, a Pulitzer.

And even when the police commissioner and the mayor demanded the name of the kid, the *Post* refused to tell the reporter to divulge it.

They talked about protecting sources, the role of the press, and all the things editors love to get somber about.

Now, I'll tell you what I would have done if I had been an editor and a young reporter came to me with that same story. I would have said something like this:

"I want the name of the kid now. I want the name of the mother. I want the name of the guy giving the kid heroin.

"We're going to call the cops right now, and we're going to have that sonofabitch put in jail, and we're going to save that kid's life.

"After we do that, then we'll have a story."

And if she refused, I would have told her that she would either give me the information or she'd be fired. And I'd have done it.

They were talking about the life of a child. Or, at least, they thought they were, the editors not knowing that the story was a fake.

How could they sit there and say, yes, we will keep our word to a mother who is letting her child be destroyed? How could they say that we will protect the identity of a man who is slowly murdering a child?

What would the *Post* have done if it had discovered that a congressman knew an eight-year-old child was being murdered, but had given the killer his word that he wouldn't reveal his identity?

I know what the *Post* would have done. It would have demanded that congressman's scalp.

The *Post* and other newspapers love to deplore the covering-up of wrongdoing. At just a hint of a cover-up, they begin baying like beagles.

So what does Mrs. Kay Graham, *Washington Post* CEO, have to say about her editors covering up the slow murder of an eight-year-old child?

C'mon, Kay. Speak up. We might need snappy dialogue for another movie.

JANUARY 29, 1992

Star Gives Public Just What It Wants

A group of scientists has made the amazing discovery that there is a direct relationship between the size of a man's sexual organ and the size of his nose.

For a long time, this was thought to be just folklore or the subject of locker room or barracks jokes.

But now, by using measuring devices on the noses and sexual organs of 15,000 men who volunteered for the study, the scientists have found that . . .

Have you read this far? Sure you did. I can't be certain, but I suspect that the above three paragraphs had a bigger and more intense readership than anything I've ever written.

And not just by guys with big noses.

But don't be embarrassed. It is perfectly normal for you to read on when something is titillating and holds out the promise of being prurient or downright smutty.

However, I must confess with regret that there is no such scientific study. I made it up. Why? Because I wanted to know what it would be like to have 100 percent of the people who begin a column get beyond the third or fourth paragraph.

And the easiest way to do that is to toss off something that has to do with sex.

Of course, if you found the subject of sexual organs so boring or so offensive that you didn't read those paragraphs, you can drop me a note and say so. But that will just prove you read far enough to accept my invitation to drop me a note. So you were interested, you scamp.

So what's my point? (My columns are supposed to make a point, although there are days when I can't find it.)

My point is that we shouldn't be so hard on the *Star*, the unspeakably vile supermarket tabloid that has been trying to dirty up Governor Bill Clinton.

During the last few days, just about every reputable, responsible, thoughtful, and fair columnist in America has condemned the *Star* for its unspeakably vile conduct.

And many have gone on to condemn the so-called mainstream media—broadcast and print—for writing about the *Star*'s unspeakably vile conduct, thus engaging in unspeakably vile conduct themselves.

Of course, by writing about the unspeakably vile conduct of the *Star* and the go-along mainstream media, the columnists are helping pass the vile story on, which means they're engaging in unspeakably vile conduct themselves.

So I guess I am, too. But by now, everyone else has done it, so what's one more unspeakably vile column?

Besides, I'm not going to write about what the cheap floozie said she and Clinton did, or what Clinton said he and the cheap floozie didn't do. I doubt if they did anything that isn't on my cable movie channel. Besides, his wife says she believes him, and in such matters, hers is the only vote that counts.

But it is the reaction to the *Star* that I find interesting. Cheap, sleazy, rotten, beneath contempt. It's been called all that and more.

And you would think that if every paper and TV network ignored the *Star,* the Clinton story would have escaped notice by the American reading public.

Those who believe that must think that the *Star* is some mimeograph sheet put out in somebody's basement.

It isn't. The *Star* is one of the biggest-selling publications in this country, with 3.5 million sales a week. That's close to its sleaze sister, the *National Enquirer,* which sells 3.8 million copies. They're owned by the same company and have a combined circulation of more than 7 million.

That's big-time trash. Only a few newspapers in America sell that many papers in a week. But they have to publish every day to do it.

And while other publishing companies are laying off help, cutting back on their news coverage, and scrambling for ad revenue and circulation, the *Star* and *Enquirer* are prospering. The *Wall Street Journal* just quoted a stock analyst as saying the *"Enquirer/Star* has more upside than any media stock we cover."

What does that tell us? What we already know: In this country, trash sells. Just look at the best-seller lists. Or listen to the hit records. Check out the most successful movies or the freak-show guests on the most popular TV talk shows.

So is the *Star* to be condemned for giving 3.5 million Americans the trash they crave? (More with the famous Clinton issue; the *Star* says it sold an extra 500,000 copies. Who says Americans aren't interested in politics?)

We're a society with an appetite for trash. While fine small magazines struggle to survive, honorable newspapers fold, good books end up in the wholesale bin, and thoughtful TV shows get a .0001 rating, we gorge on sex and blood in movies, transom-peeking on TV, and tell-all scandals in books and magazines.

Then, after indulging our taste for the unspeakably vile in one form or another, we sit back and cluck about how terrible it is and what this country is coming to. And the line forms down the block for an autograph from some aging bimbo who is selling a book about how many stars she bedded.

In the 19th century, Marshall Field launched Chicago's most successful department store with the motto: "Give the lady what she wants."

It may peddle sleaze, but the *Star* knows as much about today's buying public as Marshall Field did about that of his day.

And looking at those circulation figures, I have to wonder—just what is mainstream journalism?

APRIL 7, 1993

Rodney King and a Double Standard

Let's have a brief current events quiz. It's simple. Tell me who the following people are:

1. Rodney King
2. Barbara Meller Jensen

Your time is up. I can probably guess your score. Fifty percent.

You know who Rodney King is because he has become world famous as the videotaped victim of police brutality.

But you don't know who Barbara Meller Jensen is, correct?

That's understandable. Mrs. Jensen has been in the news only a tiny fraction of the time that Rodney King has.

Yet, she is a victim of a crime far more horrifying than the one allegedly committed against Rodney King.

Mrs. Jensen, 39, a citizen of Germany, recently flew to Miami with her mother and two children.

They picked up a rental car at the airport and set off for their hotel.

But she made a traffic mistake, lost her direction, became confused, and left the highway.

This put her in the ironically named Liberty City, a low-income, high-crime area.

Her car was bumped from behind. She stopped and got out to check for damage.

The men who bumped her got out, beat her, took her purse, then ran her over with their car and killed her.

It was a crime so despicable that it almost defies description.

Yet, Mrs. Jensen is already yesterday's news. Within 48 hours, her cruel death was no longer the story. Instead, the news focus was on whether the German consul general in Miami would urge his fellow countrymen to stay away from Florida, thus damaging the tourist trade. From life and death to dollars and cents.

At the same time, the trial of the policemen accused of depriving Rodney King of his civil rights was still getting prime coverage in the news media.

Why the difference in emphasis? Because in the minds of those who run the news business, the Rodney King beating has social significance.

It is about Rodney King, symbolic of a black man beaten by white cops. It is about oppression, victimization, economic and social deprivation, legal discrimination, and any other ". . . ion" you want to toss in.

But Mrs. Jensen? She's just a tourist who happened to be in the wrong place at the wrong time. What else is new?

So Mrs. Jensen will quickly fade from sight, since her death is of little social significance. But Rodney King will remain a presence. Will the jury's verdict bring us new rioting and looting? If so, will the president and the Congress of the United States respond to the rioting and looting with new social programs for the socially disadvantaged rioters and looters?

And other such curbstone sociology.

If I may part company with the mainstream of American journalistic thought, Mrs. Jensen's murder is every bit as significant as the beating of Rodney King.

First: Rodney King is alive. Not only alive, but he will become a millionaire when his suits against the City of Los Angeles are settled or tried.

Mrs. Jensen is dead. Her husband, children, and other family members and friends will never see her again. And there is nobody for them to sue for this catastrophic loss.

Second: Despite his troubles, Rodney King is a lucky guy. He is a criminal by trade, having served time for armed robbery. He was beaten after driving drunk and being chased at dangerously high speeds, putting innocent motorists at risk. He was a social menace.

In contrast, Mrs. Jensen was a law-abiding, useful person: a therapist for handicapped children. She had gone to Florida because her husband, a biologist, needed solitude to complete a book. She wasn't a threat to anyone.

Third: Those L.A. cops are on trial because the government believes the beating was a racist act. Maybe they're right. White cops have never been known for their liberal views.

But is anyone going to say, with a straight face, that race was not a factor in Mrs. Jensen's murder? Would those black thugs have rammed a car driven by Rodney King? Of course not. They saw a white family in a helpless situation. And they turned what should have been a routine robbery into an unspeakably cruel murder. Was Mrs. Jensen's skin color a factor? Could race hatred be why they mauled her after they had her money? "Black rage," as the rap stars put it. If so, doesn't that make it a racial crime?

I think it was. If white cops beating up Rodney King was a racial crime, then why not black thugs turning a simple robbery into a pointlessly brutal murder?

And if people like Mrs. Jensen are being murdered because of their skin color, isn't that socially significant? Or is it necessary for vote-hustling politicians to make that decision?

Something really strange has happened to our sense of right and wrong. People like Mrs. Jensen are murdered, and we view it as something socially predictable—the result of social injustice, black rage, etc.

How about plain, simple, mindless, brutal murder? Is anyone in this country so deprived, so hungry, so maladjusted, that his condition justifies beating and running over an innocent woman? What's next—maybe a plea of justifiable homicide for cannibalism?

As you may have gathered, I'm a little tired of the hand-wringing and soul-searching over Rodney King and the prospect of rioting in Los Angeles.

There are more Mrs. Jensens being murdered in cold blood by urban predators than there are Rodney Kings being abused by cops. But you wouldn't know it, the way the two stories are treated.

Next week, we will have Rodney King: The Verdict.

There will be no riots for Mrs. Jensen. Only a tombstone.

That's the luck of the videotape. And the social conscience of a socially numb society.

JUNE 8, 1994

Second Thought on That Invite: Oh, Forget It

The morning stress began with a call from a woman expressing outrage at what she called "the most arrogant piece of journalistic tripe I have ever read."

"I cannot believe you could write anything this stupid," she said.

Well, if it is on page 3 with my lopped-head picture, the stupidity must be mine.

"You should be ashamed of yourself," she said. "The president of the United States invites you to dinner, and you treat it as a joke.

"Don't you realize what an honor that invitation is? The average American would be thrilled just to shake a president's hand. You are typical of today's media arrogance. Shame on you."

It was an impressive tirade, and I thanked her and said I would reread what I had written and reconsider my arrogant position.

Which I have done. And now I realize that she has a point. The fault was mine for not having explained more clearly why I turned down a dinner invitation at the White House.

Stated as simply as possible: Politicians are enormously charming.

I've been talking to, reporting on, and writing about politicians for almost 40 years.

And I have to admit, I have never met a politician I didn't like.

That might sound odd, coming from someone who has made a cottage industry out of bashing politicians.

But it's true. From Chicago aldermen—the lowest of the political food chain—on up to presidents and ex-presidents, I've pummeled them: Democrats, Republicans, liberals, conservatives, independents, the brilliant, and the harebrained.

And I have yet to meet a politician who didn't have some redeeming qualities.

I like politicians because they put it on the line. In a society of salesmen and pitchmen, they are the ultimate hustlers. To succeed, they need approval of 50.01 percent of the customers. That is one tough sales rate.

They do it with charm. In my lifetime, FDR had it in excess. Truman in a spunky way. Ike, the hero, by being bigger than life. Kennedy was the ultimate youth-vigor symbol. Nixon because he was Everyman, the mope who somehow makes it. Carter because he was so decent. Reagan, who had it all. And Clinton . . . Clinton?

I don't doubt that Clinton has a brilliant mind and that his wife exceeds him. You don't get to be president of the United States unless you are smarter than about 99 percent of the people who voted for or against you.

And you don't get to be president, governor, mayor, senator, congressman, or even a schnook alderman in Chicago unless you can ooze charm and shake a hand as though you love the other end of that appendage.

So that's the main reason I declined the invitation to dine at the White House.

There is no doubt that if I spent the evening with Bill and Hillary, they would charm me out of my shoes. And I would be inhibited every time I decided to write something mean about them. And if I can't be mean, what the heck good am I?

Journalists are human. At least some of us older ones. So if I sit down for dinner with a president, I feel like an "in-person." I am no longer some guy who grew up along Milwaukee Avenue. I am a VIP, big heat, or why else would a prez invite me to chow down at the White House?

Which is ridiculous. If I was my friend Big John, an expert on the printing industry and many other things, or my friend Danny, who went from laying bricks to running his own construction company, I wouldn't be invited to the White House.

I was invited because by dumb luck, an editor's folly, and my willingness to work cheap, I ended up writing a newspaper column.

And that is why President Clinton or one of his flunkies decided to invite me to dine in that great transient home in our capital. It ain't me, it's my job.

But if I went, I would be charmed. Hillary would smile and I would melt. Bill would give me that stiff lower-lip grin and I would be saluting.

That's why I have had my own rule of journalistic ethics: Don't get chummy with pols because you will like them, and when that happens, you can't beat them up.

It's why my favorite politician was the late Richard J. Daley, mayor of Chicago from 1955 until his death in 1976. He was the last of America's great municipal politicians.

I wrote countless columns and a best-selling book about him. But any time he was asked about something I wrote, he would put on a stone face and say: "Who's he?"

That was his way of saying that he didn't care what some goof with a typewriter wrote. He had the votes, and that's what counted. I admired him for it then, and I do so even more today.

So as much as I like politicians, I keep my distance. It's the only way I can keep whatever scruffy integrity I have.

And any politician who feels the same way—and many do—has my respect. I wouldn't have me over for dinner, either.

MAY 21, 1996

Will "Gotcha" Crowd Go After Questions in Admiral's Death?

Admiral Jeremy Boorda killed himself with a bullet to the chest, and there is little mystery as to why he did it.

The Navy's top man knew it was likely he would soon end his remarkable career in embarrassment, shame, or even disgrace.

The reason: Until a year ago, he had worn two tiny ribbons on his chest that indicated he had been in combat in Vietnam.

Military experts now differ as to whether he was entitled to wear these ribbons. Some say "no" because he had not been directly involved in combat. Others say "yes" because he served on ships that were in the combat zone. And others say "maybe."

But the admiral knew that the matter was being pursued by a major news organization—*Newsweek* magazine—with nudging from a small news agency known as the National Security News Service, which specializes in military matters.

Which meant that Admiral Boorda, 56, was almost certain to be on the media hot seat, and his reputation would be tarnished, if not destroyed, by "gotcha" journalism.

So he went home, wrote farewell letters to his family and the Navy, and put a bullet where he once wore those ribbons.

A simple story with few unanswered questions, right?

No, wrong. There are many fascinating questions that have yet to be answered. And I hope that some of the thousands of Washington-based journalists will hotfoot after the answers.

It's a safe guess that someone wanted to stick it to Admiral Boorda. Maybe those who had an ax to grind, jealous colleagues, or someone with a grudge.

It took someone with more than a fleeting interest in Admiral Boorda's chest ornaments to have blown the whistle to these news organizations. The questions are who and why.

It could have been some of the Navy's many elite Annapolis grads, some of whom are said to have resented the amazing success of a 16-year-old high school dropout who lied about his age to join the Navy and rise from the enlisted ranks to four stars and the top job.

That person should really step forward. After all, it isn't just every day you set out to destroy the career of a remarkable man and end up driving him to suicide. Take a bow.

There also are questions that should be answered by *Newsweek* and the tiny National Security News Service.

Such as: Why were they pursuing the business of the ribbons?

Almost a year ago, the National Security News Service began asking the Navy questions about whether the admiral should be wearing them.

So the admiral took them off and kept them off. It isn't known whether he thought he knowingly or unwittingly had done something wrong or if he simply wanted to avert a conflict with the press.

And that might have been the end of it, as the admiral surely hoped it would be.

But, no. Like an itch that has to be scratched, a nasty little news nugget about a prominent person has to be made public. That's one of the rules of modern "gotcha" journalism: If you got it, baby, use it.

So *Newsweek* got the dirt from the tiny military news service and set up an interview with the admiral. They told the Navy that they wanted to ask him to explain the two tiny ribbons he no longer wore.

Instead of explaining, he killed himself.

In its latest issue, *Newsweek*'s media writer does an oily piece, raising the usual soul-searching clichés about journalism's handling of stories involving public figures, but basically taking *Newsweek* off the hook.

He points out that *Newsweek* had not yet done the interview, so it had not yet decided if it would write about the ribbons.

Of course, he also admits that the magazine's Washington bureau chief saw it as "a big story."

Sure he did. Washington is a journalistic jungle with a limited food supply. So while the story might not have caused more than a shrug out here, in Washington it was red meat.

Imagine the headlines, if not in *Newsweek* then in the many other publications that would have leaped on the story: "Top Admiral Wore Fake Hero Medals."

It wouldn't have mattered what Admiral Boorda said, so long as *Newsweek* and other media outlets could find those who would say he wasn't entitled. And the little military news service could provide all sorts of eager finger pointers.

So Admiral Boorda had to realize that he was already dead meat. If *Newsweek* didn't do the story, which is unlikely, the eager little news service would have peddled it elsewhere—the networks, the big papers, other magazines—and in time found a taker.

It was too juicy a story for today's "gotcha" journalists to resist: A man of prominence and achievement—ah, but with a hidden and embarrassing secret and flaw.

Gotcha, admiral, gotcha.

And it would be justified by that most lofty of journalistic trusts—fulfilling the public's "right to know." But did Americans really yearn to know about the admiral's ribbons?

Some good did come out of this for Admiral Boorda. Until last week, most Americans had never heard of him.

Now they know he was one heck of a good guy.

Fine job.

NOVEMBER 7, 1996

If Media Say It's Over, Why Should Voters Play Around?

During a break in the action on Election Day, Dan Rather announced on the CBS evening news that fewer than half of the nation's eligible voters would cast ballots. And he declared that the low turnout was "a national disgrace."

That's the traditionally stern position many media people take whenever great numbers of Americans choose to exercise their precious right NOT to vote.

Commentators on the air and in print love to slip into their civics-teacher mode and lecture listeners and readers on why it is essential to take part in the democratic process.

Not me. I'm proud that in more than 30 years at this job I have never once urged people to vote or chided them for failing to do so.

My belief is that someone who must be nagged into voting hasn't been paying attention and doesn't have any idea what the issues are or what the candidates will or won't be trusted to do. In other words, a civic klutz.

So why is it important to the future of this nation for a klutz, or millions of klutzes, to go punch holes in a ballot?

Think about that. If you are the kind of thoughtful, involved person who really studies the issues and the candidates, do you want your vote canceled out by some klutz who doesn't even bother to say eenie, meenie, miney, mo?

But what bothered me most about Rather's "national disgrace" remark was that he didn't bother to explain why so many Americans decided to sit this one out.

If he had, he would have been required to say: "It is a national disgrace—and media creatures like me must bear a big part of the blame."

It's true that this election featured two presidential candidates who didn't exactly remind anyone of Dwight Eisenhower and Adlai Stevenson or even John Kennedy and Richard Nixon.

But how can Rather expect people to flock to the voting booths when for months they have been bombarded with pollsters and pundits telling them: "Forget it. Dole is dead in the water. Clinton has an insurmountable lead."

Hardly a day passed without some network or big newspaper or news magazine coming out with a new set of numbers showing that Bob Dole was like a movie character in swampy quicksand with only his hand showing above the muck.

So after the news industry beats people over the head with one message—it's all over but the funeral—how can the media then tell these same people that it is their civic duty to show up as pallbearers?

America is a nation of sports addicts. And what makes any sports event exciting is not knowing how it will turn out, the genuine possibility of an upset, the outcome being in doubt until the final whistle or the last-second pitch, serve, putt, bell, or swing of the bat.

Consider the Chicago Bulls, who, at their best, appear almost invincible.

When the Bulls play the Toronto Raptors, a feeble crew, the stadium is still packed and the TV ratings are high, despite the fans knowing that the game will almost surely be a blowout and that a perfunctory last quarter will be mopped up by bench players instead of Michael Jordan, Scottie Pippen, and Dennis Rodman.

Fans turn out or tune in for so predictable a game because they get to see Jordan and the other great stars perform.

But what if the Bulls played every game of the long season against the Raptors? What if fans picked up a paper the morning of every game and read: "The only question is whether the Bulls will be bored and win by 20 points or make an effort and give us a 30- or 40-point blowout?"

Even Jordan might not show up. And Rodman might call in to say that he had a bad-hair day.

That, in effect, is what America's punditry did in this campaign. It became a daily competition to see which paper, network, or blabbermouth could bury Dole the earliest or the deepest.

Almost since the first primary, we've been told that he is too old, too vague or wobbly in his message, too lacking in vision, and too this, that, and everything else to make it a genuine contest.

And there were the polls, the laziest, dumbest, cheapest form of journalism. You hire some pollster to bounce a few questions off a few hundred people and you headline these few hundred opinions as big news.

Then the pundits and other deep thinkers of the media see the poll results and say: "Ah, the poor sap doesn't have a prayer."

Of course, when you take polls months before the campaigns actually get going and people aren't paying much attention, it's unlikely that you'll get meaningful answers.

And if for months you keep telling people: "Oh my, this is so dull, so lopsided, so pathetic, we barely have anything to jabber at you about," you can't very well turn around on Election Day and say: "See here, Citizen Mope, while we may have told you that this was dull, lopsided, and a sure thing, that is no excuse for you to fail to take it all seriously.

"If you don't vote, you are a national disgrace. And I am a pompous ass."

HERE'S LOOKING
AT ME, KID

Tchaikovsky's "1812 Overture"?

I like it. It's wonderfully noisy, and it has cannons and bells and when I play it loud, my stereo woofers have convulsions and my tweeters go berserk; my cats run up the drapes, my dogs howl and foam at the mouth, and nails pop out of the walls of my house. It is my kind of classical music.

—*Chicago Sun-Times,* June 28, 1979

Casino Gambling?

I love gambling casinos. It's as simple as that. I want to put on a midnight blue suit, a silk shirt, a white-on-white tie, dark sunglasses, and with a thin Italian cigar between my teeth, I want to walk cat-like into a casino and let my cool gaze pass slowly over the thickly carpeted gaming room before sitting down at the baccarat table, placing my silver lighter next to my gold cigaret case, ordering a bottle of champagne, nodding to the croupier, and saying to Sinatra and Martin and Jimmy the Greek: "Thank you for waiting; deal the cards."

—*Chicago Sun-Times,* September 13, 1979

Wearing Jeans?

I'm aware that some men wear jeans into their middle years. But I assume that they are making a personal statement. The only statement I make with clothing is that I am not naked.

—*Chicago Tribune,* June 21, 1995

Riverview Park: A Coward's Tale

It was the red badge of courage, the moment of truth. It was put up or shut up.

There could be no conscientious objection—no draft card burning—when you faced the Parachute in Riverview Park.

This was it. You had what it took or you didn't.

And for those who didn't, the chance is gone forever. They will have to live with the knowledge that they couldn't do it.

Oh, you can say: "But I rode the Bobs, and the Bobs was really something."

I once rode the Bobs eight times without getting off.

Sure, it was rough, that first dip, and it took extraordinary courage.

But it wasn't the Parachute. You couldn't see it from miles away. It didn't rise into the sky, warning you that soon you must look deep into your soul to see what, if anything, was there.

I'd start thinking about the Parachute even before I left the neighborhood. That's a lie. I thought about it the night before. Sometimes I'd pace the floor. That's what got me smoking at the age of 12.

When we walked through the front gate, I'd try to stall. One of my tricks was to ride every ride. Sometimes, if I had the money, I'd ride them twice, or more.

I was the only kid in the neighborhood who rode the Tunnel of Love seven times straight—alone.

One time I stayed in the freak house so long that Slats Grobnik told everybody I had a crush on the reptile girl.

There used to be a thing called "The African Dip." You threw balls and if you hit the target a Negro fell from his perch into water. They got rid of the thing when Negroes learned how to throw things back. But to delay the Parachute confrontation, I once knocked the same guy into the water 23 times. The effect of that on my youthful conscience contributed to my liberal tendencies, I'm sure.

My Parachute fears caused me to have my weight guessed by the same man four times. And he was right the first time.

Actually, that's the reason I stayed on the Bobs for eight straight rides. If Slats Grobnik hadn't got sick to his stomach, I'd still be on the Bobs, trying to duck the Parachute.

Then, finally, I'd be standing there. They would have dragged me away from the monkey races, off the merry-go-round, out of the Flying Turns. I'd ride the Shoot the Chutes so often that my clothes would be soaked.

And there it would be—14 miles high, the top of it up in the clouds. My mouth would hang open, my eyes would pop, and the only thing that would keep me from running was a temporary paralysis of the body.

But my nimble mind would be working.

ME: "I'm out of money."

SLATS: "I'll borrow you some."

ME: "I can't never pay you back."

SLATS: "I don't care."

ME: "I hear that thing is ready to keel over."

CHESTER: "No it ain't."

ME: "My foot hurts."

NORBERT: "You're chicken."

ME: "I rode that thing before with some other guys."

BIG RED: "Then you can ride it now with us."

ME: "No."

ALL: "You're chicken."

ME: Silence.

After that, even the darkness of Aladdin's Castle wasn't enough to hide the mocking smiles. Even looking bored on the Silver Streak couldn't remove the stain of cowardice.

On the way home, I'd be last on the crowded streetcar so I could stand on the platform step, dangling by one arm and a leg, hoping to regain some face.

Much later, I discovered the secret of riding the Parachute: Go there with a girl.

A boy has to suggest the Parachute to prove he is a dashing fellow. A girl has to say yes to prove she is a good sport. I'm told they still have this sort of arrangement, except now it is sex instead of the Parachute.

So I went there with a girl. We went to the Parachute. I bought two tickets. We got in line and waited. I looked cool. Our turn finally came and we walked toward the empty, dangling seats.

Then she screamed and screamed.

I can't really blame her for screaming, what with me falling over in a dead faint even before we got on!

So that's as close as I came. I've been back almost every summer to give it another try. But something always comes up. I run out of money, I have a sore foot, I'm chicken.

And now Riverview Park is being closed forever. The Parachute will be gone, along with the old ladies who were experts at spotting counterfeit money and shortchanging people, the Bobs, the dumpy old beer garden, and the rest.

Now I won't get another chance. But I know down deep that I would have made it.

It was just a matter of getting into the right frame of mind. I'm positive it would have been next summer.

I wish I could have another chance.

MARCH 21, 1969

How to Beat an Aching Back

When it comes to pain and suffering, I can endure as much as the next sissy.

There was the time I got hurt, but refused to go to the hospital until I had written my column. Later, when the doctor brought the X-rays into the room, he said:

"You were lucky. Your little finger is sprained, not broken."

Sometimes I choose the more painful way. It keeps a person tough. For instance, the last time I sat down in the dentist's chair, I said:

"No gas or Novocaine this time, doc. I can take it. So go ahead and clean 'em."

But some things are almost too much for even this body—a body that was once known all along the North Avenue Beach as "The Rib."

A few days ago, I wrenched my lower back.

At first the pain wasn't too bad and I got around OK except when the copy boys jiggled my stretcher.

But that night, after 45 minutes in rush-hour traffic, I pulled into the driveway and found that my body was virtually locked in the driving position.

The slightest movement was painful. And getting out of the car would be much worse. But I didn't panic. I just sat there for awhile, whimpering.

Finally, I had to decide: Move slowly, try for less intense pain but over a longer period, or move fast and take a real jolt all at once.

It's something like removing a bandage: Some people yank it off, others peel slowly.

Actually, with bandages I've always taken another approach. I remember going down for my first draft physical and the doctor asking me why I had a bandage on my knee.

"I skinned it," I told him.

"When?" he asked.

"In fourth grade."

So I considered just sitting there several days until my back was mended. But I ruled it out. Someone might have mistaken me for a Chicago street department foreman.

There was no easy way out. The human spine isn't designed, even when healthy, to be the center of weight for a large mass spinning out of a bucket seat.

Finally, I opened the door and let myself go limp, tumbling sideways onto the grass along my driveway.

Two people screamed. I recognized one voice as being mine. The other belonged to a woman who happened to be walking by with her dog.

Apparently she had never seen anyone get out of a car that way.

She stood and stared while I moaned and rolled over onto my chest.

That shows how city life is changing. In my old neighborhood, you didn't just stand there if someone fell out of a parked car. You did something.

If it was your father, you ran and told your mother that he had finally made it home. If it wasn't your father, you went for his wallet.

"Is something wrong?" she finally asked.

"Back!" I mumbled.

She apparently took this for a belligerent command to "get back," because she retreated, saying, "Well!"

With a sprained back, the best way to walk is on all fours. It is probably the best way to walk under any conditions. How many goats or dogs have aching backs?

That is how I crossed the front lawn, trying to look as casual as was possible.

A group of teenagers walked by, and one could not resist showing his wit by giggling: "Lose something, mister?"

"No," I said, "but a teenager did, and I'm trying to find it. His brain fell out of his ear."

At the front steps, it got even tougher because I had to try to stand erect.

A monkey-like crouch was all I could manage. A moan must have escaped my lips, because all over the neighborhood dogs began barking.

Moaning is said to be beneficial because it relieves pain tensions. But swearing is even better, so I swore all the way up the steps. I recall hearing a voice across the street say: "Same to you, fella."

But I made it. And now I tell this story because it shows how indomitable the human spirit can be.

Also, that woman deserves some kind of explanation.

JUNE 2, 1969

Who Actually Creates Gaps?

A student berated me recently for the failure of my generation to stamp out war, poverty, injustice, and prejudice.

He said we were do-nothings when we were his age. And because of us, his generation now had so much evil-curing to do.

I couldn't think of any excuses, so I just mumbled that I'd been busy and couldn't get around to everything.

But the truth is, I had never given any thought to being part of a particular generation, so I couldn't say much about its accomplishments.

That's a mistake. We must speak up for our own generations. With all the generation gaps that exist, we need clearly defined generations to fit around them.

So from now on, I'm going to be ready to defend my generation.

Unfortunately, I'm not sure what to say about it. There aren't many generations that were less exciting. I'm not even sure of its name.

It's the group that was born just before and after the Great Depression began. People who are part of it are now saying: "Forty? The prime of life."

If any generation had an inferiority complex, mine did.

For one thing, it was really small. Today's young generation is enormous because everybody wanted babies after World War II, and just about everybody had them.

Half the kids born in my generation were "accidents." That's a hearty welcome for you.

A Depression childhood left its mark. Maybe we were too young to have to scratch for a living, but everyone we knew did.

That's why we have different economic attitudes than the young generation.

They spend money foolishly and they enjoy doing it.

We spend money foolishly, too, and we enjoy doing it. But then our stomachs hurt.

Then came World War II, and everybody had a brother, uncle, or father in it. But as adolescents, we did nothing but collect old fat, old papers, and old tires, and give dirty looks to neighborhood 4-Fs.

A few years later, our war came along. And those of us who took part were pioneers. It was the first time our country took half a loaf.

But were we viewed as victims or martyrs? No. We were hailed as losers. Coming back from Korea, and expecting people to be interested, was about like coming back from a Wisconsin vacation with color slides.

Many members of my generation are still haunted by the question of why we didn't rebel against our dirty little war, why we didn't march in the streets, burn draft cards, and all that. It was just as bad a war.

The question doesn't haunt me. I know why we didn't.

By then, the country was firmly in the hands of those who had scraped through a depression and won a popular war.

Actually, they are still running things. But today's young protesters are their children and they have become tolerant and understanding.

My generation wasn't their children. We were their young brothers, maybe, or their nephews. I think they would have punched us in the mouth. Besides, we were outnumbered. We were always outnumbered. Even in politics.

Today's young generation has had several political leaders they could follow, beginning with John F. Kennedy, and followed by his brother and Senators McCarthy, Muskie, and McGovern.

We, too, had a forward-thinking, exciting, charismatic political figure. The trouble was, Adlai Stevenson kept losing.

Today's generation has even had its political villain in President Johnson. It could stand in Chicago's Grant Park and chant an obscenity: "[beep-beep] LBJ," and feel good about it.

We had only Ike, and it was inconceivable that anyone could chant "[beep-beep]" at Ike. We would have chewed on soap.

And so we slid comfortably into something resembling maturity, without doing a thing. At least, that is what the young student radical told me.

But you have to wonder where some of today's righteous movements would be without a few members of my generation—such as Martin Luther King Jr., Robert F. Kennedy, Malcolm X, and Lenny Bruce, all heroes to today's generation.

In fact, it makes you wonder exactly who is creating the gaps.

FEBRUARY 8, 1972
Acute Crisis in Identity

The "identity crisis" has become a common ailment in our society. People wonder who they really are. Sometimes they have to go off and find themselves.

This occurs most often among young people. When it happens, they sing sad songs about it, or renounce their parents' central air conditioning, smoke strange things, put flowers in their hair, eat an organically grown peanut, or assume the lotus position.

It happens to adults, too, although not as often.

Grown women seldom have an identity crisis while raising small children. When a woman has diapers to change, she knows who she is: She is the person who changes diapers.

But when the children get older and go to school, she isn't sure anymore. So she might go back to college and study philosophy, great literature, or ceramics. Or she might get involved in Women's Lib, which can make her even more confused.

For a man, it is simpler. His identity crisis might hit him at about 7:45 a.m. while stuck on an expressway with the sun in his left eye. Then he might think: "Why am I here? Why was I here yesterday? Will I be here tomorrow?" In most cases, the man manages to change lanes, and he feels better.

But if it becomes acute, he could clean out the joint savings account and go off to find himself, maybe to Las Vegas and in the arms of a painted woman.

Until recently, my knowledge of the identity crisis came from reading advice columnists and other scientific journals, and from talking to my 17-year-old nephew, who is a guru and is into a diet of organically grown guitar picks.

As for myself, I never had an identity crisis. I have always known who I am, which, while deeply depressing, saved me a lot of running around looking for me.

But now it has happened to me. I have had my identity crisis. It came about in a strange way.

Hoping to be one of the American journalists accompanying President Nixon to China, I decided to get a passport.

The State Department said I would need a birth certificate to get a passport. It is a rule.

I didn't have one and did not remember ever seeing it. Few occasions arise in which you must have written proof that you were born.

So I went to the office of Cook County Clerk Edward J. Barrett, where all Chicago births are kept on file. I made out the form and paid the man $2.

In a few minutes, he had gone through the files, found the old document, and handed me a Xeroxed copy.

As I read it, my identity crisis exploded.

Almost everything on the document was correct. The hospital, the date, the parents.

But it said my name was Mitchell.

Not Michael. Not Mike. Not any of the names I have been known by—Goofy, Stop Thief, Hey You, Creep, Obnoxious—but Mitchell.

I went back to the counter and pointed to the name and asked the clerk: "What does this mean?"

He said: "Is this your birth certificate?"

"Yes."

He studied it a moment, then said: "It means your first name is Mitchell."

I said: "But nobody has ever called me Mitchell."

He nodded. "I suppose they call you Mitch."

My head swam. At least it swam faster than it usually swims.

How could my name have been Mitchell all of these years without my knowing it? And if it was Mitchell, why have I always thought it was Michael?

Several ideas came to me. Maybe the real Mitchell Royko had been misplaced by a nurse. And somebody named Michael put in his crib by mistake. You hear about hospitals doing such things. If that had happened, who was I? And where was he?

I pondered this awhile, then concluded that it made no sense.

Then it occurred to me that maybe twins had been born—one named Mike and one named Mitch. But I would have noticed him as we grew up. We had a small flat.

Whatever the explanation was, one thing was perfectly clear: I wasn't me. According to the office of Edward J. Barrett, county clerk, I was somebody named Mitchell. But I could not be Mitchell, since my name is Michael on my Playboy Club key. Yet, there was no record of the birth of Michael, so I wasn't either Michael or Mitchell.

Then, who was I?

I began feeling like a teenager.

Despite the panic, I saw obvious benefits in having a new name. I could put an ad in the personals: "Responsible for my own debts only and not that other guy's. Mitchell Royko." Then off to Las Vegas.

But that would not clear up the mystery and ease my identity crisis. So I went to older relatives and asked them if they remembered anything strange about my birth.

"Only you," one of them said.

But there was something. A relative remembered it, and I'm convinced it is the answer.

"The doctor was called to St. Mary's Hospital from a wedding on Milwaukee Avenue," he said. "So he walked funny.

"I think when he slapped you, like they slap newborn babies to make them breathe, he might have slapped you in the head."

That explains many things, but not the name.

"Yes, but afterwards the doctor and your father went over to a place on North Avenue to have a couple of drinks."

To celebrate?

"There are other reasons to drink. And after they had a few, the doctor wasn't thinking too clearly, and he didn't know much English anyway, so he probably wrote in the wrong first name."

I'm satisfied that is the explanation, undramatic as it may be.

If the doctor had to make a mistake, though, I wish it had been in the date. A change in one figure, and I could be 19—officially. But then I'd just brood about why a young kid like me has got falling hair.

DECEMBER 20, 1976

That Old, Gray Area

It can be infuriating the way minor government officials take their power and flaunt it.

For example, my driver's license expired, so the other day I went to the Illinois secretary of state's office on Elston Avenue to get renewed.

A little lady behind the counter was filling out the application form. Height . . . weight . . .

"Color of eyes?" she asked.

"Brown."

"Color of hair?"

"Brown."

She glanced at my head. "Brown?"

"Uh-huh. Brown. I've always had brown hair."

She looked dubious and said: "I'd say it is, uh, gray."

"Well, in this light, I suppose there's a little gray mixed in with the brown."

She squinted her eyes, studied my head more intensely, and said:

"No, it's mostly gray."

"On the sides, yes. I'm probably getting a little gray along the sideburns."

"Sir, you don't have much hair anywhere but on the sides."

"Look," I said, "what's the big deal? This is just a form."

"I know, sir, but we're supposed to try to get it right. For identification purposes. So I'll put down . . ."

"How about grayish brown?"

"I'm sorry, we can use only one color."

"That's a ridiculous rule. There are many colors that can't be described in one word."

"I don't make the rules, sir."

"Well, this is silly."

Which it was, of course. All my life, on every piece of identification I have ever had, the color of my hair has been listed as brown.

And suddenly this woman, who obviously had weak eyes, the way she squinted, was being arbitrary.

I showed her my company identification card. "See, right there it says brown."

"That's not official, sir."

"Look at my company ID photograph. Does that hair look gray? It's brown. Almost jet black, as a matter of fact."

"Is that you?"

"Of course it's me."

"My, you used to be a nice-looking man."

"Oh, for Pete's sake," I said, which is all a person can say when they are dealing with someone that negative.

A supervisor walked over and said: "Some kind of problem here?"

"Yes," I said. "I don't want my driver's license to contain inaccurate information."

The woman looked indignant and said: "Just a moment, sir."

The supervisor said: "What kind of inaccurate information?"

"Oh, it's not that important," I said. "Let's get on with it."

"This gentleman says his hair is brown," the woman said.

The supervisor gawked at my hair, shook his head, and said: "It is gray. What there is of it."

"Ha!" I said. "My father always told me that you can't fight City Hall."

"This isn't City Hall," the supervisor said. "This is a state office."

"Look, I don't have all day," I said. "Can't we get this over with?"

(I knew there was no point in arguing. These government people always band together against us. My hair could have been purple and he would have agreed with her.)

"All right," the lady said, "I'll put down gray."

"You couldn't make it pale brown?"

"I'm sorry, sir, but it's really . . ."

"Oh, go ahead."

And she did. She actually wrote it down. Gray. GRAY! On my driver's license.

Not that I care. Who is ever going to see it, really? Nobody. Except maybe a traffic policeman.

What is the policeman going to think, seeing "gray" on a driver's license that belongs to a guy with all that thick, bushy brown hair?

And what if it is a policewoman?

Later that evening I was having dinner with some friends and told them about the incredibly color-blind license clerk.

"Don't feel bad," one of my friends said. "Paul Newman is almost entirely gray."

I felt better.

"And Marlon Brando is getting fat," another friend said.

"And Steve McQueen is getting all wrinkled," someone else said.

I felt really good.

"So," one of my friends concluded, "you've got it all—gray, fat, and wrinkled. You're a superstar."

OCTOBER 24, 1978

He's Loser by a Nose

After seeing the amazing results Betty Ford got from her cosmetic surgery, more and more youth-hungry people are rushing to have the same thing done to their bags and wrinkles.

It's been described by *Newsweek* magazine as a nationwide "plastic explosion" and is probably the biggest trend in the youth craze since millions of men began sticking hairpieces to their scalps.

Some people have criticized Mrs. Ford for her facelift, saying she is silly to try undoing nature's aging process. But I disagree. If a person feels happier spending a few thousand dollars to make themselves feel younger, why not? Anything that makes it easier to look in the mirror in the morning has to be good.

However, not all cosmetic operations give perfect results. And I speak from personal experience.

During my recent vacation, I decided that I, too, would like a more youthful appearance. So I underwent cosmetic surgery.

Like Betty Ford, I'm being frank and open about it because things like this have a way of getting in the gossip columns anyway.

The doctor I chose happened to be a recent arrival from an Iron Curtain country. I mention this because it has significance in what happened.

We discussed the parts of my face that needed improvement. I said the eye bags had to go, as well as the increasingly sagging jaw and some wrinkles.

But the part of me that was the number one priority was my rather outsized nose, which I've always disliked.

"The nose," I said, as he slid the anesthetic into my head, "has to go."

That was my mistake. Having trained in a Communist country, he was accustomed to following orders precisely as they are given. And he did exactly as I said.

That's right. He removed my entire nose.

As you can see in the picture that accompanies this column, where my nose once protruded there is now nothing but a smooth, flat surface. He didn't even leave a nostril, the lack of which now causes me to breathe entirely through my mouth.

After my initial surprise wore off, I realized that there was no point in complaining, since it was my own fault. So I decided that I would just have to make the best of it and face my friends and hope that they wouldn't be unnerved by my new appearance.

The first person I ran into was a neighbor, who stared at me for a moment and said: "You look different."

"Yes," I said, "I've had cosmetic surgery."

"Ah, that's it," he said. "You don't have bags under your eyes anymore."

"Right. I had them removed."

"Amazing. It's altered your entire appearance. Funny, but having the bags removed gives the impression that you don't have a nose."

"To tell the truth, I don't have a nose anymore. It was removed."

"That's what I thought, but I didn't want to mention it. Why did you do that?"

"I didn't like my nose to begin with. Even when I was an infant, the nurses in the maternity ward called me 'little eagle beak.' I didn't see any reason to have a nose that I disliked. I'm tired of blowing it, and having it freeze up in winter, and being punched in it. And as I got older, it would have probably turned red and bulbous."

"Yeah, I can see your point. I mean, I can't see your point anymore, but I know what you mean."

"Well, be brutally frank with me—do you think it makes me look younger?"

He pursed his lips and studied me from several angles, then said: "Actually, it's hard to say how old you are now. A nose is part of the frame of reference in telling someone's age. So not having one creates an interesting visual effect. You could be any age. Before I can judge, I'd have to see other people of different ages who don't have noses."

"Well, then, some people will probably think I'm younger."

"Very possible, but I imagine a few people won't think about your age as much as they will about your lack of a nose. It's kind of unusual, and I think that's what will catch their eye first."

"Do you think it is unattractive? Be honest."

"I'll be honest, it does take a little getting used to. But the main thing is not what other people think, because many people are suspicious of any change. They might even be resentful because you had the courage to try to improve your appearance this way."

"That's true. Especially if they think I now look younger than they do."

"Right. The important question is whether it makes you happy. That's the whole point of cosmetic surgery—does the person feel more confident, vital, youthful, and content with his or herself. That's really where we are at today, isn't it—really being madly, passionately in love with ourselves? So do you feel better not having a nose?"

"Yeah, I think I do. And I'll tell you, it makes shaving easier. I've always had trouble getting the razor in close to the nose. Now I just start shaving right under my eyes and zip straight down."

"I hadn't thought of that benefit."

"And besides looking more youthful, I won't be sneezing anymore, especially at hay fever time."

"Then you should be happy with the way it turned out."

"Yeah, I think I am."

"Terrific. That's what counts. Now, all you have to do is get yourself a hairpiece. You're getting thin on top."

"A hairpiece. Never."

"Why not?"

"They don't look natural. I don't want people staring at me."

OCTOBER 26, 1978

Lookin' Fine? He Nose It

I'm deeply touched by the dozens and dozens of people who have phoned to express concern and sympathy because my nose was inadvertently removed during cosmetic surgery.

"I really feel sorry about that," said Kenneth Bradshaw, of Chicago.

"It's unbelievable that this could happen," said Helen Safirstein, of Chicago.

"This shows that you can't trust doctors," said Adelle Jackson, of Chicago.

For those who missed the column describing the loss of my nose, the mishap occurred when I was inspired by Betty Ford to seek a more youthful appearance through cosmetic surgery, a trend that is sweeping the nation.

But when I told the surgeon "the nose has to go," he took my command literally and removed the whole thing.

After that surprising experience, you might think that I would have nothing more to do with cosmetic surgery. And that was my intention.

But at the urging of friends, who felt that I looked better with a nose, I have just undergone a second cosmetic surgical procedure.

This time I have had a nose transplant, hoping to undo the mistake of the first doctor.

The kind donor for the transplant was my fellow *Sun-Times* columnist Kup. He graciously offered me part of his fine nose, since he has enough for both of us.

But once again, I made a serious error. Because of my frugal nature, I sought out a man who does cosmetic surgery for only a fraction of the fee

charged by the better-known plastic surgeons.

Most such surgeons charge several thousand dollars. However, this man said he would do the job for $99.50. He works cheap because he is ambitious and wants to make a name for himself.

Well, if you look at the picture that accompanies today's column, you will see that the transplant was only partially successful.

Once again I have a nose. But now it is attached to my forehead.

Naturally, when the doctor held up a mirror to show me how I looked, I was surprised. I asked him why he put the nose on my forehead, rather than in the middle of my face.

He said: "You didn't tell me you wanted it in the middle of your face."

"That's true," I said, "but I assumed you would put it there."

"Then you should have said so. I'm not a mind reader, you know. That's the trouble with so many people. They want cosmetic surgery to improve their appearance, but they really don't have a realistic idea of how they will look when it is over."

"Well, I sure didn't expect my nose to be on my forehead."

"Why not? It looks fine there."

"You really think so?"

"Of course. I wouldn't have put it there if I didn't think so."

"But most people have their nose in the middle of their face."

He sneered and said: "Ah, but why in the middle of their face? You haven't thought of that, have you?"

"No, I honestly haven't."

"Then I'll tell you why. Because they have no choice. That's where their noses are when they are born, and so they are stuck with it. It never occurs to them that they might look better if the nose was somewhere else."

"I guess that's true."

"Of course it is. But who says the middle is the most attractive place for a nose? I happen to believe the nose looks much better on the forehead. It gives you a more balanced appearance."

"I hadn't thought of it that way."

"Nobody has, except me and Pablo Picasso."

"Picasso?"

"Sure, Picasso. Look at some of his paintings. He puts noses in the forehead, just as I've done with you. And everybody knows he is a great genius. In fact, it was Picasso's paintings that inspired me to do this for you. I wanted to create a living work of art."

"You mean me?"

"Yes. In a sense, you are now a living, breathing version of a Picasso painting. And knowing how valuable his paintings are, that probably makes you worth a lot of money."

"Gee. And art usually keeps up with inflation."

"Right."

"And besides your improved appearance and value, you'll find that having your nose on your forehead has practical aspects."

"Such as?"

"When you go swimming, you can be almost entirely underwater and still breathe. You are your own snorkel."

"Yeah, that's handy."

"And your eyebrows now serve a double purpose. They're also a mustache."

"Hey, and I was thinking of growing one anyway."

"Sure. And now nobody can ever accuse you of looking down your nose at them."

"Now that you've explained it, I feel better about this whole thing."

"Good. Let me know if you ever want your ears rearranged. I have some ideas about that, too."

So that's the story of my nose. I'll probably get used to my new appearance, but it will take a while. The worst part of it is that I'm the kind of person who worries a lot, and when I worry, I wrinkle my brow. Now when that happens, I sneeze.

JANUARY 11, 1980

Farewell to Fitness

At least once a month, the office jock will stop me in the hall, bounce on the balls of his feet, plant his hands on his hips, flex his pectoral muscles, and say: "How about it? I'll reserve a racquetball court. You can start working off some of that. . . ." And he'll jab a finger deep into my midsection.

It's been going on for months, but I've always had an excuse.

"Next week, I've got a cold." "Next week, my back is sore." "Next week, I've got a pulled hamstring." "Next week, after the holidays."

But this is it. No more excuses. I've made one New Year's resolution, which is that I will tell him the truth.

And the truth is that I don't want to play racquetball, or handball, or tennis, or jog, or pump Nautilus machines, or do push-ups or sit-ups or isometrics, or ride a stationary bicycle, or pull on a rowing machine, or hit a softball, or run up a flight of steps, or engage in any other form of exercise more strenuous than rolling out of bed.

This may be unpatriotic, and it is surely out of step with our muscle-flexing times, but I am renouncing the physical fitness craze.

Oh, I was part of it. Maybe not as fanatically as some. But about 15 years ago, when I was 32, someone talked me into taking up handball, the most punishing court game there is.

From then on it was four or five times a week, up at 6 a.m., on the handball court at 7, run, grunt, sweat, pant until 8:30, then in the office at 9.

And I'd go around bouncing on the balls of my feet, flexing my pectoral muscles, poking friends in their soft guts, saying: "How about working some of that off? I'll reserve a court," and being generally obnoxious.

This went on for years. And for what? I'll tell you what it led to:

I stopped eating pork shanks, that's what. It was inevitable. When you join the physical fitness craze, you have to stop eating wonderful things like pork shanks because they are full of cholesterol. And you have to give up eggs Benedict, smoked liverwurst, Italian sausage, butter pecan ice cream, Polish sausage, goose liver pate, Sara Lee cheesecake, Twinkies, potato chips, salami and Swiss cheese sandwiches, double cheeseburgers with fries, Christian Brothers brandy with a Beck's chaser, and everything else that tastes good.

Instead, I ate broiled skinless chicken, broiled whitefish, grapefruit, steamed broccoli, steamed spinach, unbuttered toast, yogurt, eggplant, an apple for dessert, and Perrier water to wash it down. Blah. That's right—blahhhhh!

You do this for years, and what do you get? What is your reward for panting and sweating around a handball/racquetball court, and eating yogurt and the skinned flesh of a dead chicken?

- You can take your pulse and find that it is slow. So what? Am I a clock?
- You buy pants with a narrower waist line. Big deal. The pants don't cost less than the ones with a big waistline.
- You get to admire yourself in the bathroom mirror for about 10 seconds a day after taking a shower. It takes five seconds to look at your flat stomach from the front, and five more seconds to look at your flat stomach from the side. If you're a real creep of a narcissist, you can add another 10 seconds for looking at your small behind with a mirror.

That's it.

Wait, I forgot something. You will live longer. I know that because my doctor told me so every time I took a physical. My fitness-conscious doctor was very slender, especially the last time I saw him, which was at his wake.

But I still believe him. Running around a handball court or jogging five miles a day, eating yogurt, and guzzling Perrier will make you live longer.

So you live longer. Have you been in a typical nursing home lately? Have you walked around the low-rent neighborhoods where the geezers try to survive on Social Security?

If you think living longer is rough now, wait until the 1990s, when today's Me Generation potheads and coke sniffers begin taking care of the elderly (today's middle-aged joggers). It'll be: "Just take this little happy pill, Gramps, and you'll wake up in heaven."

It's not worth giving up pork shanks and Sara Lee cheesecake.

Nor is it the way to age gracefully. Look around at all those middle-aged jogging chicken-eaters. Half of them tape hair pieces to their heads. That's what comes from having a flat stomach. You start thinking you should also have hair. And after that comes a face-lift. And that leads to jumping around a disco floor, pinching an airline stewardess, and other bizarre behavior.

I prefer to age gracefully the way men did when I was a boy. The only time a man over 40 ran was when the cops caught him burglarizing a warehouse. Their idea of exercise was to walk to and from the corner tavern, mostly to. A well-rounded health food diet included pork shanks, dumplings, and Jim Beam and a beer chaser.

Anyone who was skinny was suspected of having TB or an ulcer. A fine figure of a man was one who could look down and not see his knees, his feet, or anything else in that vicinity. What do you have to look for anyway? You ought to know if anything is missing.

A few years ago, I was in Bavaria and I went to a German beer hall. It was a beautiful sight. Everybody was popping sausages and pork shanks and draining quart-sized steins of thick beer. Every so often, they'd thump their magnificent bellies and smile happily at the booming sound they made.

Compare that with the finish line of a marathon, with all those emaciated runners sprawled on the grass, tongues hanging out, wheezing, moaning, writhing, throwing up.

If that is the way to happiness and a long life, pass me the cheesecake.

May you get a hernia, Arnold Schwarzenegger.

And here's to you, Orson Welles.

JUNE 24, 1982

Why Rude Is Shrewd

The short lady with graying hair, wearing a jogging suit, was already in the elevator when I got on early one recent morning.

I assume she lives in one of the apartments above mine, but I don't know her and don't remember ever having seen her before.

Just as the door slid shut, she spoke:

"Tell me, are you shy or just rude?"

"Huh?" I said. At 7 a.m. I don't say much more than that.

In a stern tone of voice she said: "You *never* say hello to anyone."

I think I answered: "Well, I think I say hello to . . ."

But she bored right in, sounding quite angry as she said: "*I've* said hello to you *many* times. But you've *never* said hello."

I had run out of coffee that morning. Without two cups of coffee, my mind doesn't function at its usual nimble, turtle-like pace. So I wasn't prepared for a heated exchange on an elevator with the kind of person who goes out to jog at 7 o'clock in the morning. She probably had eaten granola with natural honey, too. I know the type. Their minds are moving at full speed when they open their eyes. They leap into the shower. They don't understand the kind of person who sometimes crawls on all fours to the kitchen.

If I had had even one cup of coffee, I would have at least been quick-witted enough to stick out my tongue at her. Or belch.

Instead, I said something like: "Uh, well, I, you see, I, uh . . ."

By then we had arrived at the lobby and she stepped out and went bouncing toward the street and the jogging path.

On the way to work, I thought about what she had said. And I regretted that I had not had time to explain why I sometimes appear rude.

Part of it is that before becoming a High Rise Man, I spent many years as a Bungalow Man.

That meant that I would go directly from my front door to my driveway and into my car every morning. And from the car to the door in the evening.

So I seldom ran into any graying ladies in jogging suits, chirping "good morning, good morning." That wasn't the social style of my neighborhood. Once in awhile the neighbor's little dog would run up and nip at me, but I didn't have to say anything to him; a kick in the ribs did the trick.

Also, I'm a habitual mumbler. Sometimes I do say hello. But as a mumbler with a deep voice, the hello doesn't get any higher than somewhere around my esophagus.

As a result people sometimes think I'm being rude when I'm actually being friendly. I can say something like: "Good morning, miss. Looks like it will be a fine, fine day. Tell me, do you play around?" But because of my habit of mumbling, they mistake my lengthy response for mere stomach growlings.

And I have to admit that after almost 19 years of writing a daily column, I'm a bit wary of people I don't know. I've had conversations that have gone like this:

"Good morning."

"Good morning."

"I hate your column."

"Looks like a nice day."

"Your opinions are disgusting."

"Of course, it could rain."

"Do they really pay you for that garbage?"

"Well, see you again."

"Drop dead."

And there is one other reason, more important than the others, why I failed to say hello to that gray-haired lady in the jogging suit.

I've never told anyone this story before, but because I want her to understand my apparent rudeness, I'm going to relate it now.

It happened many years ago. I got on an elevator in a high-rise building where I had been talking to a news source.

There was a short, graying lady on the elevator. I nodded and said cheerfully: "Hello, and how are you?"

She whipped a .45 out of her purse and snarled: "Your money or your life, big boy!"

I was so shocked I just stood there. So she rapped me across the brow with the pistol, knocking me to the floor.

Then she put her foot (she was wearing an old gym shoe) on my throat, aimed the gun at my nose, and said: "Looks like it's the end of the road, laddy."

My life flashed before my eyes. It was very depressing. I hadn't realized what a wastrel I had been. That's no way to go, I assure you. It would be more humane if a good movie flashed before your eyes at such moments.

Just as she cocked the weapon, the elevator door opened.

Two women were standing there. One was a redhead, about 5-9, long legs, and 38-24-36. The other was a blond. Maybe 5-10, longer legs, and 40-25-37.

They quickly sized up the situation, sprang into the elevator, grabbed her arm, wrestled the weapon away from her, and pinned her to the floor, and my life was saved.

"It's the notorious gray-haired granny elevator robber," the cops said when they came to take her away.

So, I think my upstairs neighbor, if she reads this, will understand.

After that long-ago trauma, I'm understandably nervous and withdrawn when I get on an elevator and meet a short, graying lady.

On the other hand, if I get on an elevator and encounter a tall, leggy redhead, or a tall, leggy blond, I'm an entirely different person.

Why, to this day, I still feel so grateful I want to give them a big hug.

OCTOBER 9, 1985

Condo Man Back Down to Earth

I suppose the tomato was a factor. I like tomatoes. But the kind sold in most stores tastes like the plastic it's wrapped in. So I figured that if I wanted a good tomato, I'd have to grow my own. To do that, I'd need a back yard.

And that's why I am no longer Condo Man. About a week ago the moving truck came, and I have reverted to my natural state of Bungalow Man.

As I explained four years ago when I moved from a house on a side street into a lakefront condo, I was launching an anthropological study of those relatively new urban creatures, Condo Man, High-Rise Man, Lake-front Man, Health Club Man, Singles Bar Man, and all the others.

To do this, I knew I couldn't watch from afar. I had to immerse myself in their native cultures, as social anthropologist Margaret Mead used to do. I had to become one of them.

Now the study is over, and I have to admit that it was a complete flop.

Oh, I tried. One of the first things I did was buy a genuine Bargongini 34-speed racing bike with a talitanium frame that weighed only 4½ ounces.

Slipping on my designer bike suit, I walked my bike into Lincoln Park, swung aboard, and began pedaling along the lake. The bike creaked once or twice, then collapsed under me.

I carried the twisted wreckage into the bike shop and demanded a re-fund. The proprietor said: "We are not responsible. You are too heavy. It says right in the warranty: 'To be ridden only by the fashionably lean.'"

So I joined the New Vo Reesh Health Club and, in my velour running suit and my Nike shoes, set about creating a lean Lakefront Man body.

"This," the hulking instructor said as he patted the derrick-like ma-chine, "is the state of the art in exercise equipment. It will develop your quadrafeds, reduce your blats, strengthen your flipadids, and do wonders for your claphs."

I strapped myself in and began lifting and pumping and kicking every which way. I found myself gasping and everything suddenly turned black.

When I came to, the instructor was standing over me with smelling salts, saying: "A close call. You caught your gold neck chain in the weight rack. Maybe you ought to try jogging."

So it was back to Lincoln Park, where I tried to learn the ways of Jog-ging Man. And many of the experienced runners were generous in shar-ing their wisdom, such as the lean runner who said, "I don't want to intrude, but it really isn't good form to jog with a Pall Mall dangling from your lips."

Within a week I had increased my distance from 10 yards to almost half a block. And I checked my pulse and found that, at the height of my workout, my rate went from its normal 100 beats a minute to almost 400.

When I mentioned that to my doctor, he turned pale and said: "Why don't you just try walking? It's just as good for you, and it reduces the odds of your collapsing while running and the momentum carrying you into the lake."

So I took to taking brisk walks along Sheridan Road, Lake Shore Drive, and Lakeview Avenue.

But after only two days I displaced my hip socket and sprung a kneecap while leaping to avoid the sidewalk droppings of a pair of 200-pound mastiffs. Their owner, a facelift under blue hair, said, "I'll thank you not to frighten my dogs."

During my recuperation, I decided to check out the scene at the singles bars. But I quickly left when a man appeared from behind a fern and said, "Looking for your runaway daughter?"

But it wasn't all bad. From my living room window I had a splendid view of the sun coming up over the lake. And over the Dopemobile, a camper that arrived in the park each morning to sell strange herbs and spices while a nearby policeman slipped tickets under windshield wipers.

And I fulfilled one goal: I found the elusive perfect pesto sauce for pasta.

When I told a neighbor of mine about my triumph, she waved her copy of *Chicago* magazine at me and said: "You're so out of date. Nobody cares about pesto sauce anymore. We're into Ethiopian cuisine. No silverware. You scoop up the yak stew with pieces of round bread."

So that was it for me. If I'm going to eat stews without silverware, I might as well do it somewhere in the direction of Milwaukee Avenue.

And if somebody runs past my front door, I'll expect to see a cop chasing him.

AUGUST 21, 1987

Windshield-Wiper Lets In Some Light

There are some mornings so lousy that you know the rest of the day is going to stink.

This one began with nature as the enemy in the form of a flooded basement. Nature is a frustrating enemy because no matter how much you rant and swear, it doesn't listen.

Then came the writing of a large check to the Internal Revenue Service. The IRS is a dangerous enemy because if you rant and swear you might be audited and have even more to rant and swear about.

And before the morning was half over, there was technology, an old and hated foe. It took the form of the Ohio Street bridge going up, then getting stuck and not coming down for 30 minutes, trapping thousands of us in our cars with nowhere to go.

There's not much point in cursing a Chicago bridgetender. If anything, we should have been grateful that he was sober enough not to raise the bridge while any of us were on it.

By the time the bridge lowered, and the traffic crept forward, I was hopelessly late for an interview with a source, my teeth were grinding, and I was sure the entire world was plotting against me.

At Clark Street, I just caught the red light. That got me even angrier.

Suddenly, water was being sloshed across my windshield. At first, I didn't know where it was coming from.

Then I saw that a teenager had stepped from the curb with one of those gas-station tools, a combination sponge and squeegee, for cleaning windshields.

And he got me mad, too. My windshield was already spotless, so why was he cleaning it? Who asked him to? The light might change and I could lose a few more precious seconds.

Before he could use the squeegee, I gave him an angry glare, waved him off, and turned on my wipers.

He stepped back on the sidewalk, shrugged, shook his head slightly, and turned away.

About 16 and very skinny. His T-shirt was a grimy gray and his trousers looked like the kind that might have sold for $8 new a long time ago.

The light turned green, and I drove ahead. By the time I got to the next corner, I realized what I had just done.

That wasn't one of my sons on a corner, washing the windshields of strangers' cars, hoping some of them would be generous enough to hand him two bits. My sons never had to do anything that demeaning to put a few dollars in their pockets. They were fortunate enough to have been born Caucasian Americans, with an overpaid father.

And there I sat, in my big, black, fat-cat car, with air-conditioning blasting, stereo playing, and enough electronic doodads to do everything but blow my nose.

I had enough money in my pocket to buy that skinny kid a suit, pay his family's rent for a month, and maybe fill up their refrigerator and pantry.

But I hadn't the decency to let him squeegee the windshield, then touch the button that lowers a window and give him a buck and a smile. I had given him a scowl and a wave-off, gestures that said he was a nothing.

And all the while, do you know what was playing on my stereo cassette? Peter, Paul, and Mary singing that if they had a hammer, they'd hammer out love between their brothers and their sisters, all over the world—that's what was playing.

While I'm telling some ghetto kid to get lost.

Statistics ran through my mind. What's the teenage black unemployment rate—40 or 50 percent? And we wonder why so many are into crime?

But there was a kid who wasn't snatching my hubcaps, smashing and grabbing, mugging or heisting. All he was doing was cleaning windshields and hoping people like me might appreciate it.

Sure, it was a form of panhandling. But with that sponge and squeegee, he gave dignity to it. He was saying: "Look, I'm trying to work, I'm doing *something*."

And I tell him to bug off.

So I made a right turn at the next corner, then another one. I figured I'd double back and catch him a second time, and this time I'd give him a five-spot.

By the time I got back to the corner, he was gone. Maybe he moved to another corner. So I went around again, tried a couple more streets. But I couldn't find him.

So I drove to the office and parked. When I walked past my assistant, she said, "Good morning."

I told her it was a lousy, stinking morning.

Then I went into the men's room, looked in the mirror, and saw the biggest reason for it being a lousy, stinking morning.

JUNE 13, 1995

Oh, the Humiliation a Dad Must Endure

Standing by the golf course pond with a fishing rod in his hand, the man felt foolish and nervous.

Not that there is anything foolish about dangling a night crawler in a golf course pond. It's more relaxing and less costly than hacking a ball into the water, and you can eat what you catch. Who eats a score card?

But catching fish wasn't his real reason for being there.

He was engaged in what detectives, spies, or journalists would call a stakeout.

In other words, while he appeared to be spending some quiet time in the shade of an old oak tree, pulling out an occasional bluegill or small bass, he was really furtively watching and waiting for a certain person to walk by.

When that person appeared, the man would do something that he had never done in his entire life and never thought he would do. He would ask a celebrity for an autograph.

The prospect filled him with shame. He would have preferred to dive into the pond or run to his car and roar away with his pride intact.

But he couldn't. The reason was standing next to him and holding a fishing pole—his eight-year-old son.

The boy was dressed in his Sunday best, his Monday best, Tuesday best, and 24-hour-a-day best.

Deep red Chicago Bulls shorts. The very latest in black basketball shoes. And a Bulls jersey with the number 45 on the back.

A few days earlier, the man had been tipped off that the world's greatest basketball player and a few friends might be playing golf that morning on that golf course.

The course and clubhouse would be closed that day for weekly maintenance with only a few workers there.

The basketball star and his group would have something rare and precious—total privacy. No gawkers or intruders and no autograph hounds.

The man had casually mentioned this to his wife, and the boy had overhead them talk.

From that moment on it was, "Dad, can we? Can we, Dad? Mom, ask Dad, please? Dad, Mom says it's up to you. Dad, puleeze?"

There are things a parent must do. Cheerfully change fragrant diapers. Smile happily while burping a child who drools milk down your shirt collar. Sit through musical assemblies.

And that's what had the man squirming more than the worms he put on the hooks. He was asked to barge in on a privacy-seeking celebrity, to be the gawker, the intruder, the autograph hound.

But how do you say no to a kid who, since he was 3, has been chanting along with the team introductions: *"And from . . . North Carolina . . ."*

So there the man stood, already feeling like an ass, while hopefully telling himself: "Maybe when he sees the fishing rods, he'll ask how we're doing. People always ask fishermen how they're doing. And that will be the conversational ice-breaker and . . ."

Suddenly they were there, teeing off, then walking briskly down a path near the pond, not 10 feet from the man and his son.

The man blurted, "Good morning." Surely they'd pause and ask how they're biting.

Not a word. Not a glance. Eyes squinting, long strides, the Great One nodded once he was past them. It was something he's had to learn to do instinctively, or he'd never get where he was going. Even on a near-deserted golf course, there was some bozo coming out from under a tree with a felt-tip marker in his hand.

The man took a deep breath and said, "Michael?" The Great One stopped, turned, and gave him a cold look that might have been taken to mean: "Person, just what is it that you want?"

"Uh, Michael, could I have a second of your time?"

Without hesitating, he said: "You've already had a second."

It wasn't exactly a slap in the face. More like a little poke in the eye. The man had an urge to back off and grab a fellow worm.

But the smiling, wide-eyed boy was looking up, as if at a god. So the man stammered: "Look, he hasn't worn anything else since you came back. He sleeps in that outfit. Could you maybe just initial . . . ?"

A slight hesitation, then he stepped forward, took the marker, and made a long squiggle on the jersey. A celebrity signature is not expected to be legible. I suppose that the touch and the moment are what matter.

With a slight smile, he said: "There you go, my little man. Nice uniform." Then he shook the boy's hand, turned, and headed up the fairway.

The boy looked down at his jersey, then looked up with a huge smile and moist eyes. "I'll never wash this. I'll never wash my hand. Dad, let me have the marker. I'll never let anyone write with it. Wow, Dad, wow."

Later, in the car, the man told his wife: "He said, 'There you go, my little man.'"

"Why, that's really nice," she said.

"Yeah. But I wonder if he was talking to me."

[Editors' note: Michael Jordan briefly wore number 45 when he returned to the Chicago Bulls in 1995 after two seasons of minor-league baseball. The Bulls had retired his famous number 23, but he soon wore it again.]